The 2012

Go-Ah

Bus Hand

British Bus Publishing

Body codes used in the Bus Handbook series:

Type:
A   Articulated vehicle
B   Bus, either single-deck or double-deck
BC   Interurban - high-back seated bus
C   Coach
M   Minibus with design capacity of 16 seats or less
N   Low-floor bus (Niederflur), either single-deck or double-deck
O   Open-top bus (CO = convertible - PO = partial open-top)

Seating capacity is then shown. For double-decks the upper deck quantity is followed by the lower deck.

Please note that seating capacities shown are generally those provided by the operator. It is common practice, however, for some vehicles to operate at different capacities when on certain duties.

Door position:-
C   Centre entrance/exit
D   Dual doorway.
F   Front entrance/exit
R   Rear entrance/exit (no distinction between doored and open)
T   Three or more access points

Equipment:-
T	Toilet	TV	Training vehicle.
M	Mail compartment	RV	Used as tow bus or engineers' vehicle.

Allocation:-
s   Ancillary vehicle
t   Training bus
u   out of service or strategic reserve; refurbishment or seasonal requirement
w   Vehicle is withdrawn and awaiting disposal.

          e.g. - B32/28F is a double-deck bus with thirty-two seats upstairs, twenty-eight down and a front entrance/exit., N43D is a low-floor bus with two or more doorways.

Re-registrations:-
Where a vehicle has gained new index marks the details are listed at the end of each fleet showing the current mark, followed in sequence by those previously carried starting with the original mark.

Annual books are produced for the major groups:
The Stagecoach Bus Handbook
The First Bus Handbook
The Arriva Bus Handbook
The Go-Ahead Bus Handbook
The National Express Coach Handbook (bi-annual)
Some editions for earlier years are available. Please contact the publisher.

Regional books in the series:
The Scottish Bus Handbook
The Welsh Bus Handbook
The Ireland & Islands Bus Handbook
English Bus Handbook: Smaller Groups
English Bus Handbook: Notable Independents
English Bus Handbook: Coaches

Associated series:
The Hong Kong Bus Handbook
The Malta Bus Handbook
The Leyland Lynx Handbook
The Postbus Handbook
The Mailvan Handbook
The Toy & Model Bus Handbook - Volume 1 - Early Diecasts
The Fire Brigade Handbook (fleet list of each local authority fire brigade)
The Police Range Rover Handbook

Some earlier editions of these books are still available. Please contact the publisher on 01952 255669.

The 2012-13 Go-Ahead Bus Handbook

The *2012-13 Go-Ahead Bus Handbook* part of the Bus Handbook series published by British Bus Publishing, an independent publisher of quality books for the industry and bus enthusiasts. Further information on these may be obtained from the address below.

Although this book has been produced with the encouragement of, and in co-operation with, Go-Ahead management, it is not an official fleet list and the vehicles included are subject to variation, particularly as the vehicle investment programme continues. Some vehicles listed are no longer in regular use on services but are retained for special purposes. Also, not all out of use vehicles awaiting disposal are listed. The services operated and the allocation of vehicles to subsidiary companies are subject to variation at any time, although accurate to September 2012.

To keep the fleet information up-to-date we recommend the Key publication, *Buses*, published monthly, or for more detailed information, the PSV Circle monthly news sheets.

Principal Editors: Stuart Martin and Bill Potter

Acknowledgments: We are grateful to Tom Johnson, Malcolm Jones, Keith Lee, Colin Lloyd, Peter Marley, David Thomas, the PSV Circle and the management and officials of Go-Ahead Group and their operating companies for their kind assistance and co-operation in the compilation of this book.

The cover photograph is by Richard Godfrey, while the frontispiece and rear cover views are by Mark Bailey and Dave Heath.

Earlier editions of the Go-Ahead Group book, available on the web site:

2004	ISBN: 9781897990964
2005	ISBN: 9781904875352
2006-07	ISBN: 9781904875369
2007-08	ISBN: 9781904875376
2008-09	ISBN: 9781904875385
2009-10	ISBN: 9781904875394
2010-11	ISBN: 9781904875406
2011-12	ISBN: 9781904875413

ISBN 9781904875 42 0   © Published by British Bus Publishing Ltd, September 2012

British Bus Publishing Ltd, 16 St Margaret's Drive, Telford, TF1 3PH

Telephone: 01952 255669

web; www.britishbuspublishing.co.uk
e-mail: sales@britishbuspublishing.

Contents

Successful Evolution: History	5
Go North East	8
Oxford Bus Company	19
Konectbus	26
Hedingham	28
Chambers	32
Anglian	33
Go-Ahead London	36
Metrobus	57
Brighton & Hove	64
Plymouth Citybus	70
Go South Coast	74
Vehicle index	*90*

Green Street Green is the location for this view of Metrobus 174, YX61ENR, one of sixteen Enviro 200 buses for London tenders to join the fleet in 2011. *Dave Heath*

Successful evolution: a brief history of the Go-Ahead Group

Go-Ahead was initially formed twenty-five years ago as the Gateshead-based Go-Ahead Northern when the management team acquired that company during the privatisation of the National Bus Company in 1987. Early expansion saw the acquisition of a number of smaller bus operators in the north east, including Gypsey Queen and Low Feel Coaches.

In November 1993 Brighton and Hove buses was acquired. This was quickly followed by the Oxford Bus Company in March 1994. The privatisation of London Buses in the mid-nineties saw Camberwell-based London Central acquired in November 1994, and this purchase was built upon in June 1996, when fellow London bus operator London General was taken over from the management and employee team that acquired the business at privatisation.

In a further move, one of the North East's oldest, largest, and most respected independents had been purchased in March 1995 adding 225 vehicles. OK Motors of Bishop Auckland had roots dating back to 1912. More recently further expansion in London has seen Docklands Minibuses and Blue Triangle join Go-Ahead London bus operations in 2006 and 2007 respectively. Other acquisitions have seen Brighton & Hove, the Oxford Bus Company, Metrobus, Wilts & Dorset, Southern Vectis and Solent Blue Line join the Go-Ahead family. Outside London and the south, the most recent acquisition was in the West Midlands where Go-Ahead purchased the Birmingham Coach Company and Probus Limited, operating the combined business under the Go West Midland brand. In March 2008 Go-ahead sold Go West Midlands to Rotala's Central connect. In July 2009, Go-Ahead entered into an agreement to acquire East Thames Buses, giving Go-Ahead a 21.5% share of London bus operations. Of Go-Ahead's fifteen key operating companies, eleven are based in London and the south of England.

In 1997 the successful blue, red and yellow colours of the Metro Supershuttle were taken as the basis for the new livery for the North Eastern operations of Go-Northern, Go-Wear Buses and Go-Gateshead local operations under the umbrella brand of Go North East. From 2006 a change of focus has been marked by the emergence of locally route branded services, with names such as the Red Kite, The Magic Roundabout, The Black Cats, The Prince Bishops and the Doxford Clipper.

In recent times, a move to increase comfort levels has become apparent too. The new trend in bus design is the low-floor bus. For elderly passengers or parents shepherding children, vastly improved access is offered. London put the first of the new buses into service. Go North East became the next company to follow suit in 1994 and it now runs one of the UK's largest fleets that meet the latest low-floor standards.

Go-Ahead acquired Plymouth CityBus in 2009 and KonectBus in Norwich in March 2010 and also entered into a joint venture with yellow

Go North East uses route branding extensively and operates a large selection of liveries as a result. West Durham Swift scheme has been applied to Scania OmniCity 5249, NK56KHV, seen leaving Gateshead for Consett. *Richard Godfrey*

school bus operator Cook-Illinois in the United States in 2009. During 2011 the company acquired Thames Travel which is now managed by The Oxford Bus Company.

Rail privatisation has presented another opportunity for the group. Through its Govia joint venture with French transport operator Keolis, the Thameslink franchise was gained in 2006/07 and Go-Ahead took on Thames Trains. Both benefited from modern rolling stock. Thames Trains worked out of Paddington and covered the country as far out as Hereford and Stratford-upon-Avon. Both this franchise and Thameslink were awarded to First Group following competitions in 2005 and 2006.

In 2001 Govia took over the operation of the South Central rail from Connex. A new franchise was signed in 2003, to run until 2009, with the railway branded as 'Southern' and on retendering in 2009, Govia retained the franchise until 2015. The Gatwick Express service is now part of the South Central services and is operated by Govia. Govia is currently shortlisted to bid for the new combined Thameslink, Southern and Geat Northern franchise which is due to start in September 2013.

In 2005 Govia was awarded the Integrated Kent Franchise which had been in public ownership since Connex were stripped of this in 2003. Renamed as Southeastern, this new franchise commenced in April 2006, runs until March 2014 and includes the operation of new high speed trains on the domestic Channel Tunnel Rail Link into St Pancras which was launched in December 2009. The service provided Javelin Shuttle service for spectators during the London Olympic and Paralympic Games in 2012.

The 2012-13 Go-Ahead Bus Handbook

In 2007 Go-Ahead, again through the Govia joint venture partnership, was awarded the newly created West Midlands Franchise which began operations in November the same year. Known as London Midland, it combines the former Silverlink County franchise and the West Midlands regional services of the former Central Trains network.

In 1998 the aviation services company GHI joined the group. The company was merged with other Go-Ahead aviation acquisitions and rebranded as 'aviance UK'. In early 2010, Go-Ahead sold the majority of its ground handling and cargo operations, as part of its strategy of focusing on its core bus and rail operations. The remainder was sold in early 2011.

Go-Ahead became the first UK transport operator to receive Carbon Trust Standard accreditation for its efforts to reduce its carbon emissions. The business was re-accredited in 2011. The company has set a target to reduce its emissions by twenty per cent per passenger journey by 2015. To date, Go-Ahead has achieved a twelve per cent reduction by focusing on a range of initiatives including fuel efficient training for its 10,000 bus drivers, introducing regenerative braking on its train fleets and reducing energy consumptions in its depots, offices and rail stations.

In October 2011, Go-Ahead won the National Transport Award for its introduction of its smartcard ticket known as The Key. The smartcard is being rolled out across the company's bus and rail divisions and aims to make travel easier for passengers, as well as giving them access to value for money fares.

2012 got off to a good start with Smartcard ticket machines being installed on all Go-Ahead's 2,000 buses outside London and The Key is successfully up and running across most of its bus network and on parts of its Southern and London Midland rail franchises.

On March 3rd 2012, Go-Ahead Group acquired Carousel Buses Limited, based in High Wycombe. Carousel operates around fifty buses in the Wycombe area and runs services to Heathrow Airport, Uxbridge, Chesham and Watford. Two days later, Go-Ahead Group announced the acquisition of Essex-based company Hedingham Omnibuses. Founded in 1960, the company is based in Colchester and operates eighty-six buses in Essex. The business has five depots, at Clacton, Hedingham, Kelvedon, Sudbury and Tollesbury. It principally operates a mix of school and local bus contracts and commercial routes. Also in March Go-Ahead acquired First London East's Northumberland Park bus depot in Tottenham, north-east London.

In April the company acquired Anglian Buses. Based in Beccles, Suffolk Anglian operates seventy-one buses and runs services from the Suffolk coast to, from and within Norwich, as well as in Yarmouth, Lowestoft and along the Suffolk coast as far as Ipswich.

On June 2nd 2012, The Go-Ahead Group acquired HC Chambers & Son Limited, a small bus company operating on the Essex/Suffolk border. All four of the new acquisitions outside London will retain their individual brands.

GO NORTH EAST

Go-North East Ltd - Go Northern Ltd
117 Queen Street, Gateshead, NE8 2UA

Go-Ahead was initially formed as the Gateshead based Go-Ahead Northern, when the management team acquired that company during the privatisation of the National Bus Company in 1987.

Early expansion saw the acquisition of a number of smaller bus operators in the north east, including Gypsy Queen and Low Fell Coaches. Further expansion occurred in March 1995, with the acquisition of OK Motor Services of Bishop Auckland which had roots dating back to 1912.

In 1997 the successful blue, red and yellow colours of the Metro Supershuttle were taken as the new livery for Go Northern, Go Wear Buses, Go Coastline and Go Gateshead under the umbrella brand of Go North East.

From 2006 a change of focus has seen the emergence of locally route branded services, with names such as the Coaster, TEN, Prince Bishops', the angel, the laser, Doxford Clipper, the Red Kite, Toon link, fab fiftysix, TYNEDALE links, the LOOP, East Durham, MetroLINK, Venture, red arrows and Fast Cats.

During 2012 several hybrid vehicles have entered the fleet including Optare Solo SRs at Sunderland and Volvo B5LHs with Wrightbus bodywork for the Angel 21 between Durham and Newcastle.

501-522 Dennis Dart SLF 8.8m — Plaxton Pointer MPD — N25F — 2001

501	PE	X501WRG	506	WA	X506WRG	515	CT	NK51MJU	519	PE	NK51MKA
502	PE	X502WRG	510	PE	X551FBB	516	CT	NK51MJV	520	PE	NK51MKC
503	PE	X503WRG	512	SR	X512WRG	517	PM	NK51MJX	521	CT	NK51MKD
504	PM	X504WRG	513	HM	X513WRG	518	CT	NK51MJY	522	PE	NK51MKE
505	PM	X595FBB	514	PM	X514WRG						

523-548 Dennis Dart 8.8m — TransBus Mini Pointer — N25F — 2002

523	WA	NA52AWF	530	WA	NA52AWP	537	PE	NA52AWZ	543	PE	NA52AXH
524	WA	NA52AWG	531	WA	NA52AWR	538	PE	NA52AXB	544	CT	NA52AXJ
525	WA	NA52AWH	532	CT	NA52AWU	539	PE	NA52AXC	545	CT	NA52AXK
526	WA	NA52AWJ	533	CT	NA52AWV	540	PE	NA52AXD	546	CT	NA52AXM
527	WA	NA52AWM	534	CT	NA52AWW	541	PE	NA52AXF	547	SD	NA52AXN
528	WA	NA52AWN	535	PE	NA52AWX	542	SD	NA52AXG	548	PM	NA52AXO
529	WA	NA52AWO	536	PE	NA52AWY						

549-574 TransBus Dart 8.8m — TransBus Mini Pointer — N29F — 2003

549	PM	NK53TKD	557	HM	NK53TKV	563	SR	NK53TLN	569	WA	NK53TMO
550	PM	NK53TKE	558	HM	NK53TKX	564	SR	NK53TLO	570	WA	NK53TMU
551	PM	NK53TKF	559	HM	NK53TKY	565	SD	NK53TLU	571	CK	NK53TMV
553	PM	NK53TKN	560	HM	NK53TKZ	566	WA	NK53TLV	572	CK	NK53TMX
554	PM	NK53TKO	561	HM	NK53TLF	567	WA	NK53TLX	573	PE	NK53TMY
555	HM	NK53TKT	562	PM	NK53TLJ	568	WA	NK53TLY	574	PE	NK53TMZ
556	HM	NK53TKU									

603-606 ADL Dart 8.8m — ADL Mini Pointer — N29F — 2004

603	SD	NK54NTX	604	SD	NK54NTY	605	SD	NK54NUA	606	SD	NK54NUB

618	CT	NK55RUV	ADL Dart 8.8m	ADL Mini Pointer	N29F	2005	Redby, Hendon, 2008
619	CT	NK55RUW	ADL Dart 8.8m	ADL Mini Pointer	N29F	2005	Redby, Hendon, 2008

Arriving in Durham is Mini Pointer Dart 501, X501WRG. It is seen in East Durham route colours.
Richard Godfrey

625-628

			Optare Solo M880 SR			Optare		N27F	2011		
625	SR	NK11HBB	**626**	SR	NK61DBX	**627**	SR	NK61DBY	**628**	SD	NK61DBZ

629	SD	NK61EFY	Optare Solo M880 SR Hybrid	Optare		N27F	2011			
630	SD	NK61EGY	Optare Solo M880 SR Hybrid	Optare		N27F	2011			

631-636

			Optare Solo M880 SR			Optare		N27F	2011-12		
631	SR	NK61FEU	**633**	SR	NK61FEX	**635**	SD	NK61FJP	**636**	SD	NK61FMD
632	SR	NK61FEV	**634**	SR	NK61FJO						

637	SR	NK12HCD	Optare Solo M900 SR	Optare		N30F	2012	
638	SR	NK12HCE	Optare Solo M900 SR	Optare		N30F	2012	
639	SR	NK12HCF	Optare Solo M900 SR	Optare		N30F	2012	
640	-	-	Optare Solo M900 SR Hybrid	Optare		-	2012	
3801	SY	V801EBR	Dennis Trident 10.5m	East Lancs Lolyne		N47/30F	2000	
3802	SY	V802EBR	Dennis Trident 10.5m	East Lancs Lolyne		N47/30F	2000	
3803	CS	V803EBR	Dennis Trident 10.5m	East Lancs Lolyne		N47/30F	2000	
3804	CS	V804EBR	Dennis Trident 10.5m	East Lancs Lolyne		N47/30F	2000	

3811-3833

			Volvo Olympian			Northern Counties Palatine II	B47/30F	1998			
3811	GD	S811FVK	**3817**	PM	S817FVK	**3823**	PM	S823OFT	**3829**	SY	S829OFT
3812	GD	S812FVK	**3818**	PM	S818OFT	**3824**	SY	S824OFT	**3830**	WA	S830OFT
3813	GD	S813FVK	**3819**	PM	S819OFT	**3825**	GD	S825OFT	**3831**	PM	S831OFT
3814	GD	S814FVK	**3820**	PM	S820OFT	**3826**	GD	S826OFT	**3832**	WI	S832OFT
3815	PM	S815FVK	**3821**	PM	S821OFT	**3827**	GD	S827OFT	**3833**	GD	S833OFT
3816	PM	S816FVK	**3822**	PM	S822OFT	**3828**	SY	S828OFT			

3858-3880

			Dennis Trident 10.5m			East Lancs Lolyne		N47/30F*	2000	*3866/7 are N47/24F	
3858	PM	V858EGR	**3864**	CS	W864PNL	**3870**	PM	W174SCU	**3876**	SY	W186SCU
3859	CS	W859PNL	**3865**	CS	W865PNL	**3871**	GD	W181SCU	**3877**	CS	W187SCU
3860	SD	W806PNL	**3866**	PM	W866PNL	**3872**	GD	W182SCU	**3878**	CS	W188SCU
3861	SD	W861PNL	**3867**	PM	W177SCU	**3873**	CS	W183SCU	**3879**	CS	W189SCU
3862	GD	W862PNL	**3868**	CS	W178SCU	**3874**	WI	W184SCU	**3880**	PM	W176SCU
3863	SD	W863PNL	**3869**	CS	W179SCU	**3875**	SY	W185SCU			

The Metrocentre in Gateshead is not only a major shopping venue but also a transport interchange. Seen heading there is 4924, X924WGR, a Volvo B10BLE with Wright Renown bodywork. *Richard Godfrey*

3885-3891
Dennis Trident 10.5m Plaxton President N47/28F* 2001 *3890/1 are N47/24F

3885	CS	NK51UCN	3887	CS	NK51UCP	3889	CS	NK51UCS	3891	PM	NK51UCU
3886	SD	NK51UCO	3888	CS	NK51UCR	3890	PM	NK51UCT

3897-3940
Volvo Olympian Northern Counties Palatine B47/31F 1997-98 Go-Ahead London, 2002

3897	CS	R255LGH	3916	CS	R274LGH	3922	WI	R281LGH	3931	SY	R390LGH
3899	u	R257LGH	3923	WI	R282LGH	3932	SD	R391LGH	3936	SD	R395LGH
3904	CS	R262LGH	3917	CS	R556LGH	3924	WI	R283LGH	3937	SD	R396LGH
3906	SY	R264LGH	3918	CS	R276LGH	3925	SY	R284LGH	3938	SD	R397LGH
3910	SY	R553LGH	3919	WI	R557LGH	3926	SY	R285LGH	3939	SY	R398LGH
3914	SY	R554LGH	3920	WI	R558LGH	3927	SY	R286LGH	3940	SY	R399LGH
3915	SY	R355LGH	3921	WI	R559LGH

3941	WI	NK05GZO	Volvo B7TL 10.1m	Wrightbus Eclipse Gemini	NC45/29F	2005
3942	WI	NK05GZP	Volvo B7TL 10.1m	Wrightbus Eclipse Gemini	NC45/29F	2005
3943	WI	NK05GZR	Volvo B7TL 10.1m	Wrightbus Eclipse Gemini	NC45/29F	2005

3962-3965
Volvo B7TL 10.1m Wrightbus Eclipse Gemini NC45/29F 2005

3962	CS	NK06JXE	3963	GD	NK06JXD	3964	GD	NK06JXC	3965	CS	NK06JXB

3966-3983
Volvo B7TL East Lancs Vyking N45/22D 2002 Go-Ahead London, 2009

3966	CS	PN02XCF	3971	SD	PJ02PYX	3976	SD	PJ02PZC	3980	CS	PJ02PZG
3967	SD	PN02XCL	3972	CS	PJ02PYY	3977	CS	PJ02PZD	3981	SD	PJ02PZH
3968	CS	PJ02PYU	3973	CS	PJ02PYZ	3978	CS	PJ02PZE	3982	CS	PJ02PZK
3969	CS	PJ02PYV	3974	CS	PJ02PZA	3979	SD	PJ02PZF	3983	CS	PJ02PZL
3970	SD	PJ02PYW	3975	CS	PJ02PZB

4820-4825
DAF SB220 Northern Counties Paladin N42F 1997

4820	WI	P320AFT	4822	WI	P322AFT	4824	WI	P324AFT	4825	WA	P325AFT
4821	WI	P321AFT	4823	WI	P323AFT

4837-4855
Volvo B10BLE Wright Renown N44F 1998

4837	GD	R837PRG	4842	GD	R842PRG	4847	SY	R847PRG	4852	CS	R852PRG
4838	GD	R838PRG	4843	GD	R843PRG	4848	SY	R848PRG	4853	CS	R853PRG
4839	GD	R839PRG	4844	GD	R844PRG	4849	SY	R849PRG	4854	CS	R854PRG
4840	GD	340GUP	4845	GD	R845PRG	4850	CS	R856PRG	4855	CS	R855PRG
4841	GD	R841PRG	4846	GD	R846PRG	4851	CS	R851PRG

The Angel of the North is a large sculpture located near the A1 road and is now depicted on the vehicles used between Durham and Chester-le-Street. Displaying the scheme is 3968, PJ02PYU, one of eighteen Volvo B7TLs with East Lancs bodywork initially used by Go-Ahead London. *Richard Godfrey*

4862-4895   DAF SB220   Plaxton Prestige   N40F   1998-99

| 4862 | CS | S862ONL | 4864 | CS | S864ONL | 4866 | CS | S866ONL | 4894 | CS | S894ONL |
| 4863 | WI | S863ONL | 4865 | CS | S865ONL | 4867 | HM | S867ONL | 4895 | CS | S895ONL |

4896-4925   Volvo B10BLE   Wright Renown   N44F   2000

4896	CS	V986ETN	4904	GD	W904RBB	4912	GD	X912WGR	4919	GD	X919WGR
4897	SY	V987ETN	4905	CS	W905RBB	4913	GD	X913WGR	4920	GD	X492WGR
4898	SY	V988ETN	4906	GD	W906RBB	4914	GD	X914WGR	4921	GD	X921WGR
4899	SY	V989ETN	4907	GD	W907RBB	4915	GD	X915WGR	4922	WI	X922WGR
4900	SY	V990ETN	4908	GD	W908RBB	4916	GD	X916WGR	4923	WI	X923WGR
4901	SY	W901RBB	4909	GD	W909RBB	4917	GD	X917WGR	4924	GD	X924WGR
4902	SY	W902RBB	4910	WI	W491SCU	4918	GD	X918WGR	4925	GD	X925WGR
4903	SY	W903RBB	4911	PM	W411SCU						

4926-4949   Scania L94UB   Wrightbus Solar   N42F   2001

4926	CS	Y926ERG	4932	SD	Y932ERG	4938	WA	NK51OKX	4945	PM	NK51OLJ
4927	CS	Y927ERG	4933	SD	Y933ERG	4940	WA	NK51OLB	4946	PM	NK51OLM
4928	CS	Y928ERG	4934	SD	Y934ERG	4941	GD	NK51OLC	4947	PM	NK51OLN
4929	CS	Y929ERG	4935	SD	Y935ERG	4942	SD	NK51OLE	4948	PM	NK51OLO
4930	CS	Y493ETN	4936	SD	Y936ERG	4943	SD	NK51OLG	4949	GD	NK51OLP
4931	CS	Y931ERG	4937	SD	NK51OKW	4944	PM	NK51OLH			

4950-4953   Scania L94UA   Wrightbus Solar Fusion   AN56D   2001

| 4950 | u | NK51OLR | 4951 | u | NK51OLT | 4952 | u | NK51OLU | 4953 | u | NK51OLV |

4954-4966   Scania L94UB   Wrightbus Solar   N42F   2002

4954	SD	NL02ZRX	4958	WA	NL52WVO	4961	WA	NL52WVS	4964	WA	NL52WVV
4955	SD	NA02NVL	4959	WA	NL52WVP	4962	WA	NL52WVT	4965	WA	NL52WVW
4956	WA	NL52WVM	4960	WA	NL52WVR	4963	WA	NL52WVU	4966	WA	NL52WVX
4957	WA	NL52WVN									

4967-4976   Scania L94UB   Wrightbus Solar   N42F   2004

4967	GD	NK53UNT	4970	SD	NK53UNW	4973	SD	NK53UNZ	4975	SD	NK53UOB
4968	SD	NK53UNU	4971	SD	NK53UNX	4974	SD	NK53UOA	4976	SD	NK53UOC
4969	SD	NK53UNV	4972	SD	NK53UNY						

4978-4982 — Volvo B7RLE — Wrightbus Eclipse Urban — N43F — 2005

4978	WI	NK54NUH	4980	WI	NK54NUM	4981	WI	NK54NUO
4979	WI	NK54NUJ						

4982 WI NK54NUP

4983-4988 — DAF SB220 — Northern Counties Paladin — N42F — 1997 — BAA Edinburgh, 2005

4983	CS	R971FNW	4985	CS	R975FNW	4987	CS	R982FNW
4984	CS	R972FNW	4986	CS	R979FNW			

4988 CS R983FNW

4989	SD	YN51MKV	Scania L94UB	Wrightbus Solar	N43F	2001	Ludlows, Halesowen, 2005
4990	SD	YN51MKX	Scania L94UB	Wrightbus Solar	N43F	2001	Ludlows, Halesowen, 2005
4991	SD	YR02ZYK	Scania L94UB	Wrightbus Solar	N43F	2002	Anglian, Beccles, 2006
4992	SD	YR02ZYM	Scania L94UB	Wrightbus Solar	N43F	2002	Anglian, Beccles, 2006
4993	CS	S590KJF	Volvo B10BLE	Alexander ALX300	N45F	1998	Felix, Stanley, 2006

5144-5150 — Volvo B10BLE — Wright Renown — N44F — 1999 — Arriva North East, 2010

5144	WI	V530GDS	5146	WI	V532GDS	5148	WI	V534GDS
5145	WI	V531GDS	5147	WI	V533GDS	5149	WI	V535GDS

5150 WI V536GDS

5151-5160 — Volvo B10BLE — Wright Renown — N39D — 1999 — Oxford Bus Company, 2010

5151	WI	T801CBW	5154	WI	T804CBW	5157	WI	T807CBW
5152	WI	T802CBW	5155	WI	T805CBW	5158	WI	T808CBW
5153	WI	T803CBW	5156	WI	T806CBW			

5159 WI T809CBW
5160 WI T810CBW

5161-5171 — Volvo B10BLE — Wright Renown — N39D — 1999-2000 — Oxford Bus Company, 2011

5161	WI	T811CBW	5164	WI	T814CBW	5167	GD	W817FBW
5162	WI	T812CBW	5165	WI	T815CBW	5168	GD	W818FBW
5163	WI	T813CBW	5166	GD	W816FBW	5169	GD	W819FBW

5170 GD W20FWL
5171 GD W821FBW

5201-5228 — Scania L94 UB — Wrightbus Solar — N43F — 2004-05

5201	SD	NK54NUU	5208	SD	NK54NVC	5215	SD	NK54NVL
5202	SD	NK54NUV	5209	SD	NK54NVD	5216	SD	NK54NVM
5203	SD	NK54NUW	5210	SD	NK54NVE	5217	SD	NK54NVN
5204	SD	NK54NUX	5211	SD	NK54NVF	5218	GD	NK54NVO
5205	SD	NK54NUY	5212	SD	NK54NVG	5219	GD	NK54NVP
5206	SD	NK54NVA	5213	SD	NK54NVH	5220	GD	NK54NVT
5207	SD	NK54NVB	5214	SD	NK54NVJ	5221	GD	NK54NVU

5222	GD	NK54NVV
5223	GD	NK54NVW
5224	GD	NK54NVX
5225	GD	NK54NVY
5226	GD	NK54NVZ
5227	GD	NK54NWA
5228	SD	NK54NWB

5229-5233 — Scania L94 UB — Wrightbus Solar — N43F — 2006

5229	CK	NK55OLG	5231	CK	NK55OLJ	5232	CK	NK55OLM
5230	CK	NK55OLH						

5233 CK NK55OLN

5234-5274 — Scania OmniCity CN230 UB — Scania — N41F — 2006-07

5234	SY	NK56KHB	5245	SY	NK56KHP	5255	PM	NK56KJE
5235	SY	NK56KHC	5246	SY	NK56KHR	5256	PM	NK56KJF
5236	SY	NK56KHD	5247	SY	NK56KHT	5257	PM	NK56KJJ
5237	SY	NK56KHE	5248	SY	NK56KHU	5258	PM	NK56KJN
5238	SY	NK56KHF	5249	SY	NK56KHV	5259	PM	NK56KJO
5239	SY	NK56KHG	5250	SY	NK56KHW	5260	PM	NK56KJU
5240	SY	NK56KHH	5251	PM	NK56KHX	5261	SY	NK56KJV
5241	SY	NK56KHJ	5252	PM	NK56KHY	5262	PM	NK56KJX
5242	SY	NK56KHL	5253	PM	NK56KHZ	5263	PM	NK56KJY
5243	SY	NK56KHM	5254	PM	NK56KJA	5264	PM	NK56KJZ
5244	SY	NK56KHO						

5265	PM	NK56KKA
5266	PM	NK56KKB
5267	PM	NK56KKC
5268	PM	NJ07GJO
5269	PM	NK56KKE
5270	PM	NK56KKF
5271	PM	NK56KKG
5272	PM	NK56KKH
5273	SY	NK56KKJ
5274	SY	NK56KKL

5275-5283 — Mercedes-Benz Citaro O530 N — Mercedes-Benz — N40F — 2007

5275	WA	NK07KPG	5278	WA	NK07KPN	5280	WA	NK07KPP
5276	WA	NK07KPJ	5279	WA	NK07KPO	5281	WA	NK07KPR
5277	WA	NK07KPL						

5282 WA NK07KPT
5283 SD NK07KPU

5284-5309 — Mercedes-Benz Citaro O530 N — Mercedes-Benz — N40F — 2008

5284	SY	NK08CFP	5291	SY	NK08CGG	5298	SD	NK08CHC
5285	SY	NK08CFU	5292	SY	NK08CGO	5299	SD	NK08CHD
5286	SY	NK08CFV	5293	SY	NK08CGU	5300	SD	NK08CHF
5287	SY	NK08CFX	5294	SY	NK08CGV	5301	SD	NK08CHG
5288	SY	NK08CFZ	5295	SY	NK08CGX	5302	SD	NK08CHH
5289	SY	NK08CGE	5296	SY	NK08CGY	5303	SD	NK08CHJ
5290	SY	NK08CGF	5297	SY	NK08CGZ			

5304	SD	NK08CHL
5305	SD	NK08CHN
5306	SD	NK08CHO
5307	SD	NK08CHV
5308	SD	NK08CHX
5309	SD	NK08CHY

Recent double-deck arrivals with Go-North East are Volvo B9TLs with Wrightbus Gemini 2 bodywork. Seen at the Gateshead Interchange is 6005, NK11BHF, from the 2011 delivery. A further batch is being delivered as we go to press. *Richard Godfrey*

5310-5327

Mercedes-Benz Citaro O530 N — Mercedes-Benz — N40F — 2008

5310	WI	NK08MXY	5315	WI	NK08MYD	5320	SD	NK58DVW	5324	SD	NK58DWA
5311	WI	NK08MXZ	5316	WI	NK08MYF	5321	SD	NK58DVX	5325	SD	NK58DWC
5312	WI	NK08MYA	5317	WI	NK08MYG	5322	SD	NK58DVY	5326	SD	NK58DWD
5313	WI	NK08MYB	5318	HM	NK08MZV	5323	SD	NK58DVZ	5327	SD	NK58DWE
5314	WI	NK08MYC	5319	HM	NK08MZW						

5328-5336

Mercedes-Benz Citaro O530 N — Mercedes-Benz — N40F — 2010

5328	HM	BJ10VUN	5331	PM	BJ10VUR	5333	PM	BJ10VUT	5335	PM	BJ10VUV
5329	HM	BJ10VUO	5332	HM	BJ10VUS	5334	PM	BJ10VUU	5336	PM	BJ10VUW
5330	HM	BJ10VUP									

5337	PM	HF06FUA	Mercedes-Benz Citaro O530 N	Mercedes-Benz	N41F	2006	Go South Coast, 2010
5338	PM	HF06FUB	Mercedes-Benz Citaro O530 N	Mercedes-Benz	N41F	2006	Go South Coast, 2010

5339-5348

Mercedes-Benz Citaro O530G — Mercedes-Benz — AN53T — 2008 — Go-Ahead London, 2011

5339	GD	BL57OXJ	5342	GD	BP57UYE	5345	GD	BP57UYH	5347	GD	BP57UYK
5340	GD	BL57OXK	5343	GD	BP57UYF	5346	GD	BP57UYJ	5348	GD	BP57UYL
5341	GD	BL57OXP	5344	GD	BP57UYG						

5349-5356

Mercedes-Benz Citaro O530G — Mercedes-Benz — AN52T — 2004 — Go-Ahead London, 2012

5349	GD	BX54UCP	5351	GD	BX54UCU	5353	GD	BX54UCW	5355	GD	BX54UDB
5350	GD	BX54UCR	5352	GD	BX54UCV	5354	GD	BX54UCZ	5356	GD	BX54UDD

6001-6007

Volvo B9TL — Wrightbus Gemini 2 — N43/28F — 2011

6001	WA	NK11BGZ	6003	WA	NK11BHD	6005	WA	NK11BHF	6007	WA	NK11BHL
6002	WA	NK11BHA	6004	WA	NK11BHE	6006	WA	NK11BHJ			

6008-6042

Volvo B7TL 10m — Plaxton President — N41/24D — 2000 — Go-Ahead London, 2011

6008	CS	V308LGC	6017	SY	V317LGC	6026	CS	V226LGC	6035	CK	V335LGC
6009	CS	V209LGC	6018	CS	V218LGC	6027	WI	V327LGC	6036	CS	V336LGC
6010	CS	V310LGC	6019	CS	V319LGC	6028	CS	V228LGC	6037	CK	V337LGC
6011	WA	V311LGC	6020	CS	V220LGC	6029	WA	V329LGC	6038	CS	V338LGC
6012	SY	V312LGC	6021	CK	V921KGF	6030	CS	V330LGC	6039	CS	V302LGC
6013	WA	V313LGC	6022	CS	V322LGC	6031	SY	V331LGC	6040	CK	V304LGC
6014	SY	V314LGC	6023	WI	V923KGF	6032	WA	V332LGC	6041	CK	V305LGC
6015	SY	V315LGC	6024	CK	V324LGC	6033	CS	V233LGC	6042	CS	V306LGC
6016	CS	V816KGF	6025	CS	V325LGC	6034	CK	V334LGC			

Houghton-le-Spring provides the location for this view of Prince Bishops liveried 5230, NK55OLH, a Scania L94 with Wrightbus Solar bodywork. The Prince Bishops service runs every ten minutes on Monday to Saturday daytimes providing links between Sunderland and Durham city centres. *Richard Godfrey*

6043-6055   Volvo B9TL   Wrightbus Gemini 2   NC43/30F*   2012   *6043-8 are NC43/28F

6043	GD	NK12GCO	6047	GD	NK12GCY	6050	WA	NK12GDE	6053	WA	NK12GDO
6044	GD	NK12GCU	6048	GD	NK12GCZ	6051	WA	NK12GDF	6054	WA	NK12GDU
6045	GD	NK12GCV	6049	WA	NK12GDA	6052	WA	NK12GDJ	6055	WA	NK12GDX
6046	GD	NK12GCX									

6056-6070   Volvo B5LH   Wrightbus Gemini 2   N-/-F   2012

6056	-	NK62CBV	6060	-	NK62CFN	6064	-	NK62CLZ	6068	-	NK62CYF
6057	-	NK62CBV	6061	-	NK62CJE	6065	-	NK62CME	6069	-	NK62CZA
6058	-	NK62CCY	6062	-	NK62CJJ	6066	-	NK62CYC	6070	-	NK62CXL
6059	-	NK62CEN	6063	-	NK62CKC	6067	-	NK62CYE			

7087	CS	NA52RMZ	Volvo B12M			Plaxton Paragon		C49FT	2002
7090	CS	CU6860	Volvo B12B			Plaxton Panther		C49FT	2004
7092	CS	K2VOY	Volvo B12B			Plaxton Panther		C49FT	2006
7093	CS	K3VOY	Volvo B12B			Plaxton Panther		C49FT	2006

7094-7102   Scania K340 EB6   Caetano Levanté   C53FT   2008

7094	CS	FJ08KLF	7097	CS	FJ08KLX	7099	CS	FJ08KMU	7101	CS	FJ08KNV
7095	CS	FJ08KLS	7098	CS	FJ08KLZ	7100	CS	FJ08KMV	7102	CS	FJ08KNW
7096	CS	FJ08KLU									

| 7103 | CS | JCN822 | Volvo B9R | | | Caetano Levanté | | C48FT | 2012 |
| 7104 | CS | 574CPT | Volvo B9R | | | Caetano Levanté | | C48FT | 2012 |

8158-8173   Dennis Dart SLF 11.3m   Plaxton Pointer SPD   N41F   1999

| 8158 | SY | S358ONL | 8160 | u | S360ONL | 8172 | SD | S372ONL | 8173 | SD | S373ONL |
| 8159 | u | S359ONL | 8161 | u | S361ONL | | | | | | |

8201-8222   Dennis Dart SLF 11.3m   Plaxton Pointer SPD   N41F   1999-2000

8201	SR	V201ERG	8207	PM	V207ERG	8213	PM	V213ERG	8218	GD	V218ERG
8202	SR	V202ERG	8208	PM	V208ERG	8214	PM	V214ERG	8219	GD	V219ERG
8203	u	V203ERG	8209	PM	V209ERG	8215	PM	V215ERG	8220	GD	V210ERG
8204	SR	V204ERG	8210	PM	V210ERG	8216	PM	V216ERG	8221	SD	V221ERG
8205	SR	V205ERG	8211	PM	V211ERG	8217	GD	V217ERG	8222	WA	V822ERG
8206	PM	V206ERG	8212	PM	V212ERG						

2009 saw the arrival of a batch of sixteen 11m Optare Versa buses which are equally allocated to Gateshead and Sunderland. Carrying Saltwell Park livery which is used on buses operating routes 53 and 54, is Gateshead's 8301, NK09FVB. *Norman Price*

8223-8241 — Dennis Dart SLF 11.3m — Plaxton Pointer SPD — N41F — 2001

8223	PM	X223FBB	8228	HM	X228FBB	8233	SD	X233FBB	8238	PM	NK51MKM
8224	SD	X224FBB	8229	GD	X229FBB	8234	SD	NK51MKF	8239	PM	NK51MKN
8225	GD	X822FBB	8230	GD	X823FBB	8235	SD	NK51MKG	8240	PM	NK51MKO
8226	PM	X226FBB	8231	SD	X231FBB	8236	SD	NK51MKJ	8241	PM	NK51MKP
8227	PM	X227FBB	8232	SD	X232FBB	8237	SD	NK51MKL			

8242-8252 — DAF SB120 — Wrightbus Cadet — N39F — 2003

8242	SR	NA52BUU	8245	SD	NA52BVB	8248	WA	NA52BVE	8251	WA	NA52BVH
8243	SD	NA52BUV	8246	SD	NA52BVC	8249	WA	NA52BVF	8252	WA	NA52BVJ
8244	SD	NA52BUW	8247	WA	NA52BVD	8250	WA	NA52BVG			

8253-8273 — VDL Bus SB120 — Wrightbus Cadet 2 — N39F — 2004

8253	WA	NK04FOP	8260	WA	NK04FPE	8265	GD	NK04ZND	8270	SD	NK54NKX
8254	WA	NK04FOT	8261	GD	NK04ZNC	8266	GD	NK04ZNE	8271	SD	NK54NKZ
8255	WA	NK04FOU	8262	GD	NK04ZKY	8267	SD	NK54NKT	8272	SD	NK54NLC
8258	SD	NK04FPC	8263	GD	NK04ZKZ	8268	SD	NK54NKU	8273	SD	NK54NLD
8259	SD	NK04FPD	8264	GD	NK04ZLE	8269	SD	NK54NKW			

8281	SD	T428LGP	Dennis Dart SLF 10.7m	Caetano Compass	N38F	2001	Elcock Reisen, Telford, '05
8289	SD	Y558KUX	Dennis Dart SLF 10.7m	Plaxton Pointer 2	N38F	2001	Elcock Reisen, Telford, '05
8291	u	S783RNE	Dennis Dart SLF 10.7m	Plaxton Pointer 2	N37F	1998	Supertravel, Speke, 2006
8292	u	T438EBD	Dennis Dart SLF 10.7m	Plaxton Pointer 2	N40F	1999	Supertravel, Speke, 2006
8293	HM	NK54PHV	Volvo B6BLE	Plaxton Concept	N40F	2005	Northumbria MC., 2007

8294-8309 — Optare Versa V1110 — Optare — N39F — 2009

8294	GD	NK09FUP	8298	GD	NK09FUW	8302	SD	NK09FVC	8306	SD	NK09FVG
8295	GD	NK09FUT	8299	GD	NK09FUY	8303	SD	NK09FVD	8307	SD	NK09FVH
8296	GD	NK09FUU	8300	GD	NK09FVA	8304	SD	NK09FVE	8308	SD	NK09FVJ
8297	GD	NK09FUV	8301	GD	NK09FVB	8305	SD	NK09FVF	8309	SD	NK09FVL

8310-8318   Optare Versa V1110   Optare   N39F   2010

8310	SR	NK10GNY	8313	SR	NK10GOC	8315	SR	NK10GOH	8317	SR	NK10GOP
8311	SR	NK10GNZ	8314	SR	NK10GOE	8316	SR	NK10GOJ	8318	SR	NK10GOU
8312	SR	NK10GOA									

8319-8338   Optare Versa V1110   Optare   N38F   2011

8319	SD	NK11FXB	8324	SD	NK11FXG	8329	SD	NK11HDN	8334	GD	NK11HJE
8320	SD	NK11FXC	8325	SD	NK11FXH	8330	GD	NK11HDO	8335	GD	NK11HJF
8321	SD	NK11FXD	8326	SD	NK11GWX	8331	GD	NK11HJX	8336	GD	NK11HJG
8322	SD	NK11FXE	8327	SD	NK11GWY	8332	GD	NK11HJC	8337	GD	NK11HJP
8323	SD	NK11FXF	8328	SD	NK11HBC	8333	GD	NK11HJV	8338	GD	NK11HJT

Ancillary vehicles:

7060	t	N760RCU	Volvo B10M-62	Plaxton Expressliner II	TV	1996
7076	t	YSU876	Volvo B10M-60	Plaxton Expressliner II	TV	1997
7077	t	S977ABR	Volvo B10M-62	Plaxton Expressliner II	TV	1998
7078	t	S978ABR	Volvo B10M-62	Plaxton Expressliner II	TV	1998
7079	t	S979ABR	Volvo B10M-62	Plaxton Expressliner II	TV	1998
7080	t	Y808MFT	Volvo B10M-62	Plaxton Paragon	TV	2001
7082	t	Y782MFT	Volvo B10M-62	Plaxton Paragon	TV	2001

Previous registrations:

574CPT	FJ61CGD		N760RCU	N760RCU, CU6860
JCN822	FJ61GZC		NA52RMZ	FCU190

Depots and allocations:

Chester-le-Street (Picktree Lane) - CS

DAF SB220	4862	4864	4865	4866	4894	4895	4983	4984
	4985	4896	4987	4988				
Volvo B10BLE	4850	4851	4852	4853	4854	4855	4896	4905
Scania L94	4926	4927	4928	4929	4930	4931		
Volvo B12M	7087							
Volvo B12B	7090	7091	7092	7093				
Scania K340	7094	7095	7096	7097	7098	7099	7100	7102
Volvo B9R	7103	7104						
Olympian	3897	3904	3916	3917	3918			
Trident	3803	3804	3859	3868	3869	3872	3873	3877
	3878	3879	3885	3887	3888	3889		
Volvo B7TL	3962	3965	3966	3968	3969	3972	3973	3974
	3975	3977	3978	3980	3982	3983	6008	6009
	6010	6016	6018	6019	6020	6022	6025	6026
	6028	6030	6033	6036	6038	6039	6042	

Consett (Delves Lane) - CT

Dart	515	516	518	521	532	533	534	544
	545	546	618	619				

Crook (Prospect Road) - CK

Dart	571	572					
Scania L94	5229	5230	5231	5232	5233		
Volvo B7R	6021	6024	6034	6035	6037	6040	6041

Gateshead (Sunderland Road) - GD

Dart	8217	8218	8219	8220	8225	8229	8230	
SB120	8261	8262	8263	8264	8265	8266		
Versa	8294	8295	8296	8297	8298	8299	8300	8301
	8330	8331	8332	8333	8334	8335	8336	8337
	8338							

Volvo B10BLE	4837	4838	4839	4840	4841	4842	4843	4844
	4845	4846	4904	4606	4907	4908	4909	4912
	4913	4914	4915	4916	4917	4918	4919	4920
	4921	4924	4925	5166	5167	5168	5169	5170
	5171							
Mercedes-Benz O530G	5339	5340	5341	5342	5343	5344	5345	5346
	5347	5348	5349	5350	5351	5352	5353	5354
	5355	5356						
Scania	4941	4949	4967	5218	5219	5220	5221	5222
	5223	5224	5225	5226	5227			
Olympian	3811	3812	3813	3814	3825	3826	3827	3833
Trident	3862	3871	3872					
Volvo B7TL	3963	3964						
Volvo B9TL	6043	6044	6045	6046	6047	6048		

Gateshead (Saltmeadows Road) - SR

Solo	625	626	627	631	632	633	634	
Dart	512	563	564	8201	8202	8204	8205	8219
	8220	8223	8226	8227	8242			
Versa	8310	8311	8312	8313	8314	8315	8316	8317
	8318							

Hexham (Tyne Green Road) - HM

Dart	513	555	556	557	558	559	560	561
	8228							
Volvo B6LE	8293							
SB220	4867							
Citaro	5318	5319	5328	5329	5330	5332		

Percy Main (Rothbury Terrace) - PM

Dart	504	505	514	517	548	549	550	551
	553	554	562	8206	8207	8208	8209	8210
	8211	8212	8213	8214	8215	8216	8222	8223
	8226	8227	8238	8239	8240	8241	8276	8277
	8278	8279	8285	8286	8287			
Volvo B10BLE	4911							
Scania L94	4944	4945	4946	4947	4948			
Scania OmniCity	5251	5252	5253	5254	5255	5256	5257	5258
	5259	5260	5262	5263	5264	5265	5266	5267
	5268	5269	5270	5271	5272			
Citaro	5331	5333	5334	5335	5336	5337	5338	
Olympian	3815	3816	3817	3818	3819	3820	3821	3822
	3823	3831						
Trident	3858	3866	3867	3870	3880	3890	3891	

Peterlee (Cook Way) - PE

Dart	501	502	503	510	519	520	522	535
	536	537	538	539	540	541	543	573
	574							

Stanley (High Street) - SY

Dart	8158							
Volvo B10BLE	4847	4848	4849	4897	4898	4899	4900	4901
	4902	4903						
Scania OmniCity	5234	5235	5236	5237	5238	5239	5240	5241
	5242	5243	5244	5245	5246	5247	5248	5249
	5250	5261	5273	5274				
Mercedes-Benz Citaro	5284	5285	5286	5287	5288	5289	5290	5291
	5292	5293	5294	5295	5296	5297		
Volvo B7R	6012	6014	6015	6017	6031			
Olympian	3824	3828	3829	3906	3910	3914	3915	3925
	3926	3927	3931	3939	3940			
Trident	3801	3802	3875	3876				

Sunderland (Deptford Terrace) - SD

Optare Solo	628	629	630	635	636			
Dart	542	547	565	603	604	605	606	8172
	8173	8221	8224	8231	8232	8233	8234	8235
	8236	8237	8281	8289				
SB120	8243	8244	8245	8246	8258	8259	8260	8267
	8268	8269	8270	8271	8272	8273		
Optare Versa	8302	8303	8304	8305	8306	8307	8308	8309
	8319	8320	8321	8322	8323	8324	8325	8326
	8327	8328	8329					
Scania	4932	4933	4934	4935	4936	4937	4942	4943
	4954	4955	4968	4969	4970	4971	4972	4973
	4974	4975	4976	4989	4990	4991	4992	5201
	5202	5203	5204	5205	5206	5207	5208	5209
	5210	5211	5212	5213	5214	5215	5216	5217
Mercedes Citaro	5283	5298	5299	5300	5301	5302	5303	5304
	5305	5306	5307	5308	5309	5320	5321	5322
	5323	5324	5325	5326	5327			
Olympian	3932	3936	3937	3938				
Trident	3860	3861	3863	3886				
Volvo B7TL	3967	3970	3971	3976	3979	3981		

Washington (Industrial Road) - WA

Dart	506	523	524	525	526	527	528	529
	530	531	566	567	568	569	570	8222
DAF SB120	8247	8248	8249	8250	8251	8252	8253	8254
	8255	8260						
DAF SB220	4825							
Scania	4938	4940	4956	4957	4958	4959	4960	4961
	4962	4963	4964	4965	4966	5228		
Mercedes Citaro	5275	5276	5277	5278	5279	5280	5281	5282
Olympian	3830							
Volvo B7TL	3943	6011	6013	6029	6032			
Volvo B9TL	6001	6002	6003	6004	6005	6006	6007	6049
	6050	6051	6052	6063	6054	6055		

Winlaton (Cromwell Place) - WI

SB220	4820	4821	4822	4823	4824	4863		
Volvo B10BLE	4910	4922	4923	5144	5145	5146	5147	5148
	5149	5150	5151	5152	5153	5154	5155	5156
	5157	5158	5159	5160	5161	5162	5163	5164
	5165							
Mercedes Citaro	5310	5311	5312	5313	5314	5315	5316	5317
Volvo B7RLE	4978	4979	4980	4981	4982			
Olympian	3832	3919	3920	3921	3922	3923	3924	
Trident	3874							
Volvo B7TL	3941	3942	6023	6027				

Unallocated or stored - u

Remainder

OXFORD BUS COMPANY

The City of Oxford Motor Services Ltd, Cowley House, Watlington Road, Oxford, OX4 6GA

Thames Travel (Wallingford) Ltd., Lester Way, Hithercroft Road, Wallingford, OX10 9TD

Carousel Buses Ltd, Unit 2, Hughenden Avenue, High Wycombe, Bucks, HP13 5SG

The Oxford company can trace its roots back to 1881 as the operator of horse tramways in the city. Attempts to electrify the system did not succeed, and after a short period of competition with buses operated by William Morris (later Lord Nuffield) motor buses were introduced in 1913. Through an agreement with Oxford City Council, the company was the only operator of local bus services in the city, although it expanded into other areas during the 1930s to cover an operating territory of approximately thirty kilometres radius of Oxford. In the 1940s longer distance services were introduced to Newbury, Stratford and Swindon.

The ownership of the company was changing, too. It was owned by the National Electric Company (and the Great Western Railway bought an interest in 1930), until 1931 when BET took over NEC. It remained in BET ownership until the creation of the National Bus Company in 1969. The company was not directly involved in express work until after the formation of NBC. It then took over the Oxford-based services of Thames Valley to London, Southsea and Worcester. In the 1973, the company began to work closely with local authorities, including operation of the UK's first permanent Park & Ride service.

In 1984, the company was split into two: The City of Oxford Motor Services took Oxford City, local services to the east of Oxford and the former express operations, whilst a new company, South Midland, took over the remaining rural routes. Both companies were sold to their respective management teams under NBC privatisation, with Oxford becoming part of the Go-Ahead Group in 1994.

Since 1994, the company has been at the forefront of innovation and has established a network of high frequency services in the Oxford and Abingdon area operated by environmentally friendly vehicles. It also runs express services to Gatwick and Heathrow airports and to central London. In 2011 and 2012, Go-Ahead expanded in the Thames Valley with the acquisition of Thames Travel of Wallingford in south Oxfordshire and Carousel Buses of High Wycombe in south Buckinghamshire and these were placed in the care of the Oxford business, although retaining their legal status and identities. A common fleet numbering system is used across all three companies.

During the last year the Oxford Bus Company has expanded to encompass the operations of Thames Travel and Carousel's services from High Wycombe. The express coach network has also been upgraded. Seen at Marble Arch is 84, DB07OXF, a Plaxton Panther-bodied Volvo which carries route X90 livery. *Richard Godfrey*

1-18
Scania K360 EB4 — Plaxton Panther — C44FT — 2011

1	OX	AF61OXF	6	OX	FF61OXF	11	OX	LF61OXF	15	OX	RF61OXF
2	OX	BF61OXF	7	OX	GF61OXF	12	OX	MF61OXF	16	OX	SF61OXF
3	OX	CF61OXF	8	OX	HF61OXF	13	OX	OF61OXF	17	OX	TF61OXF
4	OX	DF61OXF	9	OX	JF61OXF	14	OX	PF61OXF	18	OX	UF61OXF
5	OX	EF61OXF	10	OX	KF61OXF						

29-34
Volvo B12B — Jonckheere Mistral 50 — C46FT — 2002

29	w	OA02OXF	31	w	OC02OXF	33	w	OE02OXF	34	w	OF02OXF
30	w	OB02OXF	32	w	OD02OXF						

35-41
Scania K114EB4 — Irizar Century 12.35 — C46FT — 2003

35	w	J1OXF	37	w	L1OXF	39	w	N1OXF	41	w	R1OXF
36	w	K1OXF	38	w	M1OXF	40	w	P1OXF			

42-46
Scania K114EB4 — Irizar Century 12.35 — C46FT — 2004

42	w	AF53OXF	44	w	CF53OXF	45	w	DF53OXF	46	w	EF53OXF
43	w	BF53OXF									

51-90
Volvo B12B — Plaxton Panther — C44FT — 2007

51	OX	AB07OXF	84	OX	DB07OXF	87	OX	GB07OXF	89	OX	JB07OXF
52	OX	BB07OXF	85	OX	EB07OXF	88	OX	HB07OXF	90	OX	KB07OXF
83	OX	CB07OXF	86	OX	FB07OXF						

91-99
Volvo B12B — Plaxton Panther — C44FT — 2008

91	OX	AA08OXF	94	OX	DD08OXF	96	OX	FF08OXF	98	OX	HH08OXF
92	OX	BB08OXF	95	OX	EE08OXF	97	OX	GG08OXF	99	OX	JJ08OXF
93	OX	CC08OXF									

Oxford boasts one of the more environmentally-friendly bus services with both principal operators selecting modern hybrid buses. The Oxford Bus Company now operates seventeen of the BAE Systems-powered Enviro 400 double-decks on its Park & Ride services. Illustrating the model is the first of the batch 301, HY11BRD, seen in the city. *Dave Heath*

101-120
Dennis Trident 10.5m — Alexander ALX400 — N47/24D* — 1999 — *109 is N47/27F

101	OX	T101DBW	106	OX	T106DBW	113	OX	T113DBW	117	OX	T117DBW
102	OX	T102DBW	108	OX	T108DBW	114	OX	T114DBW	118	OX	T118DBW
103	OX	T103DBW	109	TT	T109DBW	115	OX	T115DBW	119	OX	T119DBW
104	OX	T104DBW	110	OX	T110DBW	116	OX	T116DBW	120	OX	T120DBW
105	OX	T105DBW	111	OX	T111DBW						

201-211
Scania N230 UD — ADL Enviro 400 — N51/29F — 2009

201	OX	AF09OXF	204	OX	DF09OXF	207	OX	GF09OXF	210	OX	KF09OXF
202	OX	BF09OXF	205	OX	EF09OXF	208	OX	HF09OXF	211	OX	OF09OXF
203	OX	CF09OXF	206	OX	FF09OXF	209	OX	JF09OXF			

212-231
Scania N230 UD — ADL Enviro 400 — N51/29F — 2010

212	OX	AF10OXF	217	OX	FF10OXF	222	OX	LF10OXF	227	OX	SF10OXF
213	OX	BF10OXF	218	OX	GF10OXF	223	OX	MF10OXF	228	OX	TF10OXF
214	OX	CF10OXF	219	OX	HF10OXF	224	OX	OF10OXF	229	OX	UF10OXF
215	OX	DF10OXF	220	OX	JF10OXF	225	OX	PF10OXF	230	OX	VF10OXF
216	OX	EF10OXF	221	OX	KF10OXF	226	OX	RF10OXF	231	OX	WF10OXF

301-317
ADL E400H — ADL Enviro 400 — N47/30F — 2011

301	OX	HY11BRD	306	OX	HF11OXF	310	OX	HK11OXF	314	OX	HP11OXF
302	OX	HB11OXF	307	OX	HG11OXF	311	OX	HL11OXF	315	OX	HR11OXF
303	OX	HC11OXF	308	OX	HH11OXF	312	OX	HM11OXF	316	OX	HS11OXF
304	OX	HD11OXF	309	OX	HJ11OXF	313	OX	HN11OXF	317	OX	HY11OXF
305	OX	HE11OXF									

401	TT	AF53EUV	MAN 14.220		MCV Stirling		N39F	2003

402-414
MAN 14.220 — MCV Evolution — N40F — 2005-08

402	TT	AE05EUX	406	TT	AE57LYJ	409	TT	AE57LYP	412	TT	AE08DLD
403	TT	AE05EUZ	407	TT	AE57LYK	410	TT	AE57LYR	413	TT	AE08DKX
404	TT	AE56OUF	408	TT	AE57LYO	411	TT	AE57LYS	414	TT	AE08DKY
405	TT	AE57LYH									

415	CB	AF53GCX	MAN 14.220			MCV Stirling		N41F	2003	NCP, Birmingham, 2009
416	CB	AF53GCY	MAN 14.220			MCV Stirling		N39F	2003	NCP, Birmingham, 2009
417	CB	AF53GCZ	MAN 14.220			MCV Stirling		N39F	2003	NCP, Birmingham, 2009
418	CB	AE59AWH	MAN 14.240			MCV Evolution		N44F	2010	
419	CB	AE59AWJ	MAN 14.240			MCV Evolution		N44F	2010	

420-424			MAN 14.240			ADL Enviro 200		N38F	2010	
420	CB	RX60DLY	**422**	CB	RX60DME	**423**	CB	RX60DMF	**424**	CB RX60FKF
421	CB	RX60DLZ								

451-454			Scania N94UB			East Lancs Esteem		N31F	2006	
451	TT	PF06ENL	**452**	TT	PF06ENM	**453**	TT	PF06ENN	**454**	TT PF06ENO

471	u	C1WYC	Irisbus Agoraline			Irisbus		N41F	2006	
472	u	C2WYC	Irisbus Agoraline			Irisbus		N41F	2006	
473	u	C3WYC	Irisbus Agoraline			Irisbus		N41F	2006	
501	TT	OU04FMV	TransBus Dart 8.8m			TransBus Mini Pointer		N29F	2004	

502-508			ADL Dart 4 8.9m			ADL Enviro 200		N29F	2007	
502	TT	OU57FGV	**504**	TT	OU57FGZ	**506**	TT	SN10CCX	**508**	TT SN10CCZ
503	TT	OU57FGX	**505**	TT	OU57FHA	**507**	TT	SN10CCY		

521	CB	CB54BUS	VDL Bus SB120			Wrightbus Cadet 2		N30F	2005	
551	TT	AJ58PZS	ADL Dart 4 8.9m			MCV Evolution		N29F	2008	
552	TT	OU57FKB	ADL Dart 4 8.9m			ADL Enviro 200		N29F	2007	
553	TT	AE59AWM	ADL Dart 4 8.9m			MCV Evolution		N29F	2009	

701-708			Optare Solo M880			Optare		N29F	2010	
701	TT	YJ10MFA	**703**	WA	YJ10MFF	**705**	WA	YJ10MFN	**707**	WA YJ10MFP
702	TT	YJ10MFE	**704**	WA	YJ10MFK	**706**	WA	YJ10MFO	**708**	WA YJ10MFU

709	TT	MX08MYV	Optare Solo M880			Optare		N29F	2008	Go South Coast, 2012
710	TT	MX08MYY	Optare Solo M880			Optare		N29F	2008	Go South Coast, 2012
711	TT	MX58AAF	Optare Solo M950			Optare		N33F	2008	Go South Coast, 2012
712	TT	MX58AAJ	Optare Solo M950			Optare		N33F	2008	Go South Coast, 2012
713	TT	MX58AAN	Optare Solo M950			Optare		N33F	2008	Go South Coast, 2012
751	CB	YX07HNO	Enterprise Plasma EB01			Plaxton Primo		N28F	2007	Rotala, Birmingham, 2011
752	CB	YX07HPJ	Enterprise Plasma EB01			Plaxton Primo		N28F	2007	Rotala, Birmingham, 2011
753	CB	RX07BNF	Enterprise Plasma EB01			Plaxton Primo		N28F	2007	

Beaconsfield is the location for this view of 421, RX60DLZ, a MAN 14.240 with an Alexander Dennis Enviro 200 body. About fifty buses are operated under the Carousel brand in the Wycombe area with services extending to Heathrow Airport, Uxbridge, Chesham and Watford. *Richard Godfrey*

Air-conditioned Mercedes-Benz Citaro buses are used on several of the key routes into Oxford with fifty of the type now operated. From the 2008 intake 865, FF57OXF is seen with lettering for the service from Abingdon to the John Radcliffe Hospital. *Richard Godfrey*

801-809

Optare Tempo X1260 · Optare · N47F · 2007 · Go-South Coast, 2012

801	CB	YJ56FXW	804	CB	YJ56WUD	806	CB	YJ56WVS	808	CB	YJ56WVU
802	CB	YJ56WUB	805	TT	YJ56WUE	807	CB	YJ56WVT	809	CB	YJ56WVV
803	CB	YJ56WUC									

822-827

Mercedes-Benz Citaro 0530 · Mercedes-Benz · N35D · 2002

| 822 | OX | MA52OXF | 824 | OX | MC52OXF | 826 | OX | ME52OXF | 827 | OX | MF52OXF |
| 823 | OX | MB52OXF | | | | | | | | | |

828-838

Mercedes-Benz Citaro 0530 · Mercedes-Benz · N42F · 2003

828	OX	X28OXF	831	OX	X31OXF	834	OX	X4OXF	837	OX	X7OXF
829	OX	X29OXF	832	OX	X2OXF	835	OX	X5OXF	838	OX	X8OXF
830	OX	X13OXF	833	OX	X3OXF	836	OX	X6OXF			

839-848

Mercedes-Benz Citaro 0530 · Mercedes-Benz · N37D · 2005

839	OX	AF55OXF	842	OX	DF55OXF	845	OX	GF55OXF	847	OX	JF55OXF
840	OX	BF55OXF	843	OX	EF55OXF	846	OX	HF55OXF	848	OX	KF55OXF
841	OX	CF55OXF	844	OX	FF55OXF						

849-859

Mercedes-Benz Citaro 0530 · Mercedes-Benz · N42F · 2006

849	OX	LF56OXF	852	TT	PF56OXF	855	OX	TF56OXF	858	OX	WF56OXF
850	OX	MF56OXF	853	TT	RF56OXF	856	OX	UF56OXF	859	OX	YF56OXF
851	TT	OF56OXF	854	TT	SF56OXF	857	OX	VF56OXF			

860-870

Mercedes-Benz Citaro 0530 · Mercedes-Benz · N40F · 2008

860	OX	AF57OXF	863	OX	DF57OXF	866	OX	GF57OXF	869	OX	KF57OXF
861	OX	BF57OXF	864	OX	EF57OXF	867	OX	HF57OXF	870	OX	LF57OXF
862	OX	CF57OXF	865	OX	FF57OXF	868	OX	JF57OXF			

| 871 | CB | CB51BUS | Mercedes-Benz Citaro 0530 | Mercedes-Benz | N42F | 2003 |
| 872 | CB | CB53BUS | Mercedes-Benz Citaro 0530 | Mercedes-Benz | N42F | 2003 |

873	CB	AE61EWO	Mercedes-Benz Touro OC500	MCV Evolution	N43F	2012	
874	CB	AE61EWP	Mercedes-Benz Touro OC500	MCV Evolution	N43F	2012	
875	CB	AE61EWR	Mercedes-Benz Touro OC500	MCV Evolution	N43F	2012	
900	OX	SN60BXW	ADL E400H	ADL Enviro 400	N45/31F	2010	
911	TT	OU54PGZ	Scania OmniDekka N94UD	East Lancs	N47/33F	2005	
912	TT	OU08HGM	Scania OmniCity N230 UD	Scania	NC45/30F	2008	
913	TT	OU08HGN	Scania OmniCity N230 UD	Scania	NC45/30F	2008	
914	TT	OU08HGO	Scania OmniCity N230 UD	Scania	NC45/30F	2008	
915	TT	T806RFG	Dennis Trident 10.5m	East Lancs	N47/31F	1999	Brighton & Hove, 2011
916	TT	T807RFG	Dennis Trident 10.5m	East Lancs	N47/31F	1999	Brighton & Hove, 2011
917	TT	T809RFG	Dennis Trident 10.5m	East Lancs	N47/31F	1999	Brighton & Hove, 2011

918-922			Volvo B7TL	East Lancs Vyking	N45/23D	2002	Go-Ahead London, 2009
918	CB	PN02XBZ	**920**	CB	PN02XCK	**921**	CB	PN02XCS	**922**	CB	PN02XCT
919	CB	PN02XCA					

923	CB	G530VBB	Leyland Olympian ON2R50C13Z4	Northern Counties	B47/27D	1990	Arriva London, 2006
924	CB	G534VBB	Leyland Olympian ON2R50C13Z4	Northern Counties	B47/27D	1990	Arriva London, 2006
925	CB	H554GKX	Leyland Olympian ON2R50C13Z4	Leyland	B47/31F	1991	Armchair, 2003
926	CB	H556GKX	Leyland Olympian ON2R50C13Z4	Leyland	B47/31F	1991	Armchair, 2003
927	CB	H563GKX	Leyland Olympian ON2R50C13Z4	Leyland	B47/31F	1991	Armchair, 2002
928	CB	R267LGH	Volvo Olympian	Northern Counties Palatine	B47/31F	1997	Go-Ahead North East, 2012
929	CB	R270LGH	Volvo Olympian	Northern Counties Palatine	B47/31F	1997	Go-Ahead North East, 2012
930	TT	R279LGH	Volvo Olympian	Northern Counties Palatine	B47/31F	1997	Go-Ahead North East, 2012
931	CB	R280LGH	Volvo Olympian	Northern Counties Palatine	B47/31F	1997	Go-Ahead North East, 2012

Ancillary vehicles:

961	OX	V284SBW	Volvo B10M-62	Plaxton Excalibur	TV	1999	
962	OX	K119BUD	Volvo B10B	Northern Counties Paladin	TV	1993	London General, 1997
963	OX	K120BUD	Volvo B10B	Northern Counties Paladin	TV	1993	London General, 1997
964	OX	R225HCD	Volvo B10BLE	Wright Renown	N39D	1998	Brighton & Hove, 2009-10
965	OX	R218HCD	Volvo B10BLE	Wright Renown	N39D	1998	Brighton & Hove, 2009-10
976	TT	R976FNW	DAF SB220	Plaxton Prestige	N30D		

Previous registrations:

OU04FMV	SN04EFW		
		V284SBW	V16OXF

Depots and allocations:

High Wycombe (Hughenden Avenue) - CB

MAN 14.220	415	416	417				
MAN 14.240	418	419	420	421	422	423	424
VDL SB120	521						
Plaxton Primo	751	752	753				
Optare Tempo	801	802	803	804	806	807	808	809
Citaro	871	872					
Mercedes-Benz OC500	873	874	875				
Olympian	923	924	928	929	931		
Volvo B7TL	918	919	920	921	922		

Oxford (Cowley House, Watlington Road) - OX

Citaro O530	822	823	824	826	827	828	829	830
	831	832	833	834	835	836	837	838
	839	840	841	842	843	844	845	846
	847	848	849	850	855	856	857	858
	859	860	861	862	863	864	865	866
	867	868	869	870				
Volvo B12B coach	51	52	83	84	85	86	87	88
	89	90	91	92	93	94	95	96
	97	98	99					
Scania coach	1	2	3	4	5	6	7	8
	9	10	11	12	13	14	15	16
	17	18	31	32	33	34	35	36
	37	38	39	40	41			

Since the last edition of this Handbook, Thames Travel vehicles have been re-numbered into the main Oxford Bus Company fleet. Seen in Reading is 452, PF06ENM, a Scania N94 with East Lancs Esteem bodywork. *Dave Heath*

Trident	101	102	103	104	105	106	108	110
	111	113	114	115	116	117	118	119
	120							
Scania dd	201	202	203	204	205	206	207	208
	209	210	211	212	213	214	215	216
	217	218	219	220	221	222	223	224
	225	226	227	228	229	230	231	
Enviro 400H	301	302	303	304	305	306	307	308
	309	310	311	312	313	314	315	316
	317	900						
Ancillary	*961*	*962*	*963*	*964*	*965*			

Wallingford (Lester Way) - TT

Outstation: Elms Farm, Grove, Wantage; Weller Way, Finchampstead, Wokingham and Lovelace Road, Bracknell

MAN 14.220	401	402	403	404	405	406	407	408
	409	410	411	412	413	414		
Scania OmniTown	451	452	453	454				
ADL Dart	501	502	503	504	505	506	507	508
	551	552	553					
Optare Solo	701	702	703	704	705	706	707	708
	709	710	711	712	713			
Optare Tempo	805							
Citaro	851	852	853	854				
Olympian	930							
Scania DD	911	912	913	914				
Trident	109	915	916	917				
Ancillary	*976*							

KONECTBUS

Konectbus Ltd, 7 John Goshawk Road, Dereham, NR19 1SY

Konectbus was set up by two former First Eastern Counties managers and began operations in August 1999 in the village of Saham Toney near Watton in Norfolk, initially with four coaches providing a mixture of market day local bus services, school contracts and private hire. Over the next few years the attention was focused on local bus service operation and as well as the introduction of commercial services, tendered work was also undertaken for Norfolk County Council.

By 2003 expansion of the local bus network meant that the original rented premises were becoming increasingly unsuitable, so a new site was purchased in the town of Dereham sixteen kilometres away and a new depot, which would allow for further growth in fleet size, opened in January 2004.

In 2005 the award of contracts to operate buses from two of Norwich's Park & Ride sites (Costessey and Thickthorn) saw the arrival of the first double deckers in the fleet and these contracts were re-awarded in 2010 along with a further Park and Ride site at Harford.

Investment in the fleet and driver training has also been an important part of the growth of the business. Coupled with attention to detail throughout the organisation and a quality culture this has helped achieve ever-increasing patronage which has seen most routes grow from two-hourly to hourly six days a week and more recently the introduction of Sunday services on routes that had not had them since the 1970s. The network consists of inter-urban and connecting routes to the west of Norwich, routes in the city itself along with Norwich Park & Ride.

The first buses in the fleet were Leyland Nationals followed by mainly new and acquired Optare products for single deck requirements and double deck VDL/Wrightbus and ADL Enviro 400s. The fleet currently stands at forty-four buses, all of which are low-floor with the exception of two Leyland Olympians used on school services and a special event vehicle, a Leyland National, which occasionally acts as a 'Thunderbird' vehicle retained as a reminder of the company's early years. Konectbus became part of Go-Ahead in March 2010.

216-229			Optare Excel L1150			Optare			N45F*	2000	Trent Buses, 2004-07
											*219 is N42F, 229 is N44F
216	DM	W216PRB	218	DM	W218PRB	219	DM	W219PRB	229	DM	X229WRA
217	DM	W217PRB									

300	DM	MX08UZT	Optare Versa V1100			Optare			N37F	2008	
301	DM	MX08UZU	Optare Versa V1100			Optare			N37F	2008	

400-413			Optare Tempo X1200			Optare			N42F*	2005-09	*409-13 are N43F
400	DM	MX05EKW	404	DM	MX05ELH	408	DM	YJ56WVB	411	DM	MX58ABV
401	DM	MX05EKY	405	DM	MX05ELJ	409	DM	YJ57EGY	412	DM	YJ09MHY
402	DM	MX05EKZ	406	DM	MX06YXU	410	DM	YJ57EGX	413	DM	YJ09MHZ
403	DM	MX05ELC	407	DM	YJ56WVA						

Konectbus was set up by two former First Eastern Counties managers and began operations in August 1999 in the Norfolk village of Saham Toney, initially with four coaches providing a mixture of market day local bus services, school contracts and private hire. Many early examples have been replaced with modern vehicles. One of fourteen Optare Tempo buses, 413, YJ09MHZ, is seen in Norwich. *Mark Doggett*

500-504

				VDL Bus DB250		Wrightbus Pulsar Gemini		N41/24F	2005	
500	DM	YJ05PXA	**502**	DM	YJ05PXC	**503**	DM	YJ05PXD	**504**	DM	YJ05PXE
501	DM	YJ05PXB								

600-609

				ADL Trident 2		ADL Enviro 400		N47/33F	2010-11	
600	DM	SN10CFD	**603**	DM	SN10CFG	**606**	DM	SN61CZW	**608**	DM	SN61CZY
601	DM	SN10CFE	**604**	DM	SN10CEX	**607**	DM	SN61CZX	**609**	DM	SN61CZZ
602	DM	SN10CFF	**605**	DM	SN61CZV					

610-614

				ADL E40D		ADL Enviro 400		N47/33F	2012	
610	DM	SN62AVG	**612**	DM	SN62AVR	**613**	DM	SN62AVY	**614**	DM	SN62AVZ
611	DM	SN62AVO								

701	DM	V301LGC	Volvo B7TL	10m		Plaxton President		N41/21D	2000	Go-Ahead London, 2011
703	DM	V303LGC	Volvo B7TL	10m		Plaxton President		N41/21D	2000	Go-Ahead London, 2011
707	DM	V307LGC	Volvo B7TL	10m		Plaxton President		N41/21D	2000	Go-Ahead London, 2011
725	DM	W825NNJ	Dennis Trident			East Lancs Lolyne		N47/31F	2000	Brighton & Hove, 2012

800-807

				Mercedes-Benz Citaro O530G		Mercedes-Benz		AN47T	2008	Go-Ahead London, 2011
800	DM	BD57WDA	**802**	DM	BD57WCZ	**804**	DM	BD57UYL	**806**	DM	BX54UDV
801	DM	BD57WCY	**803**	DM	BD57UYK	**805**	DM	BX54UDK	**807**	DM	BX54UEA

900	DM	VX51RHZ	Optare Solo M920			Optare		N33F	2002	
901	DM	VX51RJZ	Optare Solo M920			Optare		N33F	2002	

Special event vehicle:

152	DM	UFX852S	Leyland National 11351A/1R					B49F	1977	Wilts & Dorset, 2010

Seen leaving the city for a return trip to Dereham is Alexander Dennis Enviro 400 number 609, SN61CZZ. A further five of the latest variant of the E400 are expected shortly. *Mark Lyons*

Allocations:

Dereham (John Goshawk Road) - DM

Solo	900	901					
Optare Versa	300	301					
Optare Excel	216	217	218	219	229		
Optare Tempo	400	401	402	403	404	405	406	407
	408	409	410	411	412	413	
Mercedes-Benz Citaro	800	801	802	803	804	805	806	807
VDL DB250	500	501	502	503	504		
Volvo B7TL	701	703	707				
Trident	725						
Enviro 400	600	601	602	603	604	605	606	607
	608	609	610	611	612	613	614	

HEDINGHAM

Hedingham & District Omnibuses Ltd, Wethersfield Road, Sible Hedingham, Halstead, CO9 3LB

L148	TY	WPH135Y	Leyland Tiger TRCTL11/2R	East Lancs EL2000 (1994)	B55F	1982	Kentish Bus, 1988
L160	TY	H160HJN	Leyland Olympian ONCL10/1RZ	Alexander RL	B47/32F	1990	
L198	KN	K198EVW	Dennis Dart 9.8m	Alexander Dash	B43F	1992	
L207	CN	L207RNO	Volvo B6 9.9m	Alexander Dash	B40F	1994	
L208	KN	L208RNO	Volvo B6 9.9m	Alexander Dash	B40F	1994	
L210	TY	M210VEV	Dennis Dart 9m	Plaxton Pointer	B34F	1994	

Hedingham Omnibuses is an Essex bus company founded shortly after the First World War by Aubrey Ernest Letch and the company has grown through a mixture of organic growth and purchases of other companies ever since. Now itself acquired by Go-Ahead it currently retains its autonomy. Illustrating the familiar livery is Alexander Dennis Dart L339, EU05AUR. *Mark Doggett*

L211	HD	M212WHJ	Dennis Lance SLF	Wright Pathfinder 320	N40F	1995	
L212	HD	M211WHJ	Dennis Lance SLF	Wright Pathfinder 320	N40F	1995	
L241	CN	N241EWC	Dennis Dart 9m	Plaxton Pointer	B35F	1996	
L243	HD	M262KWK	Volvo B6 9.9m	Alexander Dash	B40F	1995	Volvo demonstrator, 1996
L244	CN	M988NAA	Volvo B10M-62	Plaxton Première 320	C53F	1995	Excelsior, Bournemouth, '96
L258	CN	M261KWK	Volvo B6 9.9m	Plaxton Pointer	B40F	1995	Volvo demonstrator, 1997
L282	KN	M571XKY	Volvo B10M-62	Plaxton Première 350	C53F	1995	A&R International, 1997
L286	CN	P530CLJ	Volvo B10M-62	Plaxton Première 320	C53F	1996	Excelsior, Bournemouth, '98
L290	CN	S290TVW	Volvo B10M-62	Plaxton Première 320	C53F	1998	
L291	KN	S291TVW	Volvo B10M-62	Plaxton Première 320	C53F	1998	
L295	CN	N664THO	Volvo B10M-62	Plaxton Première 320	C53F	1996	Excelsior, Bournemouth, '98
L296	w	M441CVG	Volvo B6 9.9m	Plaxton Pointer	B40F	1995	Lamberts, Beccles, 1999
L299	CN	P395AAA	Volvo B10M-62	Plaxton Première 320	C53F	1997	Excelsior, Bournemouth, '99
L300	TY	S300XHK	Volvo Olympian	Alexander RL	B51/36F	1999	
L301	HD	S376MVP	Volvo B10BLE	Alexander ALX300	N44F	1998	Volvo demonstrator, 1999
L309	CN	R453FWT	Volvo B10M-62	Plaxton Première 350	C53F	1998	Wallace Arnold, Leeds, '00
L312	TY	W312CJN	Dennis Dart SLF	Plaxton Pointer 2	N40F	2000	
L325	HD	EX02RYR	Dennis Dart SLF	Plaxton Pointer MPD	N29F	2002	
L326	HD	EJ02KYY	Dennis Dart SLF	Plaxton Pointer MPD	N29F	2002	
L328	HD	EU03BZK	TransBus Dart	TransBus Pointer	N37F	2003	
L330	HD	EU53MVZ	Volvo B7TL	TransBus President	N47/28F	2003	
L333	CN	R259LGH	Volvo Olympian	Northern Counties Palatine	B47/31F	1997	London General, 2003
L334	KN	V250BNV	Dennis Dart SLF	Plaxton Pointer MPD	N29F	1999	Zak's, Birmingham, 2004
L335	CN	PJ02RHE	Dennis Dart SLF	Plaxton Pointer 2	N39F	2002	Pete's, W Bromwich, 2004
L336	CN	N540LHG	Volvo Olympian	Northern Counties Palatine	B47/33F	1996	London General, 2004
L337	TY	R279LHG	Volvo Olympian	Northern Counties Palatine	B47/31F	1998	London General, 2004
L338	CN	EU05AUT	ADL Dart 10.1m	ADL Pointer	N34F	2005	
L339	CN	EU05AUR	ADL Dart 10.1m	ADL Pointer	N34F	2005	
L340	HD	EU05CLJ	Volvo B7RLE	Wrightbus Eclipse Urban	N43F	2005	
L342	TY	L108HHV	Dennis Dart 9m	Northern Counties Paladin	B34F	1994	Trustline, Hunsdon, 2005
L343	CN	EU55BWC	ADL Dart 10.7m	ADL Pointer	N37F	2005	
L344	TY	P104OLX	Dennis Dart SLF 9.2m	Plaxton Pointer	N31F	1997	Metroline, Harrow, 2005
L345	CN	N427JBV	Volvo Olympian	Northern Counties Palatine 2	B43/30F	1995	London General, 2006
L346	CN	EU06KCX	ADL Dart 8.8m	ADL Mini Pointer	N29F	2006	

L347	CN	W649FUM	Volvo B10M-62	Plaxton Première 350	C48FT	2000	WA Shearings, Wigan, '06
L348	CN	EU56FLR	ADL Dart 10.7m	ADL Pointer	N37F	2006	
L349	CN	EU56FLP	ADL Dart 10.7m	ADL Pointer	N37F	2006	
L350	CN	EU56FLN	ADL Dart 10.7m	ADL Pointer	N37F	2006	
L351	CN	EU56FLM	ADL Dart 10.7m	ADL Pointer	N37F	2006	
L352	TY	P494MBY	Volvo Olympian	Alexander RH	B43/30F	1996	Metroline, Harrow, 2006
L353	TY	P489MBY	Volvo Olympian	Alexander RH	B43/30F	1996	Metroline, Harrow, 2006
L354	TY	M604TTV	Volvo B10B	Alexander Strider	B51F	1995	City of Nottingham, 2006
L355	HD	EU07GVY	ADL Trident 2	ADL Enviro 400	N47/33F	2007	
L356	CN	EY57FZE	ADL Dart 4 10.7m	ADL Enviro 200	N37F	2007	
L357	CN	J838TSC	Leyland Olympian ON2R56C13Z4	Alexander RH	B51/34F	1991	Lothian Buses, 2007
L358	CN	M276UKN	Volvo Olympian	Alexander RH	B47/31F	1995	Dublin Bus, 2007
L359	CN	M273UKN	Volvo Olympian	Alexander RH	B47/31F	1995	Dublin Bus, 2007
L360	CN	M282UKN	Volvo Olympian	Alexander RH	B47/31F	1995	Dublin Bus, 2007
L361	CN	M144UKN	Volvo Olympian	Alexander RH	B47/31F	1995	Dublin Bus, 2007
L362	CN	M146UKN	Volvo Olympian	Alexander RH	B47/31F	1995	Dublin Bus, 2007
L363	CN	M294UKN	Volvo Olympian	Alexander RH	B47/31F	1995	Dublin Bus, 2007
L364	KN	K107JWJ	Volvo Olympian	Northern Counties	B47/29F	1993	Stagecoach, 2008
L365	KN	L109LHL	Volvo Olympian	Northern Counties	B47/29F	1993	Stagecoach, 2008
L366	KN	S127RLE	Volvo Olympian	Alexander RH	B47/29F	1998	Metroline, Harrow, 2008
L367	KN	K357DWJ	Leyland Olympian ON2R50C13Z4	Northern Counties	B47/29F	1992	Stagecoach, 2008
L368	TY	K508ESS	Leyland Olympian ON2R50C13Z4	Alexander RL	BC43/27F	1992	
L369	KN	K518ESS	Leyland Olympian ON2R50C13Z4	Alexander RL	BC43/27F	1992	
L370	CN	EU58JCJ	ADL Dart 4 10.7m	ADL Enviro 200	N37F	2009	
L371	TY	K510ESS	Leyland Olympian	Alexander RL	BC43/27F	1992	Stagecoach, 2009
L372	KN	R626MNU	Volvo Olympian	Northern Counties Palatine	B47/29F	1998	Arriva Midlands, 2009
L373	KN	R629MNU	Volvo Olympian	Northern Counties Palatine	B47/29F	1998	Arriva Midlands, 2009
L374	HD	R643MNU	Volvo Olympian	Northern Counties Palatine	B47/29F	1998	Arriva Midlands, 2009
L375	KN	P605CAY	Volvo Olympian	Northern Counties Palatine	B47/29F	1996	Arriva Midlands, 2009
L376	TY	P602CAY	Volvo Olympian	Northern Counties Palatine	B47/29F	1996	Arriva Midlands, 2009
L377	KN	P606CAY	Volvo Olympian	Northern Counties Palatine	B47/29F	1996	Arriva Midlands, 2009
L378	HD	P608CAY	Volvo Olympian	Northern Counties Palatine	B47/29F	1996	Arriva Midlands, 2009
L379	KN	P612CAY	Volvo Olympian	Northern Counties Palatine	B47/29F	1996	Arriva Midlands, 2009
L380	KN	EU59AFF	ADL Dart 4 8.9m	ADL Enviro 200	N29F	2009	
L381	CN	EU59AFJ	ADL Dart 4 8.9m	ADL Enviro 200	N29F	2009	
L382	CN	EU59AYM	ADL Dart 4 10.8m	ADL Enviro 200	N37F	2009	
L383	CN	EU59AYP	ADL Dart 4 10.8m	ADL Enviro 200	N37F	2009	
L384	TY	R702DNH	Leyland Olympian	Alexander RL	B51/36F	1997	Stagecoach, 2010
L385	TY	EU10AOX	ADL Dart 4 10.8m	ADL Enviro 200	N37F	2010	
L386	HD	SN10CCV	ADL Trident 2 10.5m	ADL Enviro 400	N47/33F	2010	
L387	TY	R935FNG	Optare Excell L1150	Optare	N40F	1998	Konectbus, 2012
L388	TY	S169UAL	Optare Excell L1150	Optare	N40F	1998	Konectbus, 2012
L389	TY	T789XVO	Optare Excell L1150	Optare	N40F	1998	Konectbus, 2012
L390	u	V203ENU	Optare Excell L1150	Optare	N40F	1998	Konectbus, 2012
L391	TY	V205ENU	Optare Excell L1150	Optare	N40F	1998	Konectbus, 2012

The Hedingham fleet now comprises many Volvo Olympians which displaced a large collection of Bristol VRs. One of several from Arriva Midlands is L373, R629MNU.
Mark Doggett

The latest single-deck is Enviro 200 Dart L385, EU10AOX, which is based at Tollesbury depot. It is seen working route 92 to Colchester. *Mark Doggett*

L392	HD	R227HCD	Volvo B10LE	Wright Renown	N45F	1998	Brighton & Hove, 2012
L393	HD	R229HCD	Volvo B10LE	Wright Renown	N45F	1998	Brighton & Hove, 2012
L394	TY	Y346YGU	Dennis Dart 8.8m	Plaxton Pointer MPD	N29F	2000	Brighton & Hove, 2012
L395	TY	Y347YGU	Dennis Dart 8.8m	Plaxton Pointer MPD	N29F	2000	Brighton & Hove, 2012
L396	CN	EU04BVF	TransBus Dart 10.7m	TransBus Pointer	N37F	2004	Blue Triangle, 2007
L397	CN	T801RFG	Dennis Trident 10.5m	East Lancs Lolyne	N47/32F	1999	Brighton & Hove, 2012
L398	CN	T802RFG	Dennis Trident 10.5m	East Lancs Lolyne	N47/32F	1999	Brighton & Hove, 2012
L399	u	T814RFG	Dennis Trident 10.5m	East Lancs Lolyne	N47/32F	1999	Brighton & Hove, 2012
L400	u	T817RFG	Dennis Trident 10.5m	East Lancs Lolyne	N47/32F	1999	Brighton & Hove, 2012
L401	u	W821NNJ	Dennis Trident 10.5m	East Lancs Lolyne	N47/32F	1999	Brighton & Hove, 2012
L402	u	W822NNJ	Dennis Trident 10.5m	East Lancs Lolyne	N47/32F	1999	Brighton & Hove, 2012
L403	u	W823NNJ	Dennis Trident 10.5m	East Lancs Lolyne	N47/32F	1999	Brighton & Hove, 2012
L404	CN	W828NNJ	Dennis Trident 10.5m	East Lancs Lolyne	N47/32F	1999	Brighton & Hove, 2012
L405	CN	W829NNJ	Dennis Trident 10.5m	East Lancs Lolyne	N47/32F	1999	Brighton & Hove, 2012
L406	CN	W830NNJ	Dennis Trident 10.5m	East Lancs Lolyne	N47/32F	1999	Brighton & Hove, 2012
L407	HD	Y346YGU	Dennis Dart 8.8m	Plaxton Pointer MPD	N29F	2000	Brighton & Hove, 2012

Special event vehicle:

L84	HD	RGV284N	Leyland Leopard	Willowbrook	B55F	1974

Previous registrations:

M144UKN	95D202		M988NAA	A14XEL
M146UKN	95D203		N427JBV	N427JBV, WLT527
M273UKN	95D201		N664THO	XEL158
M276UKN	95D199		P395AAA	A12XEL
M282UKN	95D200		P530CLJ	A13XEL
M294UKN	95D204		R835FNG	R400BEN

Depots and allocations:

Clacton (Stephenson Road/ Wethersfield Road) - CN

Dart	L241	L335	L346	L348	L349	L350	L351	L396
Volvo B6	L207	L258						
Volvo B10M	L244	L286	L290	L295	L299	L309	L347	
Enviro 200	L338	L339	L343	L356	L370	L381	L382	L383
Olympian	L333	L336	L337	L345	L357	L358	L359	L360
	L361	L362	L363					
Trident	L397	L398	L404	L405	L406			

Sible Hedingham (High Street) - HD

Dart	L325	L326	L328	L407
Volvo B6	L243			
Lance	L211	L212		
Volvo B10BLE	L301	L392	L393	
Volvo B7RLE	L340			
Olympian	L374	L378		
Volvo B7TL	L330			
Enviro 400	L355	L386		

Kelvedon (High Street) - KN

Dart	L198	L334						
Volvo B6	L208							
Enviro 200	L380	L385						
Volvo B10M	L282	L291						
Olympian	L364	L365	L367	L369	L372	L373	L375	L377
	L379							

Tollesbury (New Road) - TY

Dart	L210	L312	L342	L344	L394	L395		
Optare Excel	L387	L388	L389	L391				
Leyland Tiger	L148							
Volvo B10B	L354							
Olympian	L160	L300	L337	L352	L353	L368	L371	L376
	L384							

CHAMBERS

H C Chambers & Son Ltd, Meeking Road, Sudbury, CO10 2XE

C	SY	M655KVU	Volvo B10M-62	Van Hool Alizée	C49FTL	1995	Shearings, 2003
C	SY	N529LHG	Volvo Olympian	Northern Counties Palatine	B48/31F	1996	London General, 2006
C	SY	N531LHG	Volvo Olympian	Northern Counties Palatine	B48/31F	1996	London General, 2006
C	SY	N532LHG	Volvo Olympian	Northern Counties Palatine	B48/31F	1996	London General, 2006
C	SY	N465PAP	Dennis Dart 9m	Alexander Dash	BC40F	1996	Stagecoach, 2011
C	SY	P515UUG	Volvo B10B	Wright Endurance	BC47F	1997	Stagecoach, 2008
C	SY	P901RYO	Volvo Olympian	Northern Counties Palatine	B47/27F	1997	London Central, 2005
C	SY	P902RYO	Volvo Olympian	Northern Counties Palatine	B47/27F	1997	London Central, 2005
C	SY	P910RYO	Volvo Olympian	Northern Counties Palatine	B47/27F	1997	Beestons, Ipswich, 2011
C	SY	P549WGT	Volvo Olympian	Northern Counties Palatine	B47/29F	1997	London Central, 2004
C	w	P475MBY	Volvo Olympian	Alexander RH	B43/29F	1996	Metroline, Harrow, 2006
C	SY	P484MBY	Volvo Olympian	Alexander RH	B43/29F	1996	Metroline, Harrow, 2006
C	SY	P488MBY	Volvo Olympian	Alexander RH	B43/29F	1996	Metroline, Harrow, 2006
C	SY	R552LGH	Volvo Olympian	Northern Counties Palatine	B47/31F	1998	Beestons, Ipswich, 2011
C	SY	R273LGH	Volvo Olympian	Northern Counties Palatine	B47/31F	1998	Hedingham Omnibus, 2012
C	w	R112NTA	Mercedes-Benz Vario 0814	Alexander ALX100	B29F	1998	Stagecoach, 2008
C	SY	R941YOV	Volvo Olympian	Alexander RH	B47/29F	1998	UK North, Manchester, '07
C	SY	R43LHK	Volvo Olympian	Alexander RH	B47/31F	1998	Dublin Bus, 2011
C	SY	R49LHK	Volvo Olympian	Alexander RH	B47/31F	1998	Dublin Bus, 2011
C	w	R978KAR	Volvo Olympian	Alexander RH	B47/31F	1998	Dublin Bus, 2011
C	SY	R987KAR	Volvo Olympian	Alexander RH	B47/31F	1997	Dublin Bus, 2011
C	SY	R989KAR	Volvo Olympian	Alexander RH	B47/31F	1998	Dublin Bus, 2011
C	SY	S218YOO	Volvo Olympian	Alexander RH	B47/31F	1998	Dublin Bus, 2011
C	SY	S233RLH	Volvo Olympian	Alexander RH	B43/29F	1998	Metroline, Harrow, 2007
C	SY	S131RLE	Volvo Olympian	Alexander RH	B43/25D	1998	Metroline, Harrow, 2008

Chambers operates a fleet dominated by Volvo Olympians including R987KAR shown. It is expected that many of these vehicles will be displaced by low-floor buses transferred within the group. *Mark Doggett*

C	SY	BX55FYH	Mercedes-Benz Touro OC500	Mercedes-Benz	C49FT	2006	
C	SY	BX55FYJ	Mercedes-Benz Touro OC500	Mercedes-Benz	C49FT	2006	

Previous registrations:

R43LHK	98D20398		R987KAR	97D363
R49LHK	98D20401		R989KAR	98D20395
R978KAR	98D20393		S218YOO	98D20417

ANGLIAN

Anglian Bus & Coach Ltd, Beccles Business Park, Sandpit Lane, Beccles, NR34 7TH

109	RH	J127LHC	Dennis Javelin 11m	Plaxton Derwent 2	BC53F	1991	Countywide, 2001
207	RH	V227KAH	Mercedes-Benz Vario 0814	Plaxton Beaver 2	B27F	1999	
211	RH	T200CBC	Mercedes-Benz Vario 0814	Plaxton Beaver 2	B27F	1999	Coakley, Motherwell, 2002
213	BE	T400CBC	Mercedes-Benz Vario 0814	Plaxton Beaver 2	B27F	1999	Coakley, Motherwell, 2002
217	BE	V380HGG	Mercedes-Benz Vario 0814	Plaxton Beaver 2	B27F	1999	Equalstorm, 2002
218	BE	AO02LVC	Mercedes-Benz Vario 0814	Plaxton Beaver 2	B31F	2002	
221	RH	AO52LJF	Mercedes-Benz Vario 0814	Plaxton Beaver 2	B31F	2002	
300	BE	YT51EBF	Optare Solo M850	Optare	N33F	2002	Travel London, 2010
301	BE	YJ51XSK	Optare Solo M920	Optare	N33F	2001	Horsburgh, Livingston, '11
302	RH	MX53FDM	Optare Solo M920	Optare	N33F	2004	
303	BE	YJ51XSK	Optare Solo M920	Optare	N33F	2001	Horsburgh, Livingston, '11
304	RH	MX53FDO	Optare Solo M920	Optare	N33F	2004	
305	BE	MX53FDP	Optare Solo M920	Optare	N33F	2004	

Many of the buses used by Anglian were sourced from Optare, although recent arrivals have included many of the Scania OmniCity integral vehicles assembled in Poland. Several of these initially operated within Heathrow Airport including 423, YN03UVT, seen here heading for Great Yarmouth. *Mark Doggett*

306	BE	AU04JKN	Optare Solo M920	Optare	N33F	2004	
307	BE	AU54EOA	Optare Solo M780 SL	Optare	N24F	2004	
308	BE	AU54ENY	Optare Solo M780 SL	Optare	N24F	2004	
309	RH	AU07KMM	Optare Solo M950 SL	Optare	N32F	2007	
310	RH	AU07KMK	Optare Solo M950 SL	Optare	N32F	2007	
311	RH	AD57BDY	Optare Solo M950 SL	Optare	N32F	2007	
312	BE	YN57HPX	Optare Solo M950 SL	Optare	N32F	2007	
313	BE	YN57HRA	Optare Solo M950 SL	Optare	N32F	2007	
314	RH	YN57HPV	Optare Solo M950 SL	Optare	N32F	2007	
315	RH	YN57HPU	Optare Solo M950 SL	Optare	N32F	2007	
316	RH	YN57HPZ	Optare Solo M950 SL	Optare	N32F	2007	
317	RH	AD57EXA	Optare Solo M950 SL	Optare	N32F	2007	
318	BE	AU08GLY	Optare Solo M950 SL	Optare	N32F	2007	
319	BE	AU58AKK	Optare Solo M950 SL	Optare	N32F	2008	
320	BE	AU58AKN	Optare Solo M950 SL	Optare	N32F	2008	
321	BE	MX58XDB	Optare Solo M880	Optare	N32F	2008	
322	BE	MX60BWH	Wrightbus Streetlight WF	Wrightbus	N37F	2010	
323	BE	MX60BWK	Wrightbus Streetlight WF	Wrightbus	N37F	2010	
324	BE	MX60BWJ	Wrightbus Streetlight WF	Wrightbus	N37F	2010	
325	BE	MX60GXA	Wrightbus Streetlight WF	Wrightbus	N37F	2010	
326	RH	YN04LWP	Optare Solo M920	Optare	N33F	2004	Veolia, 2011
400	RH	X228WRA	Optare Excel L1180	Optare	N45F	2000	Trent-Barton, 2007
411	RH	AU08DKL	Optare Versa V1100	Optare	N38F	2008	
412	RH	AU08DKN	Optare Versa V1100	Optare	N38F	2008	
413	BE	YN07LFU	Scania OmniLink K230 UB	Scania	N45F	2007	Scania demonstrator, 2008
414	BE	YN07EZB	Scania OmniLink K230 UB	Scania	N45F	2007	Scania demonstrator, 2008
415	RH	R81EMB	Scania L113 CRL	Wight Axcess Ultralow	N42F	1997	Aintree Coachline, 2008
416	RH	R82EMB	Scania L113 CRL	Wight Axcess Ultralow	N42F	1997	Aintree Coachline, 2008
417	BE	AU58AUV	Scania OmniLink CK230 UB	Scania	N45F	2008	
419	BE	MX58KYV	Optare Versa V1100	Optare	N37F	2008	Holsworthy, Dolton, 2010

420-427			Scania OmniCity CN94UB		Scania		N42F	2003	Menzies, Heathrow, 2010
420	BE	YN03UVM	422	BE	YN03UVR	424	BE	YN03UVU	426	BE	YN03UVY
421	BE	YN03UVP	423	BE	YN03UVT	425	BE	YN03UVV	427	BE	YN03UWJ

432	BE	YJ60KGU	Optare Versa V1100		Optare		N40F	2010	
433	BE	YJ60KGV	Optare Versa V1100		Optare		N40F	2010	
434	BE	YN11LVE	Scania OmniLink K230 UB		Scania		N46F	2011	
435	BE	YN11LVF	Scania OmniLink K230 UB		Scania		N46F	2011	
436	BE	AU11EPE	Optare Versa V1070		Optare		N37F	2011	
437	BE	AU11EPF	Optare Versa V1070		Optare		N37F	2011	
438	BE	AU11ESG	Optare Versa V1070		Optare		N37F	2011	
439	BE	AN61LAN	Scania OmniLink K230 UB		Scania		N46F	2011	
440	RH	AN61BUS	Scania OmniLink K230 UB		Scania		N46F	2011	
441	RH	AU61AVK	Scania OmniLink K230 UB		Scania		N46F	2011	

442-446			Scania OmniCity CN94UB		Scania		N36F	2005	Metrobus, Crawley, 2012
442	BE	YN05HFH	**444**	BE	YN05HFF	**445**	BE	YN05HFE	**446**	BE	YN05HFG
443	BE	YN05HFJ									

502-505			Scania OmniCity CN230 UD		Scania		N47/29F	2008	
502	BE	AO57EZM	**503**	BE	AO57EZM	**504**	BE	AO57EZM	**505**	BE	AO57EZM

506	BE	P476SWC	Volvo Olympian		Alexander RH		B47/27D	1996	Dublin Bus, 2008
507	BE	P478SWC	Volvo Olympian		Alexander RH		B47/27D	1996	Dublin Bus, 2008
508	BE	X251NNO	Dennis Trident 9.9m		Alexander ALX400		B45/25F	2000	Stagecoach, 2011

509-512			Dennis Trident 10.5m		Alexander ALX400		B47/25F	1999-2001	Stagecoach, 2011
509	BE	X309NNO	**510**	BE	X386NNO	**511**	RH	X384NNO	**512**	BE	V161MEV

Previous registrations:

831HKA	B146MJU			
CSK282	E993KJF		P476SWC	96D305
HIJ6931	B152MJU		P478SWC	96D306

Depots and allocations:

Beccles (Sandpit Lane) - BE

Mercedes-Benz Vario	213	217	218					
Optare Solo	300	301	303	305	306	307	308	312
	313	318	319	320	321			
Streetlite WF	322	323	324	325				
Optare Versa	419	432	433	436	437	438		
OmniLink	413	414	417	434	435	439		
OmniCity	420	421	422	423	424	425	426	427
	442	443	444	445	446			
Olympian	506	507						
Trident	509	510	511	512				
OmniCity DD	502	503	504	505				

Rackheath (Green Lane West) - RH

Mercedes-Benz Vario	207	211	221					
Optare Solo	302	304	309	310	311	314	315	316
	317	326						
Javelin	109							
Optare Excel	400							
Optare Versa	411	412						
Scania L113	415	416						
OmniLink	440	441						

GO-AHEAD LONDON

London Central Bus Co Ltd; London General Transport Services Ltd
18 Merton High Street, London, SW19 1DN

London Central and London General are relatively new bus companies, being formed in 1989 in preparation for the privatisation of London Buses Limited. However, the origins of both companies can be traced back to one of the original pioneers of bus operations in the capital, the London General Omnibus Company Limited (LGOC).

LGOC or "General" as it was known locally, operated services throughout the capital and was absorbed into the new London Transport Executive in 1933. London Transport became synonymous with the red London bus until the bus operation was segregated in 1985, becoming London Buses Ltd and London Underground Ltd.

Upon privatisation in autumn 1994, London Central was purchased by the Go-Ahead Group. London General was initially purchased by an employee/management team led by Keith Ludeman, being subsequently acquired by the Go-Ahead Group in the summer of 1996.

London Central, London General, together with the Southeastern and Southern train companies, provide Go-Ahead with a significant presence in the capital's transport infrastructure. More recently the London companies have not only expanded through successful tendering and winning TfL contract work, but also through the acquisition of Docklands Minibuses, based in Silvertown, and Blue Triangle Buses based in Rainham.

The London bus companies account for approximately 350 million bus journeys annually on over one hundred day and night routes. The success in winning the local TfL contracts has necessitated the opening of two new bases, one at Plough Lane in Wimbledon, the other at Mandela Way off the Old Kent Road in south east London. When coupled with Metrobus, the Group's London bus operation is the largest in terms of both PVR and percentage of network (over 20%).

The first batch of Euro IV engined buses, designed with the latest development in engineering technology to reduce emissions and particulates, was delivered in 2006; by mid-2008 the company total was 99. The first Euro V EEV vehicles went into service on route 453 in February 2008; these were the first Euro V articulated buses in the country.

In line with Go-Ahead's environmental policy, the company has invested heavily in fitting CRT particulate traps and Euro II or above engines to all of its fleet; the entire fleet thus conforms to the London Low Emission Zone (LEZ) which came into force in July 2008. To minimise pollution levels the fleet now operates on Ultra Low Sulphur Diesel fuel.

The Go-Ahead Group announced in March 2012 its acquisition of First London East's Northumberland Park bus depot in Tottenham. This purchase increased Go-Ahead's share of the London bus market by a further one percent to 23%. Seen in Stratford is DWL27, FJ54ZTV, a VDL SB120 with Wrightbus Cadet bodywork. *Richard Godfrey*

DMN1	NP	LT02NUK	Dennis Dart SLF 10.7m		Marshall Capital	N25F	2002	First, 2012

DOE1-54

ADL Trident 2 10.3m · Optare Olympus · N43/21D · 2008-09

1	A	LX58CWN	15	A	LX58CXE	29	A	LX58CXV	42	A	LX09BXL
2	A	LX58CWO	16	A	LX58CXF	30	A	LX58CXW	43	A	LX09BXM
3	A	LX58CWP	17	A	LX58CXG	31	A	LX58CXY	44	A	LX09BXO
4	A	LX58CWR	18	A	LX58CXH	32	A	LX58CXZ	45	A	LX09AXU
5	A	LX58CWT	19	A	LX58CXJ	33	A	LX58CYA	46	A	LX09AXV
6	A	LX58CWU	20	A	LX58CXK	34	A	LX58CYC	47	A	LX09AXW
7	A	LX58CWV	21	A	LX58CXL	35	A	LX58CYE	48	A	LX09AXY
8	A	LX58CWW	22	A	LX58CXN	36	A	LX58CYF	49	A	LX09AXZ
9	A	LX58CWY	23	A	LX58CXO	37	A	LX58CYG	50	A	LX09AYA
10	A	LX58CWZ	24	A	LX58CXP	38	A	LX09BXG	51	A	LX09AYB
11	A	LX58CXA	25	A	LX58CXR	39	A	LX09BXH	52	A	LX09AYC
12	A	LX58CXB	26	A	LX58CXS	40	A	LX09BXJ	53	A	LX09AYD
13	A	LX58CXC	27	A	LX58CXT	41	A	LX09BXK	54	AL	LX09AYE
14	A	LX58CXD	28	A	LX58CXU						

DP193-205

TransBus Dart 10.7m · TransBus Pointer · N33D · 2003-04 · Blue Triangle, 2007

193	SW	EU53PXY	197	SW	EU53PYD	200	SW	EU53PYH	203	SW	EU53PYO
194	SW	EU53PXZ	198	SW	EU53PYF	201	SW	EU53PYJ	204	SW	EU53PYP
195	SW	EU53PYA	199	SW	EU53PYG	202	SW	EU53PYL	205	SW	BT04BUS
196	SW	EU53PYB									

DP207	SW	EU04BVF	TransBus Dart 10.7m	TransBus Pointer	N37F	2004	Blue Triangle, 2007
DP208	SW	SN56AYC	ADL Dart 10.7m	ADL Pointer	N33D	2006	Blue Triangle, 2007
DP209	SW	SN56AYD	ADL Dart 10.7m	ADL Pointer	N33D	2006	Blue Triangle, 2007

DW1-12

DAF SB120 9.4m · Wrightbus Cadet 2 · N23D · 2003 · East Thames, 2009

1	AL	LF52TKJ	4	AL	LF52TJY	7	AL	LF52TKO	10	AL	LF52TKE
2	AL	LF52TKC	5	AL	LF52TJV	8	AL	LF52TKK	11	AL	LF52TKN
3	AL	LF52TKD	6	AL	LF52TJX	9	AL	LF52TKT	12	AL	LF52TKA

DWL13-37

VDL Bus SB120 10.8m · Wrightbus Cadet 2 · N30D · 2004 · East Thames, 2009

13	BX	BX04BXL	20	BX	FJ54ZDU	26	NX	FJ54ZFA	32	NX	FJ54ZUA
14	BX	BX04BXP	21	BX	FJ54ZDV	27	NX	FJ54ZTV	33	NX	FJ54ZUC
15	BX	BX04BXN	22	BX	FJ54ZDW	28	NX	FJ54ZTW	34	NX	FJ54ZUD
16	BX	BX04BXM	23	BX	FJ54ZDX	29	NX	FJ54ZDX	35	NX	FJ54ZVA
17	BX	FJ54ZDR	24	BX	FJ54ZDY	30	NX	FJ54ZTY	36	NX	FJ54ZVB
18	BX	FJ54ZDP	25	BX	FJ54ZDZ	31	NX	FJ54ZTZ	37	NX	FJ54ZDC
19	BX	FJ54ZDT									

The Enviro 400 first entered service in 2006 and while available as a body on Volvo and Scania chassis is mostly supplied in a semi-integral form on the ADL Trident chassis and its successors the E40D and E40H. Some ### of the model have been built including E44, LX56ETK, seen arriving in North Greenwich.
Dave Heath

E1-39

						ADL Trident 2	10.1m		ADL Enviro 400			N41/26D*	2006	1-4 are N41/24D
1	SW	SN06BNA	11	SW	SN06BNV	21	PM	LX06EZR	31	PM	LX06EZF
2	SW	SN06BNB	12	SW	SN06BNX	22	PM	LX06EZS	32	PM	LX06EZG
3	SW	SN06BND	13	SW	SN06BNY	23	PM	LX06EZT	33	PM	LX06EZH
4	SW	SN06BNE	14	SW	SN06BNZ	24	PM	LX06EYY	34	PM	LX06ECT
5	SW	SN06BNF	15	SW	SN06BOF	25	PM	LX06EYZ	35	PM	LX06ECV
6	SW	SN06BNJ	16	PM	LX06EZL	26	PM	LX06EZA	36	PM	LX06FKL
7	SW	SN06BNK	17	PM	LX06EZM	27	PM	LX06EZB	37	PM	LX06FKM
8	SW	SN06BNL	18	PM	LX06EZN	28	PM	LX06EZC	38	SW	LX06FKN
9	SW	SN06BNO	19	PM	LX06EZO	29	PM	LX06EZD	39	SW	LX06FKO
10	SW	SN06BNU	20	PM	LX06EZP	30	PM	LX06EZE

E40-56

						ADL Trident 2	10.1m		ADL Enviro 400			N41/26D	2006-07
40	BX	LX56ETD	45	BX	LX56ETL	50	BX	LX56ETV	54	BX	LX56EUB
41	BX	LX56ETE	46	BX	LX56ETO	51	BX	LX56ETY	55	BX	LX56EUC
42	BX	LX56ETF	47	BX	LX56ETR	52	BX	LX56ETZ	56	BX	LX56EUD
43	BX	LX56ETJ	48	BX	LX56ETT	53	BX	LX56EUA
44	BX	LX56ETK	49	BX	LX56ETU

E57-99

						ADL Trident 2	10.1M		ADL Enviro 400			N39/25D*	2007-08	*57 is N41/26D
57	SW	LX07BYH	68	SW	LX57CJO	79	SW	LX57CKJ	90	SW	LX57CLN
58	A	LX07BYC	69	SW	LX57CJU	80	SW	LX57CKK	91	SW	LX57CLO
59	A	LX07BYD	70	SW	LX57CJV	81	SW	LX57CKL	92	SW	LX57CLV
60	A	LX07BYF	71	SW	LX57CJY	82	SW	LX57CKN	93	SW	LX57CLY
61	PM	LX07BYG	72	SW	LX57CJZ	83	SW	LX57CKO	94	NX	LX08EBP
62	SW	LX57CHV	73	SW	LX57CKA	84	SW	LX57CKP	95	NX	LX08EBU
63	SW	LX57CHY	74	SW	LX57CKC	85	SW	LX57CKU	96	NX	LX08EBV
64	SW	LX57CHZ	75	SW	LX57CKD	86	SW	LX57CKV	97	NX	LX08EBZ
65	SW	LX57CJE	76	SW	LX57CKE	87	SW	LX57CKY	98	NX	LX08ECA
66	SW	LX57CJF	77	SW	LX57CKF	88	SW	LX57CLF	99	NX	LX08ECC
67	SW	LX57CJJ	78	SW	LX57CKG	89	SW	LX57CLJ

Around fifty Enviro 400 buses joined the London operation in 2011 with more entering service in 2012. E167, SN61BGV, is seen passing Government buildings in Whitehall while working route 453 to Deptford Bridge. *Richard Godfrey*

E100-128

			ADL Trident 2 10.1M			ADL Enviro 400		N39/26D	2009		
100	Q	LX09EZU	108	Q	LX09FAO	115	Q	LX09FBF	122	Q	LX09FBV
101	Q	LX09EZV	109	Q	LX09FAU	116	Q	LX09FBG	123	Q	LX09FBY
102	Q	LX09EZW	110	Q	LX09FBA	117	Q	LX09FBJ	124	Q	LX09FBZ
103	Q	LX09EZZ	111	Q	LX09FBB	118	Q	LX09FBK	125	Q	LX09FCA
104	Q	LX09FAF	112	Q	LX09FBC	119	Q	LX09FBN	126	Q	LX09FCC
105	Q	LX09FAJ	113	Q	LX09FBD	120	Q	LX09FBO	127	Q	LX09FCD
106	Q	LX09FAK	114	Q	LX09FBE	121	Q	LX09FBU	128	Q	LX09FCE
107	Q	LX09FAM									

E129-150

			ADL Trident 2 10.1M			ADL Enviro 400		N41/26D	2010		
129	SW	SN60BZA	135	SW	SN60BZG	141	AL	SN60BZO	146	AL	SN60BZU
130	SW	SN60BZB	136	SW	SN60BZH	142	AL	SN60BZP	147	AL	SN60BZV
131	SW	SN60BZC	137	SW	SN60BZJ	143	AL	SN60BZR	148	AL	SN60BZW
132	SW	SN60BZD	138	AL	SN60BZK	144	AL	SN60BZS	149	AL	SN60BZX
133	SW	SN60BZE	139	AL	SN60BZL	145	AL	SN60BZT	150	AL	SN60BZY
134	SW	SN60BZF	140	AL	SN60BZM						

E151-204

			ADL Trident 2 10.1M			ADL Enviro 400		N41/24D	2011		
151	SW	SN11BTY	165	MW	SN61BGO	179	MW	SN61BHO	192	MW	SN61BJU
152	SW	SN11BTZ	166	MW	SN61BGU	180	MW	SN61BHP	193	MW	SN61BJV
153	SW	SN11BUA	167	MW	SN61BGV	181	MW	SN61BHU	194	MW	SN61BJX
154	SW	SN11BUE	168	MW	SN61BGX	182	MW	SN61BHV	195	MW	SN61BJY
155	SW	SN11BUF	169	MW	SN61BGY	183	MW	SN61BHW	196	MW	SN61BJZ
156	SW	SN11BUH	170	MW	SN61BGZ	184	MW	SN61BHX	197	MW	SN61BKA
157	SW	SN11BUJ	171	MW	SN61BHA	185	MW	SN61BHY	198	MW	SN61BKD
158	SW	SN11BUO	172	MW	SN61BHD	186	MW	SN61BHZ	199	MW	SN61BKE
159	SW	SN11BUP	173	MW	SN61BGE	187	MW	SN61BJE	200	MW	SN61BKF
160	SW	SN11BUU	174	MW	SN61BHE	188	MW	SN61BJF	201	MW	SN61BKG
161	SW	SN11BUV	175	MW	SN61BHF	189	MW	SN61BJJ	202	NX	SN61BKJ
162	SW	SN11BUW	176	MW	SN61BHJ	190	MW	SN61BJK	203	NX	SN61BKK
163	MW	SN61BGF	177	MW	SN61BHK	191	MW	SN61BJO	204	NX	SN61BKL
164	MW	SN61BGK	178	MW	SN61BHL						

E205-245 — ADL E40D / ADL Enviro 400 / N41/24D / 2011-12

205	NX	SN61DCV	216	NX	SN61DDU	226	NX	SN61DFF	236	BX	YX61DTK
206	NX	SN61DCX	217	NX	SN61DDV	227	NX	SN61DFG	237	BX	YX61DTN
207	NX	SN61DCY	218	NX	SN61DDX	228	NX	SN61DFJ	238	BX	YX61DPF
208	NX	SN61DCZ	219	NX	SN61DDY	229	BX	YX61DSE	239	BX	YX61DPK
209	NX	SN61DDA	220	NX	SN61DDZ	230	BX	YX61DSV	240	BX	YX61DPN
210	NX	SN61DDE	221	NX	SN61DEU	231	BX	YX61DSO	241	BX	YX61DPO
211	NX	SN61DDF	222	NX	SN61DFA	232	BX	YX61DSU	242	BX	YX61DPU
212	NX	SN61DDJ	223	NX	SN61DFC	233	BX	YX61DSY	243	BX	YX61DPV
213	NX	SN61DDK	224	NX	SN61DFD	234	BX	YX61DSZ	244	BX	YX61DPY
214	NX	SN61DDL	225	NX	SN61DFE	235	BX	YX61DTF	245	BX	YX61DPZ
215	NX	SN61DDO									

E246-260 — ADL E40D / ADL Enviro 400 / N41/24D / 2012

246	-	YX12FPA	250	-	YX12FPF	254	-	YX12FPL	258	-	YX12FPT
247	-	YX12FPC	251	-	YX12FPG	255	-	YX12FPN	259	-	-
248	-	YX12FPD	252	-	YX12FPJ	256	-	YX12FPO	260	-	-
249	-	YX12FPE	253	-	YX12FPK	257	-	YX12FPP			

ED1-8 — ADL Dart 4 10.8m / MCV Evolution / N29D / 2006

1	NX	AE06HCA	3	NX	AE06HCD	5	BE	AE06HCG	7	NX	AE06HCJ
2	NX	AE06HCC	4	NX	AE06HCF	6	BE	AE06HCH	8	NX	AE06HCK

ED9-17 — ADL Dart 4 9.2m / MCV Evolution / N23D / 2006

9	BE	AE56OUH	12	BE	AE56OUL	14	BE	AE56OUN	16	BE	AE56OUP
10	BE	AE56OUJ	13	BE	AE56OUM	15	BE	AE56OUO	17	BE	AE56OUS
11	BE	AE56OUK									

ED18-28 — ADL Dart 4 10.4m / MCV Evolution / N29D / 2007

18	BE	LX07BYJ	21	BE	LX07BYM	24	BE	LX07BYP	27	BE	LX07BYT
19	BE	LX07BYK	22	BE	LX07BYN	25	BE	LX07BYR	28	BE	LX07BYU
20	BE	LX07BYL	23	BE	LX07BYO	26	BE	LX07BYS			

EH1-5 — ADL Trident E400H 10.1m / ADL Enviro 400 / N37/25D / 2008-09

1	SW	LX58DDJ	3	SW	LX58DDL	4	SW	LX58DDN	5	SW	LX58DDO
2	SW	LX58DDK									

EH6-20 — ADL E40H 10.1m / ADL Enviro 400 / N37/25D / 2012

6	NX	SN61BLJ	10	NX	SN61DAO	14	NX	SN61DSO	18	NX	SN61DCE
7	NX	SN61BLK	11	NX	SN61DAU	15	NX	SN61DBX	19	NX	SN61DCO
8	NX	SN61BLV	12	NX	SN61DBO	16	NX	SN61DBY	20	NX	SN61DCU
9	NX	SN61DAA	13	NX	SN61DBU	17	NX	SN61DBZ			

ELS1-14 — Scania N94UB 10.6m / East Lancashire Myllennium / N32D / 2002 / East Thames, 2009

1	Q	YU02GHG	5	Q	YU02GHD	9	Q	YR52VFJ	12	Q	YR52VFL
2	Q	YU02GHH	6	Q	YU02GHA	10	Q	YR52VFH	13	Q	YR52VFM
3	Q	YU02GHJ	7	Q	YU02GHN	11	Q	YR52VFK	14	Q	YR52VFN
4	Q	YU02GHK	8	Q	YU02GHO						

EN1-24 — ADL Trident 2 11m / ADL Enviro 400 / N41/26D / 2008 / First, 2012

1	NP	SN58CDY	7	NP	SN58CEO	13	NP	SN58CFD	19	NP	LK08FLJ
2	NP	SN58CDZ	8	NP	SN58CEU	14	NP	SN58CFE	20	NP	LK08FLL
3	NP	SN58CEA	9	NP	SN58CEV	15	NP	SN58CFF	21	NP	LK08FLM
4	NP	SN58CEF	10	NP	SN58CEX	16	NP	SN58CFG	22	NP	LK08FLN
5	NP	SN58CEJ	11	NP	SN58CEY	17	NP	SN58CFJ	23	NP	LK08FLP
6	NP	SN58CEK	12	NP	SN58CFA	18	NP	LK08FLH	24	NP	LK08FLR

HOV1	Q	OP07ARE	Optare Versa V1100 Hybrid	Optare	N38F	2011	On loan from Optare
LDP183	A	Y983TGH	Dennis Dart SLF 9.3m	Plaxton Pointer 2	N28F	2001	
LDP186	PL	Y986TGH	Dennis Dart SLF 9.3m	Plaxton Pointer 2	N28F	2001	
LDP187	SW	Y987TGH	Dennis Dart SLF 9.3m	Plaxton Pointer 2	N28F	2001	

Hybrid technology continues to improve with ADL, which uses BAe Systems units, being one of the leaders in this field. Go-Ahead London now operates twenty E40H buses including EH9, SN61DAA, seen in Lewisham. *Colin Lloyd*

LDP191-227

Dennis Dart SLF 10.1m | Plaxton Pointer 2 | N30D* | 2002-03 | *seating varies

191	AL	SN51UAD	201	AL	SN51UAP	210	NX	SN51UAZ	219	PL	SK52MPF
192	AL	SN51UAE	202	BX	SN51UAR	211	PL	SK52MMU	220	PL	SK52MPO
193	AL	SN51UAF	203	u	SN51UAS	212	PL	SK52MMV	221	PL	SK52MLU
194	AL	SN51UAG	204	SW	SN51UAT	213	PL	SK52MMX	222	PL	SK52MLV
195	AL	SN51UAH	205	SW	SN51UAU	214	PL	SK52MOA	223	PL	SK52MLX
196	AL	SN51UAJ	206	PM	SN51UAV	215	PL	SK52MOF	224	PL	SK52MLY
197	SW	SN51UAK	207	BX	SN51UAW	216	PL	SK52MOU	225	PL	SK52MLZ
198	AL	SN51UAL	208	BE	SN51UAX	217	PL	SK52MOV	226	PL	SK52MMA
199	AL	SN51UAM	209	NX	SN51UAY	218	PL	SK52MPE	227	PL	SK52MME
200	AL	SN51UAO									

LDP249-262

TransBus Dart 10.1m | TransBus Pointer | N27D | 2003

249	Q	SN53KKF	253	Q	SN53KKL	257	Q	SN53KKR	260	Q	SN53KKV
250	Q	SN53KKG	254	Q	SN53KKM	258	Q	SN53KKT	261	Q	SN53KKW
251	Q	SN53KKH	255	Q	SN53KKO	259	Q	SN53KKU	262	Q	SN53KKX
252	Q	SN53KKJ	256	Q	SN53KKP						

LDP263-272

ADL Dart 8.8m | ADL Pointer | N23F | 2005

263	PL	LX05EYP	266	PL	LX05EYT	269	PL	LX05EYW	271	PL	LX05EXZ
264	PL	LX05EYR	267	PL	LX05EYU	270	PL	LX05EYY	272	PL	LX05EYA
265	PL	LX05EYS	268	PL	LX05EYV						

LDP273-280

ADL Dart 10.1m | ADL Pointer | N28D | 2006

273	NX	LX06EYT	275	NX	LX06EYV	277	NX	LX06FBD	279	NX	LX06FAA
274	NX	LX06EYU	276	NX	LX06EYW	278	NX	LX06FBE	280	NX	LX06FAF

LDP281-291

ADL Dart 8.8m | ADL Pointer | N23F | 2006

281	AF	LX06FAJ	284	AF	LX06FAO	287	SW	LX06FBB	290	SW	LX06EZV
282	AF	LX06FAK	285	AF	LX06FAU	288	SW	LX06FBC	291	SW	LX06EZW
283	AF	LX06FAM	286	AF	LX06FBA	289	SW	LX06EZU			

LDP292	PL	LX06EZZ	ADL Dart 10.1m	ADL Pointer	N28D	2006
LDP293	PL	LX06EZJ	ADL Dart 10.1m	ADL Pointer	N28D	2006
LDP294	PL	LX06EZK	ADL Dart 10.1m	ADL Pointer	N28D	2006

While the last of the articulated Mercedes-Benz Citaro buses has now departed the capital for work elsewhere, the basic model remains on the TfL approved vehicle list. Go-Ahead London operates fifty including MEC31, BD09ZVW, seen at Aldwych. *Colin Lloyd*

MEC1-50

Mercedes-Benz Citaro O530 — Mercedes-Benz — N21D — 2009

1	RA	BG09JJK	14	RA	BD09ZPU	27	RA	BD09ZVS	39	RA	BD09ZWF
2	RA	BG09JJL	15	RA	BD09ZPV	28	RA	BD09ZVT	40	MW	BD09ZWG
3	RA	BG09JJU	16	RA	BD09ZPW	29	RA	BD09ZVU	41	RA	BD09ZWH
4	RA	BG09JJV	17	RA	BD09ZPX	30	RA	BD09ZVV	42	RA	BT09GOH
5	RA	BG09JJX	18	RA	BD09ZPY	31	RA	BD09ZVW	43	RA	BT09GOJ
6	RA	BG09JJY	19	RA	BD09ZPZ	32	MW	BD09ZVX	44	RA	BT09GOK
7	RA	BG09JJZ	20	RA	BD09ZRA	33	RA	BD09ZVY	45	MW	BT09GOP
8	RA	BG09JKE	21	RA	BD09ZRC	34	RA	BD09ZVZ	46	RA	BT09GOU
9	RA	BG09JKF	22	RA	BD09ZRE	35	RA	BD09ZWA	47	RA	BT09GOX
10	RA	BG09JKJ	23	RA	BD09ZRF	36	RA	BD09ZWB	48	MW	BT09GPE
11	RA	BD09ZPR	24	RA	BD09ZRG	37	MW	BD09ZWC	49	MW	BT09GPF
12	RA	BD09ZPS	25	RA	BD09ZRJ	38	MW	BD09ZWE	50	RA	BT09GPJ
13	RA	BD09ZPT	26	RA	BD09ZRK						

NV170	AL	R370LGH	Volvo Olympian	Northern Counties Palatine II	CO47/24D	1997-98	
NV171	AL	R371LGH	Volvo Olympian	Northern Counties Palatine II	CO47/24D	1997-98	
OS1	SI	MX09HHW	Optare Solo M880SL	Optare	N28F	2009	Docklands Buses, 2009

PDN1-6

Dennis Trident 9.9m — Plaxton President 4.4m — N39/23D — 2001-02 — First, 2012

1	NP	LN51GKD	3	NP	LN51GKG	5	NP	LN51GOK	6	NP	LT52WXJ
2	NP	LN51GKE	4	NP	LN51GOJ					

PVL56-143

Volvo B7TL 10m — Plaxton President — N41/19D* — 2000 — *seating varies

56	u	W956WGH	76	Qt	W476WGH	97	BE	W497WGH	127	AL	W527WGH
57	u	W457WGH	79	Q	W479WGH	106	AL	W505WGH	128	AL	W428WGH
58	u	W458WGH	80	Qt	W408WGH	110	AL	W401WGH	129	Q	W529WGH
59	AL	W459WGH	82	Qt	W482WGH	112	AL	W512WGH	130	Qt	W403WGH
60	Qt	W996WGH	83	NX	W483WGH	113	AF	W513WGH	131	Q	W531WGH
61	SW	W461WGH	84	AL	W484WGH	114	AL	W514WGH	132	Qt	W532WGH
62	AL	W462WGH	85	NX	W485WGH	115	AL	W415WGH	133	Qt	W533WGH
63	NX	W463WGH	86	Q	W486WGH	116	AL	W516WGH	134	Qt	W534WGH
64	Qt	W464WGH	87	t	W487WGH	117	AL	W517WGH	135	Qt	W435WGH
66	u	W466WGH	88	u	W488WGH	118	AL	W518WGH	136	Qt	W536WGH
67	u	W467WGH	89	u	W489WGH	119	AL	W519WGH	137	AL	W537WGH
68	u	W468WGH	90	u	W409WGH	120	Qt	W402WGH	138	Qt	W538WGH
69	u	W469WGH	91	u	W491WGH	121	AL	W521WGH	139	Qt	W539WGH
70	AL	W578DGU	92	Qt	W492WGH	122	AL	W522WGH	140	u	W404WGH
71	u	W471WGH	93	SW	W493WGH	123	Qt	W523WGH	141	Qt	W541WGH
72	u	W472WGH	94	BE	W494WGH	124	AL	W524WGH	142	Qt	W542WGH
73	u	W473WGH	95	BE	W495WGH	125	AL	W425WGH	143	Qt	W543WGH
75	Qt	W475WGH	96	BE	W496WGH	126	AL	W526WGH			

PVL144-207 — Volvo B7TL 10m — Plaxton President — N41/20D — 2000

No		Reg	No		Reg	No		Reg	No		Reg
144	AL	X544EGK	154	AL	X554EGK	166	AL	X566EGK	189	PM	X589EGK
145	AL	X745EGK	155	AL	X615EGK	167	AL	X567EGK	190	NX	X509EGK
146	AL	X546EGK	159	Q	X559EGK	168	SW	X568EGK	201	SW	X501EGK
147	AL	X547EGK	160	AL	X616EGK	169	AF	X569EGK	202	SW	X702EGK
148	AL	X548EGK	161	AL	X561EGK	170	AF	X707EGK	203	SW	X503EGK
149	AF	X549EGK	162	AL	X562EGK	171	u	X571EGK	204	SW	X504EGK
150	Q	X599EGK	163	AL	X563EGK	175	u	X575EGK	205	SW	X705EGK
151	NX	X551EGK	164	AL	X564EGK	176	u	X576EGK	206	SW	X506EGK
152	AL	X552EGK	165	AL	X656EGK	178	u	X578EGK	207	SW	X507EGK
153	AL	X553EGK									

PVL209-272 — Volvo B7TL 10m — Plaxton President — N41/20D* — 2001-02

*263/4 are NC41/20D
*221/2 are N41/25F, 224 is O41/20D

No		Reg	No		Reg	No		Reg	No		Reg
209	BE	Y809TGH	220	PL	Y802TGH	230	SW	Y703TGH	238	SW	Y738TGH
210	u	Y801TGH	221	A	Y821TGH	231	SW	Y731TGH	244	PL	Y744TGH
211	u	Y811TGH	222	A	Y822TGH	232	SW	Y732TGH	245	A	Y745TGH
214	SW	Y814TGH	223	NX	Y823TGH	233	SW	Y733TGH	248	NX	Y748TGH
215	AL	Y815TGH	224	A	Y824TGH	234	SW	Y734TGH	263	A	PN02XBL
216	NX	Y816TGH	225	NX	Y825TGH	235	SW	Y735TGH	264	NX	PN02XBM
217	Q	Y817TGH	226	A	Y826TGH	236	SW	Y736TGH	265	A	PN02XBO
218	A	Y818TGH	229	AL	Y729TGH	237	SW	Y737TGH	272	Q	PN02XBW
219	BX	Y819TGH									

PVL276-354 — Volvo B7TL 10m — TransBus President — N41/20D — 2002-03

No		Reg	No		Reg	No		Reg	No		Reg
276	NX	PJ02RBO	298	Q	PJ02RFK	317	Q	PJ52LVU	336	PM	PJ52LWR
278	SW	PJ02RBV	299	Q	PJ02RFL	318	Q	PJ52LVV	337	PM	PJ52LWS
281	A	PJ02RBZ	300	Q	PJ02RFN	319	NX	PJ52LVW	338	PM	PJ52LWT
282	A	PJ02RCF	301	Q	PJ02RFO	320	NX	PJ52LVX	339	PM	PJ52LWU
283	A	PJ02RCO	302	Q	PJ02RFX	321	NX	PJ52LVY	340	PM	PJ52LWV
284	A	PJ02RCU	303	Q	PJ02RFY	322	NX	PJ52LVZ	341	PM	PJ52LWW
285	A	PJ02RCV	304	Q	PJ02RFZ	323	NX	PJ52LWA	342	PM	PJ52LWX
286	A	PJ02RCX	305	Q	PJ02RGO	324	NX	PJ52LWC	343	NX	PF52WPT
287	A	PJ02RCY	306	Q	PJ02RGU	325	NX	PJ52LWD	344	NX	PF52WPU
288	A	PJ02RCZ	307	Q	PJ02RGV	326	Q	PJ52LWE	345	NX	PF52WPV
289	A	PJ02RDO	308	Q	PJ02TVN	327	Q	PJ52LWF	346	BX	PF52WPW
290	A	PJ02RDU	309	Q	PJ02TVO	328	Q	PJ52LWG	347	BX	PF52WPX
291	A	PJ02RDV	310	Q	PJ02TVP	329	PM	PJ52LWH	348	BX	PF52WPY
292	A	PJ02RDX	311	Q	PJ02TVT	330	PM	PJ52LWK	349	BX	PF52WPZ
293	A	PJ02RDY	312	Q	PJ02TVU	331	PM	PJ52LWL	350	BX	PF52WRA
294	A	PJ02RDZ	313	Q	PJ52LVP	332	PM	PJ52LWM	351	BX	PF52WRC
295	A	PJ02REU	314	Q	PJ52LVR	333	PM	PJ52LWN	352	BX	PF52WRD
296	A	PJ02RFE	315	Q	PJ52LVS	334	PM	PJ52LWO	353	BX	PF52WRE
297	A	PJ02RFF	316	Q	PJ52LVT	335	PM	PJ52LWP	354	BX	PF52WRG

At the turn of the century the principal double-deck for the fleet was the President, first supplied under the Plaxton name and then TransBus. The model is represented by PVL88, W488WGH. It is expected that many of these will move to the provincial fleets in coming months.
Dave Heath

PVL355-389 — Volvo B7TL 10m — TransBus President — N41/20D — 2003

355	BX	PL03AGZ	369	BV	PJ53SRO	376	AL	PJ53NKN	383	AL	PJ53NKX
362	BX	PJ53SOF	370	BX	PJ53SRU	377	AL	PJ53NKO	384	AL	PJ53NKZ
363	BX	PJ53SOH	371	BX	PJ53NKG	378	AL	PJ53NKP	385	AL	PJ53NLA
364	BX	PJ53SOU	372	AL	PJ53NKH	379	AL	PJ53NKR	386	AL	PJ53NLC
365	BX	PJ53SPU	373	AL	PJ53NKK	380	AL	PJ53NKS	387	AL	PJ53NLD
366	BX	PJ53SPV	374	AL	PJ53NKL	381	AL	PJ53NKT	388	AL	PJ53NLE
367	BX	PJ53SPX	375	AL	PJ53NKM	382	AL	PJ53NKW	389	AL	PJ53NLF
368	BV	PJ53SPZ									

PVL390-419 — Volvo B7TL 10m — ADL President — N41/20D — 2005

390	NX	LX54HAA	398	NX	LX54GZK	406	NX	LX54GYV	413	NX	LX54GZE
391	NX	LX54HAE	399	NX	LX54GZL	407	NX	LX54GYW	414	NX	LX54GZF
392	NX	LX54HAO	400	NX	LX54GZM	408	NX	LX54GYY	415	NX	LX54GZU
393	NX	LX54HAU	401	NX	LX54GZN	409	NX	LX54GYZ	416	NX	LX54GZV
394	NX	LX54HBA	402	NX	LX54GZO	410	NX	LX54GZB	417	NX	LX54GZW
395	NX	LX54HBB	403	NX	LX54GZP	411	NX	LX54GZC	418	NX	LX54GZY
396	NX	LX54GZG	404	NX	LX54GZR	412	NX	LX54GZD	419	NX	LX54GZZ
397	NX	LX54GZH	405	NX	LX54GZT						

PVN1-17 — Volvo B7TL 10.6m — TransBus President 4.4m — N44/21D — 2003 — First, 2012

1	NP	LK03NHF	6	NP	LK03NHX	10	NP	LK03NHF	14	NP	LK03NJX
2	NP	LK03NHG	7	NP	LK03NHY	11	NP	LK03NJJ	15	NP	LK03NJY
3	NP	LK03NHP	8	NP	LK03NHZ	12	NP	LK03NJN	16	NP	LK03NJZ
4	NP	LK03NHT	9	NP	LK03NJE	13	NP	LK03NJV	17	NP	LK03NKA
5	NP	LK03NHV									

RM9 — NX — VLT9 — AEC Routemaster R2RH — Park Royal — B36/28R — 1959

RML2503-2604 — AEC Routemaster R2RH1 — Park Royal — B40/32R* — 1961-67 — *2318 is O40/32R

*2516 is B40/32R, classified DRM

2305	AL	CUV305C	2472	NX	JJD472D	2520	Q	JJD520D	2604	AL	NML604E
2318	NX	CUV318C	2516	PL	WLT516						

SE1-17 — ADL Dart 4 10.2m — ADL Enviro 200 — N29D — 2007

1	AL	LX07BXH	6	AL	LX07BXN	10	AL	LX07BXS	14	AL	LX07BXY
2	AL	LX07BXJ	7	AL	LX07BXO	11	AL	LX07BXU	15	AL	LX07BZH
3	AL	LX07BXK	8	AL	LX07BXP	12	AL	LX07BXV	16	AL	LX07BYA
4	AL	LX07BXL	9	AL	LX07BXR	13	AL	LX07BXW	17	AL	LX07BYB
5	AL	LX07BXM									

SE18-36 — ADL Dart 4 10.8m — ADL Enviro 200 — N32D — 2007-08

18	BE	SK07DZM	23	BE	SK07DWK	28	BE	SK07DWU	33	BE	SK07DWZ
19	BE	SK07DZN	24	BE	SK07DWL	29	BE	SK07DWV	34	BE	SK07DXA
20	BE	SK07DZO	25	BE	SK07DWM	30	BE	SK07DWW	35	BE	SK07DXB
21	BE	SK07DWG	26	BE	SK07DWO	31	BE	SK07DWX	36	BE	YN08DMY
22	BE	SK07DWJ	27	BE	SK07DWP	32	BE	SK07DWY			

SE37-46 — ADL Dart 4 10.2m — ADL Enviro 200 — N29D — 2010

37	BE	LX10AUP	40	BE	LX10AUU	43	BE	LX10AUY	45	BE	LX10AVC
38	BE	LX10AUR	41	BE	LX10AUV	44	BE	LX10AVB	46	BE	LX10AVD
39	BE	LX10AUT	42	BE	LX10AUW						

SE47-54 — ADL Dart 4 10.8m — ADL Enviro 200 — N29D — 2010

47	SW	YX60EOE	49	SW	YX60EOG	51	SW	YX60EOJ	53	SW	YX60EOL
48	SW	YX60EOF	50	SW	YX60EOH	52	SW	YX60EOK	54	SW	YX60EOO

SE55-84 — ADL Dart 4 10.2m — ADL Enviro 200 — N29D — 2010

55	BV	YX60DXT	63	BV	YX60FSU	71	BX	YX60FBZ	78	BX	YX60FCL
56	BV	YX60FSN	64	BV	YX60EPP	72	BX	YX60FCA	79	BX	YX60FCM
57	BV	YX60DXU	65	BV	YX60EPU	73	BX	YX60FCC	80	BX	YX60FCO
58	BV	YX60FSO	66	BV	YX60EOP	74	BX	YX60FCD	81	BX	YX60FCP
59	BV	YX60FSP	67	BV	YX60FCZ	75	BX	YX60FCE	82	BX	YX60FCU
60	BV	YX60FSS	68	BV	YX60FDA	76	BX	YX60FCF	83	BX	YX60FCV
61	BV	YX60DXW	69	BX	YX60FBU	77	BX	YX60FCG	84	BX	YX60FCY
62	BV	YX60EPO	70	BX	YX60FBY						

The Dart 4 was introduced by Alexander Dennis with a Euro 4 engine and the principal option of the Enviro 200 body, though the Dart 4 name has continued with Euro 5 and EEV engines. From the 2011 intake, SE163, YX61DVN, is seen outside Rotherhithe Police Station while heading for Surrey Quays.
Richard Godfrey

SE85-93

ADL Dart 4 9.3m   ADL Enviro 200   N24D   2011

85	Q	YX11CPE	88	Q	YX11CPN	90	Q	YX11CPU	92	Q	YX11CPY
86	Q	YX11CPF	89	Q	YX11CPO	91	Q	YX11CPV	93	Q	YX11CPZ
87	Q	YX11CPK									

SE94-103

ADL Dart 4 10.8m   ADL Enviro 200   N32D   2011

94	BE	SN11FFZ	97	BE	SN11FGD	100	BE	SN61BKV	102	BE	SN61BKY
95	BE	SN11FGA	98	BE	SN61BKO	101	BE	SN61BKX	103	BE	SN61BKZ
96	BE	SN11FGC	99	BE	SN61BKU						

SE104-119

ADL Dart 4 10.8m   ADL Enviro 200   N32D   2011

104	SI	YX61BWA	108	SI	YX61BWE	112	SI	YX61BXR	116	SI	YX61BXW
105	SI	YX61BWB	109	SI	YX61BYD	113	SI	YX61BXS	117	SI	YX61BXY
106	SI	YX61BWC	110	SI	YX61BYF	114	SI	YX61BXU	118	SI	YX61BXZ
107	SI	YX61BWD	111	SI	YX61BYG	115	SI	YX61BXV	119	SI	YX61BYA

SE120-166

ADL Dart 4 10.2m   ADL Enviro 200   N29D   2011

120	SI	YX61BWU	132	SI	YX61BWH	144	SI	YX61BXM	156	PM	YX61DVF
121	SI	YX61BWV	133	SI	YX61BWJ	145	SI	YX61BXN	157	PM	YX61DVG
122	SI	YX61BWW	134	SI	YX61BWK	146	SI	YX61BXO	158	PM	YX61DVH
123	SI	YX61BWY	135	SI	YX61BWL	147	SI	YX61BXP	159	PM	YX61DVJ
124	SI	YX61BWZ	136	SI	YX61BWM	148	SI	YX61DTO	160	PM	YX61DVK
125	SI	YX61BXA	137	SI	YX61BWN	149	SI	YX61DTU	161	PM	YX61DVL
126	SI	YX61BXB	138	SI	YX61BWO	150	SI	YX61DTV	162	PM	YX61DVM
127	SI	YX61BXC	139	SI	YX61BWP	151	SI	YX61DTY	163	PM	YX61DVN
128	SI	YX61BXD	140	SI	YX61BVY	152	SI	YX61DTZ	164	PM	YX61DVO
129	SI	YX61BXE	141	SI	YX61BVZ	153	PM	YX61DVA	165	PM	YX61DVP
130	SI	YX61BWF	142	SI	YX61BXK	154	PM	YX61DVB	166	PM	YX61DVR
131	SI	YX61BWG	143	SI	YX61BXL	155	PM	YX61DVC			

SE167-174

ADL E20D 10.2m   ADL Enviro 200   N29D   2012

167	A	YX61EKF	169	A	YX61EKH	171	A	YX61EKK	173	A	YX61EKM
168	A	YX61EKG	170	A	YX61EKJ	172	A	YX61EKL	174	A	YX61EKN

Class letters SOE are allocated to the Alexander Dennis Darts bodied by Optare at their former Blackburn facility that was previously known as East Lancs Coachbuilders. Martin Way in South Merton provides the background to this view of SOE34, LX09EVB. *Richard Godfrey*

SE175-193 — ADL E20D 10.2m — ADL Enviro 200 — N29D — 2012

175	PL	SN12AUM	180	PL	SN12AUU	185	PL	SN12AVB	190	PL	SN12AVG
176	PL	SN12AUO	181	PL	SN12AUV	186	PL	SN12AVC	191	PL	SN12AVJ
177	PL	SN12AUP	182	PL	SN12AUW	187	PL	SN12AVD	192	PL	SN12AVK
178	PL	SN12AUR	183	PL	SN12AUX	188	PL	SN12AVE	193	PL	SN12AVL
179	PL	SN12AUT	184	PL	SN12AUY	189	PL	SN12AVF			

SEN1-12 — ADL Dart 4 8.9m — ADL Enviro 200 — N26F — 2011 — First, 2012

1	NP	YX60FUA	4	NP	YX60FUE	7	NP	YX60FUH	10	NP	YX60FUO
2	NP	YX60FUB	5	NP	YX60FUF	8	NP	YX60FUJ	11	NP	YX60FUP
3	NP	YX60FUD	6	NP	YX60FUG	9	NP	YX60FUM	12	NP	YX60FUT

SEN13-20 — ADL Dart 4 9.3m — ADL Enviro 200 — N24D — 2011 — First, 2012

| 13 | NP | YX11FYS | 15 | NP | YX11FYU | 17 | NP | YX11FYW | 19 | NP | YX11FYZ |
| 14 | NP | YX11FYT | 16 | NP | YX11FYV | 18 | NP | YX11FYY | 20 | NP | YX11AGU |

SEN21-29 — ADL E20D 9.6m — ADL Enviro 200 — N25D — 2012 — First, 2012

21	NP	YX61FYT	24	NP	YX61FYW	26	NP	YX61FYZ	28	NP	YX61FZB
22	NP	YX61FYU	25	NP	YX61FYY	27	NP	YX61FZA	29	NP	YX61FZZ
23	NP	YX61FYV									

SO1-5 — Scania N94 UD 10.6m — East Lancs OmniDekka 4.4m — N45/27D — 2005 — Blue Triangle, 2007

| 1 | SI | BV55UCT | 3 | SI | BV55UCW | 4 | SI | BV55UCX | 5 | SI | BV55UCY |
| 2 | SI | BV55UCU | | | | | | | | | |

SOC1-9 — Scania OmniCity N230 UD 10.8m Scania — N41/22D — 2008

1	SI	LX08ECD	4	SI	LX08ECJ	6	SI	LX08ECT	8	SI	LX08ECW
2	SI	LX08ECE	5	SI	LX08ECN	7	SI	LX08ECV	9	SI	LX08ECY
3	SI	LX08ECF									

SOE1-40 — ADL Dart 4 10.4m — Optare Esteem — N29D — 2009

1	AL	LX09AYF	11	AL	LX09AYS	21	AL	LX09AZD	31	A	LX09BXP
2	AL	LX09AYG	12	AL	LX09AYT	22	AL	LX09AZF	32	A	LX09BXR
3	AL	LX09AYH	13	AL	LX09AYU	23	AL	LX09AZG	33	A	LX09BXS
4	AL	LX09AYJ	14	AL	LX09AYV	24	AL	LX09AZJ	34	A	LX09EVB
5	AL	LX09AYK	15	AL	LX09AYW	25	AL	LX09AZL	35	A	LX09EVC
6	AL	LX09AYL	16	AL	LX09AYY	26	AL	LX09AZN	36	A	LX09EVD
7	AL	LX09AYM	17	AL	LX09AYZ	27	AL	LX09AZO	37	A	LX09EVF
8	AL	LX09AYN	18	AL	LX09AZA	28	AL	LX09AZP	38	A	LX09EVG
9	AL	LX09AYO	19	AL	LX09AZB	29	AL	LX09AZR	39	A	LX09EVH
10	AL	LX09AYP	20	AL	LX09AXC	30	AL	LX09AZT	40	A	LX09EVJ

An interesting development vehicle currently operated by Go-Ahead London is VM1, BJ11XGZ. A product of a partnership between Volvo and MCV, it is one of only two double-deck MCV vehicle so far placed in service. It was seen near its Silvertown depot while working route 474. *Richard Godfrey*

VE1	AF	LX58CWK	Volvo B9TL	10.4m	ADL Enviro 400	N41/24D	2008	
VE2	AF	LX58CWL	Volvo B9TL	10.4m	ADL Enviro 400	N41/24D	2008	
VE3	AF	LX58CWM	Volvo B9TL	10.4m	ADL Enviro 400	N41/24D	2008	
VM1	SI	BJ11XGZ	Volvo B9TL	10.3m	MCV	N41/22D	2011	development vehicle

VP1-19

Volvo B7TL 10m — Plaxton President — N41/20D* — 2001 — *18/19 N41/23D

East Thames, 2009

1	Q	X149FBB	6	Q	X157FBB	11	Q	X163FBB	16	BX	X168FBB
2	Q	X151FBB	7	Q	X158FBB	12	Q	X164FBB	17	BX	X169FBB
3	Q	X152FBB	8	Q	X159FBB	13	Q	X165FBB	18	Qt	X171FBB
4	Q	X153FBB	9	Q	X161FBB	14	Q	X166FBB	19	Qt	X172FBB
5	Q	X154FBB	10	Q	X162FBB	15	BV	X167FBB			

VWL1-31

Volvo B7TL 10.6m — Wrightbus Eclipse Gemini — N43/22D — 2002

1	Q	LB02YWX	9	Q	LB02YXG	17	BV	LF52TGO	25	BV	LF52THN
2	Q	LB02YWY	10	Q	LB02YXH	18	BV	LF52TGU	26	BV	LF52THU
3	Q	LB02YWZ	11	BV	LB02YXJ	19	BV	LF52TGV	27	MW	LF52THV
4	Q	LB02YXA	12	BV	LB02YXK	20	BV	LF52TGX	28	MW	LF52THX
5	Q	LB02YXC	13	BV	LB02YXL	21	BV	LF52TGY	29	MW	LF52THZ
6	Q	LB02YXD	14	BV	LB02YXM	22	BV	LF52TGZ	30	MW	LF52TJO
7	Q	LB02YXE	15	BV	LB02YXN	23	BV	LF52THG	31	MW	LF52TJU
8	Q	LB02YXF	16	BV	LF52TGN	24	BV	LF52THK			

VWL32-44

Volvo B7TL 10.6m — Wrightbus Eclipse Gemini — N43/23D — 2004

32	MW	BX04AZW	36	MW	BX04BAA	39	MW	BX04BBE	42	MW	BX04BKL
33	MW	BX04AZV	37	MW	BX04BAU	40	MW	BX04BBF	43	MW	BX04BKK
34	MW	BX04AZU	38	MW	BX04BAV	41	MW	BX04BBJ	44	MW	BX04BKJ
35	MW	BX04AZZ									

WDL1	Q	LX58CWG	VDL/Wrightbus DL 10.4m	Wrightbus Gemini 2	N41/24D	2009
WHD1	SW	LX58CWJ	VDL DB300 Wrightbus Hybrid	Wrightbus Gemini 2	N41/24D	2008

WHV1-16 — Volvo B5LH — Wrightbus Gemini 2 — N41/24D — 2011

#		Reg	#		Reg	#		Reg	#		Reg
1	Q	LJ61GVW	5	Q	LJ61GWA	9	Q	LJ61GXG	13	Q	LJ61GXM
2	Q	LJ61GVX	6	Q	LJ61GWC	10	Q	LJ61GXH	14	Q	LJ61GXN
3	Q	LJ61GVY	7	Q	LJ61GXE	11	Q	LJ61GXK	15	Q	LJ61GXO
4	Q	LJ61GVZ	8	Q	LJ61GXF	12	Q	LJ61GXL	16	Q	LJ61GXP

WHV17-31 — Volvo B5LH — Wrightbus Gemini 2 — N41/24D — 2012

#		Reg	#		Reg	#		Reg	#		Reg
17	SW	LJ61NVC	21	SW	LJ61NVG	25	SW	LJ61NVM	29	SW	LJ61NVR
18	SW	LJ61NVD	22	SW	LJ61NVH	26	SW	LJ61NVN	30	SW	LJ61NVS
19	SW	LJ61NVE	23	SW	LJ61NVK	27	SW	LJ12CHH	31	SW	LJ12CHK
20	SW	LJ61NVF	24	SW	LJ61NVL	28	SW	LJ61NVP			

WHV32-41 — Volvo B5LH — Wrightbus Gemini 2 — N41/24D — On order

#			#			#			#		
32	-	-	35	-	-	38	-	-	40	-	-
33	-	-	36	-	-	39	-	-	41	-	-
34	-	-	37	-	-						

WHY1-7 — VDL Bus Hybrid 10.4m — Wrightbus Electrocity — N26D* — 2005-08 — *7 is N28D

#		Reg	#		Reg	#		Reg	#		Reg
1	Q	LX06ECN	3	Q	LX55EAE	6	Q	LX55EAJ	7	Q	LX57CLZ
2	Q	LX55EAC	4	Q	LX55EAF	5	Q	LX55EAG			

WHY8-13 — VDL Bus Hybrid 10.4m — Wrightbus Electrocity — N26D — 2011

#		Reg	#		Reg	#		Reg	#		Reg
8	Q	LX11DVA	10	Q	LX11DVC	12	Q	LX11DVG	13	Q	LX11DVH
9	Q	LX11DVB	11	Q	LX11DVF						

WS1-9 — Wrightbus StreetLite WF 8.8m — Wrightbus — N28F — 2012

#		Reg	#		Reg	#		Reg	#		Reg
1	BE	LJ12CGF	4	BE	LJ12CGO	6	BE	LJ12CGV	8	BE	LJ12CGY
2	BE	LJ12CGG	5	BE	LJ12CGU	7	BE	LJ12CGX	9	BE	LJ12CGZ
3	BE	LJ12CGK									

WVL1-121 — Volvo B7TL 10.1m — Wrightbus Eclipse Gemini 4.2m N41/22D 2002-03

#		Reg	#		Reg	#		Reg	#		Reg
1	SW	LG02KGP	32	AF	LF52ZRO	62	AF	LF52ZTG	92	AL	LF52ZND
2	SW	LG02KGU	33	AF	LF52ZRP	63	AF	LF52ZTH	93	AL	LF52ZNE
3	SW	LG02KGV	34	AF	LF52ZRR	64	AF	LF52ZTJ	94	AL	LF52ZNG
4	SW	LG02KGX	35	AF	LF52ZRT	65	AF	LF52ZTK	95	AL	LF52ZNH
5	SW	LG02KGY	36	AF	LF52ZRU	66	AF	LF52ZTL	96	AL	LF52ZNJ
6	SW	LG02KGZ	37	AF	LF52ZRV	67	AF	LF52ZTM	97	AL	LF52ZNK
7	SW	LG02KHA	38	AF	LF52ZRX	68	AF	LF52ZTN	98	AL	LF52ZNL
8	SW	LG02KHE	39	AF	LF52ZRY	69	AF	LF52ZTO	99	AL	LF52ZNM
9	SW	LG02KHF	40	AF	LF52ZRZ	70	AF	LF52ZTP	100	AL	LF52ZNN
10	SW	LG02KHH	41	AF	LF52ZSD	71	AF	LF52ZTR	101	AL	LF52ZNO
11	SW	LG02KHJ	42	AF	LF52ZPZ	72	AL	LF52ZPB	102	AL	LF52ZLZ
12	SW	LG02KHK	43	AF	LF52ZRA	73	AL	LF52ZPC	103	AL	LF52ZMO
13	SW	LG02KHL	44	AF	LF52ZRC	74	AL	LF52ZPD	104	AL	LF52ZMU
14	AF	LG02KHM	45	AF	LF52ZRD	75	AL	LF52ZPE	105	SW	LX03EXV
15	AF	LG02KHO	46	AF	LF52ZRE	76	AL	LF52ZPG	106	SW	LX03EXW
16	AF	LG02KHP	47	AF	LF52ZRG	77	AL	LF52ZPH	107	SW	LX03EXZ
17	AF	LG02KHR	48	AF	LF52ZRJ	78	AL	LF52ZPJ	108	SW	LX03EXU
18	AF	LG02KHT	49	AF	LF52ZRK	79	AL	LF52ZPK	109	SW	LX03EDR
19	AF	LG02KHU	50	AF	LF52ZRL	80	AL	LF52ZPL	110	SW	LX03EDU
20	AF	LG02KHV	51	AF	LF52ZRN	81	AL	LF52ZPM	111	SW	LX03EDV
21	AF	LG02KHW	52	AF	LF52ZPN	82	AL	LF52ZNP	112	SW	LX03EEA
22	AF	LG02KHX	53	AF	LF52ZPO	83	AL	LF52ZNR	113	SW	LX03EEB
23	AF	LG02KHY	54	AF	LF52ZPP	84	AL	LF52ZNS	114	SW	LX03EEF
24	AF	LG02KHZ	55	AF	LF52ZPR	85	AL	LF52ZNT	115	SW	LX03EEG
25	AF	LG02KJA	56	AF	LF52ZPS	86	AL	LF52ZNU	116	SW	LX03EEH
26	AF	LG02KJE	57	AF	LF52ZPU	87	AL	LF52ZNV	117	SW	LX03EEJ
27	AF	LG02KJF	58	AF	LF52ZPV	88	AL	LF52ZNW	118	SW	LX03EEM
28	AF	LF52ZSO	59	AF	LF52ZPW	89	AL	LF52ZNX	119	SW	LX03ECV
29	AF	LF52ZSP	60	AF	VLT60	90	AL	LF52ZNY	120	SW	LX03ECW
30	AF	LF52ZSR	61	AF	LF52ZPY	91	AL	LF52ZNZ	121	Q	LX03ECY
31	AF	LF52ZST									

WVL122-159 — Volvo B7TL 10.1m — Wrightbus Eclipse Gemini 4.2m N41/23D* 2003-04 — *150 is N41/21D

No.		Reg	No.		Reg	No.		Reg	No.		Reg
122	SW	LX53AZP	133	SW	LX53AZF	142	SW	LX53AYP	151	SW	LX53BJU
123	SW	LX53AZR	134	SW	LX53AZG	143	SW	LX53AYT	152	AL	LX53BEY
124	SW	LX53AZT	135	SW	LX53AZJ	144	SW	LX53AYU	153	AF	LX53BGE
125	SW	LX53AZU	136	SW	LX53AZL	145	SW	LX53AYV	154	AF	LX53BFK
126	SW	LX53AZV	137	SW	LX53AZN	146	SW	LX53AYW	155	AF	LX53BDY
129	SW	LX53AZA	138	SW	LX53AZO	147	SW	LX53AYY	156	AF	LX53BBZ
130	SW	LX53AZB	139	SW	LX53AYM	148	SW	LX53AYZ	157	AF	LX53BAA
131	SW	LX53AZC	140	SW	LX53AYN	149	SW	LX53BJK	158	AF	LX53BDO
132	SW	LX53AZD	141	SW	LX53AYO	150	Q	LX53BJO	159	AF	LX53BAO

WVL160-211 — Volvo B7TL 10.1m — Wrightbus Eclipse Gemini 4.2m N41/23D 2005

No.		Reg	No.		Reg	No.		Reg	No.		Reg
160	AF	LX05FBY	173	AF	LX05FBN	186	AF	LX05FAU	199	AF	LX05EZR
161	AF	LX05FBZ	174	AF	LX05FBO	187	AF	LX05FBA	200	AF	LX05EZS
162	AF	LX05FCA	175	AF	LX05FBU	188	AF	LX05FBB	201	AF	LX05EZT
163	AF	LX05FCC	176	AF	LX05EZJ	189	AF	LX05FBC	202	AF	LX05EZU
164	AF	LX05FCD	177	AF	LX05EYM	190	AF	LX05EZV	203	AF	LX05EYZ
165	AF	LX05FCE	178	AF	LX05EYO	191	AF	LX05EZW	204	AF	LX05EZA
166	AF	LX05FCF	179	AF	LX05FBV	192	AF	LX05EZZ	205	AF	LX05EZB
167	AF	LX05FBD	180	AF	LX05FAA	193	AF	LX05EZK	206	AF	LX05EZC
168	AF	LX05FBE	181	AF	LX05FAF	194	AF	LX05EZL	207	AF	LX05EZD
169	AF	LX05FBF	182	AF	LX05FAJ	195	AF	LX05EZM	208	AF	LX05EZE
170	AF	LX05FBJ	183	AF	LX05FAK	196	AF	LX05EZN	209	AF	LX05EZF
171	AF	LX05FBK	184	AF	LX05FAM	197	AF	LX05EZO	210	AF	LX05EZG
172	AF	LX05FBL	185	AF	LX05FAO	198	AF	LX05EZP	211	AF	LX05EZH

WVL212-273 — Volvo B7TL 10.1m — Wrightbus Eclipse Gemini 4.2m N41/21D 2006

No.		Reg	No.		Reg	No.		Reg	No.		Reg
212	Q	LX06DYS	229	Q	LX06DZM	244	Q	LX06EAG	259	Q	LX06EBK
213	Q	LX06DYT	230	Q	LX06DZN	245	Q	LX06EAJ	260	Q	LX06EBL
214	Q	LX06DYU	231	Q	LX06DZO	246	Q	LX06EAK	261	Q	LX06EBM
215	Q	LX06DYV	232	Q	LX06DZP	247	Q	LX06EAL	262	Q	LX06EBN
216	Q	LX06DYW	233	Q	LX06DZR	248	Q	LX06EAM	263	Q	LX06EBO
217	Q	LX06DYY	234	Q	LX06DZS	249	Q	LX06EAO	264	Q	LX06EBP
218	Q	LX06DZA	235	Q	LX06DZT	250	Q	LX06EAP	265	Q	LX06EBU
219	Q	LX06DZB	236	Q	LX06DZU	251	Q	LX06EAW	266	Q	LX06EBV
220	Q	LX06DZC	237	Q	LX06DZV	252	Q	LX06EAY	267	Q	LX06EBZ
222	Q	LX06DZE	238	Q	LX06DZW	253	Q	LX06EBA	268	Q	LX06ECA
223	Q	LX06DZF	239	Q	LX06DZY	254	Q	LX06EBC	269	Q	LX06ECC
224	Q	LX06DZG	240	Q	LX06DZZ	255	Q	LX06EBD	270	Q	LX06ECD
225	Q	LX06DZH	241	Q	LX06EAA	256	Q	LX06EBE	271	MW	LX06ECE
226	Q	LX06DZJ	242	Q	LX06EAC	257	Q	LX06EBG	272	BX	LX06ECF
227	Q	LX06DZK	243	Q	LX06EAF	258	Q	LX06EBJ	273	BX	LX06ECJ
228	Q	LX06DZL									

WVL274-349 — Volvo B9TL 10.1m — Wrightbus Eclipse Gemini 2 N39/23D 2009-10

No.		Reg	No.		Reg	No.		Reg	No.		Reg
274	NX	LX59CYL	293	NX	LX59CZL	312	PM	LX59CZY	331	PM	LX59DDF
275	NX	LX59CYO	294	NX	LX59CZM	313	PM	LX59CZZ	332	PM	LX59DDJ
276	NX	LX59CYP	295	NX	LX59CZN	314	PM	LX59DAA	333	PM	LX59DDK
277	NX	LX59CYS	296	NX	LX59CZO	315	PM	LX59DAO	334	BE	LX59DDL
278	NX	LX59CYT	297	NX	LX59CZP	316	PM	LX59DAU	335	BE	LX59DDN
279	NX	LX59CYU	298	NX	LX59CZR	317	PM	LX59DBO	336	BE	LX59DDO
280	NX	LX59CYV	299	NX	LX59CZS	318	PM	LX59DBU	337	BE	LX59DDU
281	NX	LX59CYW	300	NX	LX59CZT	319	PM	LX59DBV	338	BE	LX59DDV
282	NX	LX59CYY	301	NX	LX59CZU	320	PM	LX59DBY	339	BE	LX59DDY
283	NX	LX59CYZ	302	NX	LX59CZV	321	PM	LX59DBZ	340	BE	LX59DDZ
284	NX	LX59CZA	303	PM	LX59CYA	322	PM	LX59DCE	341	BE	LX59DEU
285	NX	LX59CZB	304	PM	LX59CYC	323	PM	LX59DCF	342	BE	LX59DFA
286	NX	LX59CZC	305	PM	LX59CYE	324	PM	LX59DCO	343	BE	LX59DFC
287	NX	LX59CZD	306	PM	LX59CYF	325	PM	LX59DCU	344	BE	LX59DFD
288	NX	LX59CZF	307	PM	LX59CYG	326	PM	LX59DCV	345	BE	LX59DFE
289	NX	LX59CZG	308	PM	LX59CYH	327	PM	LX59DCY	346	BE	LX59DFF
290	NX	LX59CZH	309	PM	LX59CYJ	328	PM	LX59DCZ	347	BE	LX59DFG
291	NX	LX59CZJ	310	PM	LX59CYK	329	PM	LX59DDA	348	BE	LX59DFJ
292	NX	LX59CZK	311	PM	LX59CZW	330	PM	LX59DDE	349	BE	LX59DFK

WVL350-385   Volvo B9TL 10.1m   Wrightbus Eclipse Gemini 2   N39/23D   2010-11

350	BX	LX60DVY	359	BX	LX60DWK	368	BX	LX60DWY	377	BX	LX60DXH
351	BX	LX60DVZ	360	BX	LX60DWL	369	BX	LX60DWZ	378	BX	LX60DXJ
352	BX	LX60DWA	361	BX	LX60DWM	370	BX	LX60DXA	379	BE	LX60DXK
353	BX	LX60DWC	362	BX	LX60DWN	371	BX	LX60DXB	380	Q	LX60DXM
354	BX	LX60DWD	363	BX	LX60DWO	372	BX	LX60DXC	381	Q	LX60DXO
355	BX	LX60DWE	364	BX	LX60DWP	373	BX	LX60DXD	382	Q	LX60DXP
356	BX	LX60DWF	365	BX	LX60DWU	374	BX	LX60DXE	383	Q	LX60DXR
357	BX	LX60DWG	366	BX	LX60DWV	375	BX	LX60DXF	384	Q	LX60DXS
358	BX	LX60DWJ	367	BX	LX60DWW	376	BX	LX60DXG	385	Q	LX60DXT

WVL386-421   Volvo B9TL 10.1m   Wrightbus Eclipse Gemini 2   N39/23D   2011

386	NX	LX11CVL	395	NX	LX11CVV	404	NX	LX11CWJ	413	SI	LX11CWU
387	NX	LX11CVM	396	NX	LX11CVW	405	NX	LX11CWK	414	SI	LX11CWV
388	NX	LX11CVN	397	NX	LX11CVY	406	NX	LX11CWL	415	SI	LX11CWW
389	NX	LX11CVO	398	NX	LX11CVZ	407	NX	LX11CWM	416	SI	LX11CWY
390	NX	LX11CVP	399	NX	LX11CWA	408	NX	LX11CWN	417	SI	LX11CWZ
391	NX	LX11CVR	400	NX	LX11CWC	409	NX	LX11CWO	418	SI	LX11CXA
392	NX	LX11CVS	401	NX	LX11CWD	410	NX	LX11CWP	419	SI	LX11CXB
393	NX	LX11CVT	402	NX	LX11CWE	411	NX	LX11CWR	420	SI	LX11CXC
394	NX	LX11CVU	403	NX	LX11CWG	412	NX	LX11CWT	421	SI	LX11CXD

WVL422-454   Volvo B9TL 10.1m   Wrightbus Eclipse Gemini 2   N39/23D   2011

422	SI	LX11FHV	431	SI	LX11FJJ	439	Q	LX61GWY	447	Q	LX61GWF
423	SI	LX11FHW	432	SI	LX11FJK	440	Q	LX61GWZ	448	Q	LX61GWG
424	SI	LX11FHY	433	SI	LX11FJN	441	Q	LX61GXA	449	Q	LX61GWK
425	SI	LX11FHZ	434	SI	LX11FJO	442	Q	LX61GXB	450	Q	LX61GWL
426	SI	LX11FJA	435	Q	LX61GWU	443	Q	LX61GXC	451	Q	LX61GWM
427	SI	LX11FJC	436	Q	LX61GWV	444	Q	LX61GXD	452	Q	LX61GWN
428	SI	LX11FJD	437	Q	LX61GWW	445	Q	LX61GWD	453	Q	LX61GWO
429	SI	LX11FJE	438	Q	LX61GWX	446	Q	LX61GWE	454	Q	LX61GWP
430	SI	LX11FJF									

WVL455-495   Volvo B9TL 10.1m   Wrightbus Eclipse Gemini 2   N39/23D   2012

455	BE	LJ61GVP	466	BE	LJ61NVB	476	AL	LJ61NXF	486	SW	LJ61NWV
456	BE	LJ61GVT	467	BE	LJ61NWW	477	AL	LJ61NWL	487	SW	LJ61NVZ
457	BE	LJ61NUM	468	AL	LJ61NWX	478	AL	LJ61NWM	488	SW	LJ61NWA
458	BE	LJ61NUO	469	AL	LJ12CHC	479	AL	LJ61NWN	489	SW	LJ61NWB
459	BE	LJ61NUP	470	AL	LJ61NWZ	480	AL	LJ61NWO	490	SW	LJ61NWC
460	BE	LJ61NUU	471	AL	LJ61NXA	481	SW	LJ12CHD	491	SW	LJ61NWD
461	BE	LJ61NUV	472	AL	LJ61NXB	482	SW	LJ61NWR	492	SW	LJ61NWE
462	BE	LJ61NUW	473	AL	LJ61NXC	483	SW	LJ12CHF	493	SW	LJ61NWF
463	BE	LJ61NUX	474	AL	LJ61NXD	484	SW	LJ12CHG	494	SW	LJ61NWG
464	BE	LJ61NUY	475	AL	LJ61NXE	485	SW	LJ61NWU	495	SW	LJ61NWH
465	BE	LJ61NVA									

WVL496-526   Volvo B9TL 10.1m   Wrightbus Eclipse Gemini 2   N39/23D   On order

496	-	-	504	-	-	512	-	-	520	-	-
497	-	-	505	-	-	513	-	-	521	-	-
498	-	-	506	-	-	514	-	-	522	-	-
499	-	-	507	-	-	515	-	-	523	-	-
500	-	-	508	-	-	516	-	-	524	-	-
501	-	-	509	-	-	517	-	-	525	-	-
502	-	-	510	-	-	518	-	-	526	-	-
503	-	-	511	-	-	519	-	-			

WNV1-23   Volvo B9TL   Wrightbus Eclipse Gemini 2   N41/29D   2009-10   First, 2012

1	NP	LK59FEP	7	NP	LK59FDZ	13	NP	LK59FEO	19	NP	LK59FDM
2	NP	LK59FET	8	NP	LK59FEF	14	NP	LK59FDE	20	NP	LK59FDN
3	NP	LK59FEU	9	NP	LK59FEG	15	NP	LK59FDF	21	NP	LK59FDO
4	NP	LK59FDV	10	NP	LK59FEH	16	NP	LK59FDG	22	NP	LK59FDP
5	NP	LK59FDX	11	NP	LK59FEJ	17	NP	LK59FDJ	23	NP	LK59FDU
6	NP	LK59FDY	12	NP	LK59FEM	18	NP	LK59FDL			

The principal vehicle in the Go-Ahead London fleet is the Wrightbus Eclipse Gemini-bodied Volvo double deck. North Woolwich is the location for this view of WVL420, LX11CXC, one of twenty-three Volvo B9TLs allocated to Silvertown depot. *Richard Godfrey*

WVN24-45 — Volvo B9TL — Wrightbus Eclipse Gemini 2 — N41/29D — 2009-10 — First, 2012

24	NP	BG59FXA	30	NP	BG59FXH	36	NP	BV10WVJ	41	NP	BV10WWD
25	NP	BG59FXB	31	NP	BV10WVD	37	NP	BV10WVK	42	NP	BV10WWF
26	NP	BG59FXC	32	NP	BV10WVE	38	NP	BV10WVL	43	NP	BV10WWO
27	NP	BG59FXD	33	NP	BV10WVF	39	NP	BV10WWA	44	NP	BV10WWP
28	NP	BG59FXE	34	NP	BV10WVG	40	NP	BV10WWC	45	NP	BV10WWR
29	NP	BG59FXF	35	NP	BV10WVH						

WVN46-53 — Volvo B9TL — Wrightbus Eclipse Gemini 2 — N41/29D — 2012 — First, 2012

46	NP	BL61ACY	48	NP	BL61ADU	50	NP	BL61ADV	52	NP	BL61ADX
47	NP	BL61ACX	49	NP	BL61ACZ	51	NP	BL61ADO	53	NP	BL61AD

Previous registrations:

R370LGH	R370LGH, WLT470
VLT9	VLT9, OYM374A
W425WGH	W425WGH, WLT625

W578DGU	170CLT
WLT516	CUV283C

Depots and allocations:

Belvedere (Burt's Wharf, Crabtree Manor Way, DA17 6LJ) - BV

Enviro 200	SE55	SE56	SE57	SE58	SE59	SE60	SE61	SE62
	SE63	SE64	SE65	SE66	SE67	SE68		
Volvo B7TL	PVL368	VP15	VWL11	VWL12	VWL13	VWL14	VWL15	VWL16
	VWL17	VWL18	VWL19	VWL20	VWL21	VWL22	VWL23	VWL24
	VWL25	VWL26						

Bexleyheath (Erith Road, DA7 6BX) - BX

Dart	LDP202	LDP207						
Enviro 200	SE69	SE70	SE71	SE72	SE73	SE74	SE75	SE76
	SE77	SE78	SE79	SE80	SE81	SE82	SE83	SE84
SB120	DW13	DW14	DW15	DW16	DW17	DW18	DW19	DW20
	DW21	DW22	DW23	DW24	DW25			
Volvo B7TL	PVL150	PVL159	PVL219	PVL346	PVL347	PVL348	PVL349	PVL350
	PVL351	PVL352	PVL353	PVL354	PVL355	PVL362	PVL363	PVL364
	PVL365	PVL366	PVL367	PVL369	PVL370	WVL272	WVL273	
Volvo B9TL	WVL350	WVL351	WVL352	WVL353	WVL354	WVL355	WVL356	WVL357
	WVL358	WVL359	WVL360	WVL361	WVL362	WVL363	WVL364	WVL366
	WVL367	WVL368	WVL369	WVL370	WVL371	WVL372	WVL373	WVL374
	WVL375	WVL376	WVL377	WVL378				
Enviro 400	E40	E41	E42	E43	E44	E45	E46	E47
	E48	E49	E50	E51	E52	E53	E54	E55
	E56	E229	E230	E231	E232	E233	E234	E235
	E236	E237	E238	E239	E240	E241	E242	E243
	E244	E245						

Camberwell (Warner Road, SE5 9LU) - Q

Dart	LDP249	LDP250	LDP251	LDP252	LDP253	LDP254	LDP255	LDP256
	LDP257	LDP258	LDP259	LDP260	LDP261	LDP262		
Enviro 200	SE85	SE86	SE87	SE88	SE89	SE90	SE91	SE92
	SE93							
Scania N94	ELS1	ELS2	ELS3	ELS4	ELS5	ELS6	ELS7	ELS8
	ELS9	ELS10	ELS11	ELS12	ELS13	ELS14		
Optare Versa	HOV1							
VDL/Wrightbus Hybrid	WDL1	WHY1	WHY2	WHY3	WHY4	WHY5	WHY6	WHY7
	WHY8	WHY9	WHY10	WHY11	WHY12	WHY13		
Routemaster	RML2472	RML2520						
Volvo B7TL	EVL5	EVL15	EVL17	PVL59	PVL60	PVL62	PVL64	PVL75
	PVL79	PVL129	PVL131	PVL217	PVL272	PVL298	PVL299	PVL300
	PVL301	PVL302	PVL303	PVL304	PVL305	PVL306	PVL307	PVL308
	PVL309	PVL310	PVL311	PVL312	PVL313	PVL314	PVL315	PVL316
	PVL317	PVL318	PVL326	PVL327	PVL328	VP1	VP2	VP3
	VP4	VP5	VP6	VP7	VP8	VP9	VP10	VP11
	VP12	VP13	VP14	VWL1	VWL2	VWL3	VWL4	VWL6
	VWL7	VWL8	VWL9	VWL10	WVL212	WVL213	WVL214	WVL215
	WVL216	WVL217	WVL218	WVL219	WVL220	WVL222	WVL223	WVL224
	WVL225	WVL226	WVL227	WVL228	WVL229	WVL230	WVL231	WVL232
	WVL233	WVL234	WVL235	WVL236	WVL237	WVL238	WVL239	WVL240
	WVL241	WVL242	WVL243	WVL244	WVL245	WVL246	WVL247	WVL248
	WVL249	WVL250	WVL251	WVL252	WVL253	WVL254	WVL255	WVL256
	WVL257	WVL259	WVL260	WVL261	WVL262	WVL263	WVL264	WVL265
	WVL266	WVL267	WVL268	WVL269	WVL270	WVL271	WVL272	WVL273
Volvo B9TL	WVL380	WVL381	WVL382	WVL383	WVL384	WVL385	WVL435	WVL436
	WVL437	WVL438	WVL439	WVL440	WVL441	WVL442	WVL443	WVL444
	WVL445	WVL447	WVL448	WVL449	WVL450	WVL451	WVL452	WVL453
	WVL454							
Volvo B5LH	WHV1	WHV2	WHV3	WHV4	WHV5	WHV6	WHV7	WHV8
	WHV9	WHV10	WHV11	WHV12	WHV13	WHV14	WHV15	WHV16
Enviro 400	E100	E101	E102	E103	E104	E105	E106	E107
	E108	E109	E110	E111	E112	E113	E114	E115
	E116	E117	E118	E119	E120	E121	E122	E123
	E124	E125	E126	E127	E128			

Merton (High Street, SW19 1DN) - AL

Dart	LDP191	LDP192	LDP193	LDP194	LDP195	LDP196	LDP197	LDP198
	LDP199	LDP200	LDP201					
SB120	DW1	DW2	DW3	DW4	DW5	DW6	DW7	DW8
	DW9	DW10	DW11	DW12				
Enviro 200	SE1	SE2	SE3	SE4	SE5	SE6	SE7	SE8
	SE9	SE10	SE11	SE12	SE13	SE14	SE15	SE16
	SE17	SOE1	SOE2	SOE3	SOE4	SOE5	SOE6	SOE7
	SOE8	SOE9	SOE10	SOE11	SOE12	SOE13	SOE14	SOE15
	SOE16	SOE17	SOE18	SOE19	SOE20	SOE21	SOE22	SOE23
	SOE24	SOE25	SOE26	SOE27	SOE28	SOE29	SOE30	
Routemaster	RML2305	RML2604						
Olympian	NV170	NV171						

The 2012-13 Go-Ahead Bus Handbook

Enviro 400	E138	E139	E140	E141	E142	E143	E144	
	E145	E146	E147	E148	E149	E150		
Volvo B7TL	PVL59	PVL62	PVL70	PVL84	PVL85	PVL87	PVL94	PVL106
	PVL112	PVL114	PVL115	PVL116	PVL117	PVL118	PVL119	PVL121
	PVL122	PVL124	PVL125	PVL126	PVL127	PVL128	PVL137	PVL144
	PVL145	PVL146	PVL147	PVL148	PVL152	PVL153	PVL154	PVL155
	PVL160	PVL161	PVL162	PVL163	PVL164	PVL165	PVL166	PVL167
	PVL215	PVL229	PVL371	PVL372	PVL373	PVL374	PVL375	PVL376
	PVL377	PVL378	PVL379	PVL380	PVL381	PVL382	PVL383	PVL384
	PVL385	PVL386	PVL387	PVL388	PVL389			
Volvo B7TL	WVL72	WVL73	WVL74	WVL75	WVL76	WVL77	WVL78	WVL79
	WVL80	WVL81	WVL82	WVL83	WVL84	WVL85	WVL86	WVL87
	WVL88	WVL89	WVL90	WVL91	WVL92	WVL93	WVL94	WVL95
	WVL96	WVL97	WVL98	WVL99	WVL100	WVL101	WVL102	WVL103
	WVL104							
Volvo B9TL	WVL468	WVL469	WVL470	WVL471	WVL472	WVL473	WVL474	WVL475
	WVL476	WVL477	WVL478	WVL479	WVL480			

Northumberland Park (Marsh Lane, Tottenham, N17 0XB) - NP

Dart	DMN1							
Enviro 200	SE1	SE2	SE3	SE4	SE5	SE6	SE7	SE8
	SE9	SE10	SE11	SE12	SE13	SE14	SE15	SE16
	SE17	SE18	SE19	SE20	SE21	SE22	SE23	SE24
	SE25	SE26	SE27	SE28	SE29			
Trident	PD1	PD2	PD3	PD4	PD5	PD6		
Enviro 400	EN1	EN2	EN3	EN4	EN5	EN6	EN7	EN8
	EN9	EN10	EN11	EN12	EN13	EN14	EN15	EN16
	EN17	EN18	EN19	EN20	EN21	EN22	EN23	EN24
Volvo B7TL	PVN1	PVN2	PVN3	PVN4	PVN5	PVN6	PVN7	PVN8
	PVN9	PVN10	PVN11	PVN12	PVN13	PVN14	PVN15	PVN16
	PVN17							
Volvo B9TL	WVN1	WVN2	WVN3	WVN4	WVN5	WVN6	WVN7	WVN8
	WVN9	WVN10	WVN11	WVN12	WVN13	WVN14	WVN15	WVN16
	WVN17	WVN18	WVN19	WVN20	WVN21	WVN22	WVN23	WVN24
	WVN25	WVN26	WVN27	WVN28	WVN29	WVN30	WVN32	WVN32
	WVN33	WVN34	WVN35	WVN36	WVN37	WVN38	WVN39	WVN40
	WVN41	WVN42	WVN43	WVN44	WVN45	WVN46	WVN47	WVN48
	WVN49	WVN50	WVN51	WVN52	WVN53			

New Cross (New Cross Road, SE14 5UH) - NX

Dart	DP209	LDP210	LDP273	LDP274	LDP275	LDP276	LDP277	LDP278
	LDP279	LDP280						
Enviro 200	ED1	ED2	ED3	ED4	ED7	ED8		
SB120	DWL26	DWL27	DWL28	DWL29	DWL30	DWL31	DWL32	DWL33
	DWL34	DWL35	DWL36	DWL37				
Enviro 400	E94	E95	E96	E97	E98	E99	E202	E203
	E204	E205	E206	E207	E208	E209	E210	E211
	E212	E213	E214	E215	E216	E217	E218	E219
	E220	E221	E222	E223	E224	E225	E226	E227
	E228							
Volvo B7TL	PVL63	PVL83	PVL85	PVL151	PVL190	PVL216	PVL223	PVL225
	PVL248	PVL264	PVL276	PVL319	PVL320	PVL321	PVL322	PVL323
	PVL324	PVL325	PVL343	PVL344	PVL345	PVL390	PVL391	PVL392
	PVL393	PVL394	PVL395	PVL396	PVL397	PVL398	PVL399	PVL400
	PVL401	PVL402	PVL403	PVL404	PVL405	PVL406	PVL407	PVL408
	PVL409	PVL410	PVL411	PVL412	PVL413	PVL414	PVL415	PVL416
	PVL417	PVL418	PVL419					
Routemaster	RM9	RML2318						
Volvo B9TL	WVL274	WVL275	WVL276	WVL277	WVL278	WVL279	WVL280	WVL281
	WVL282	WVL283	WVL284	WVL285	WVL286	WVL287	WVL288	WVL289
	WVL290	WVL291	WVL292	WVL293	WVL294	WVL295	WVL296	WVL297
	WVL298	WVL299	WVL300	WVL301	WVL302	WVL386	WVL387	WVL388
	WVL389	WVL390	WVL391	WVL392	WVL393	WVL394	WVL395	WVL396
	WVL397	WVL398	WVL399	WVL400	WVL401	WVL402	WVL403	WVL404
	WVL405	WVL406	WVL407	WVL408	WVL409	WVL410	WVL411	WVL412

Northumberland Park (Marsh Lane, Tottenham, N17 0HY) - NP

Dart	DMN1							
Enviro 200	SE1	SE2	SE3	SE4	SE5	SE6	SE7	SE8
	SE9	SE10	SE11	SE12	SE13	SE14	SE15	SE16
	SE17	SE18	SE19	SE20	SE21	SE22	SE23	SE24
	SE25	SE26	SE27	SE28	SE29			
Trident	PDN1	PDN2	PDN3	PDN4	PDN5	PDN6		
Volvo B7TL	PVN1	PVN2	PVN3	PVN4	PVN5	PVN6	PVN7	PVN8
	PVN9	PVN10	PVN11	PVN12	PVN13	PVN14	PVN15	PVN16
	PVN17							
Volvo B9TL	WVN1	WVN2	WVN3	WVN4	WVN5	WVN6	WVN7	WVN8
	WVN9	WVN10	WVN11	WVN12	WVN13	WVN14	WVN15	WVN16
	WVN17	WVN18	WVN19	WVN20	WVN21	WVN22	WVN23	WVN24
	WVN25	WVN26	WVN27	WVN28	WVN29	WVN30	WVN31	WVN32
	WVN33	WVN34	WVN35	WVN36	WVN37	WVN38	WVN39	WVN40
	WVN41	WVN42	WVN43	WVN44	WVN45	WVN46	WVN47	WVN48
	WVN49	WVN50	WVN51	WVN52	WVN53			
Enviro 400	EN1	EN2	EN3	EN4	EN5	EN6	EN7	EN8
	EN9	EN10	EN11	EN12	EN13	EN14	EN15	EN16
	EN17	EN18	EN19	EN20	EN21	EN22	EN23	EN24

Peckham (Blackpool Road, SE15 3SU) - PM

Dart	LDP206							
Enviro 200	SE153	SE154	SE155	SE156	SE157	SE158	SE159	SE160
	SE161	SE162	SE163	SE164	SE165	SE166		
Volvo B7TL	PVL189	PVL329	PVL330	PVL331	PVL332	PVL333	PVL334	PVL335
	PVL336	PVL337	PVL338	PVL339	PVL340	PVL341	PVL342	
Volvo B9TL	WVL303	WVL304	WVL305	WVL306	WVL307	WVL308	WVL309	WVL310
	WVL311	WVL312	WVL313	WVL314	WVL315	WVL316	WVL317	WVL318
	WVL319	WVL320	WVL321	WVL322	WVL323	WVL324	WVL325	WVL326
	WVL327	WVL328	WVL329	WVL330	WVL331	WVL332	WVL333	
Enviro 400	E16	E17	E18	E19	E20	E21	E22	E23
	E24	E25	E26	E27	E28	E29	E30	E31
	E32	E33	E34	E35	E36	E37	E61	

Putney (Chelverton Road, SW15 1RN) - AF

Dart	LDP281	LDP282	LDP283	LDP284	LDP285	LDP286		
Volvo B7TL	PVL113	PVL149	PVL169	PVL170	WVL14	WVL15	WVL16	WVL17
	WVL18	WVL19	WVL20	WVL21	WVL22	WVL23	WVL24	WVL25
	WVL26	WVL27	WVL28	WVL29	WVL30	WVL31	WVL32	WVL33
	WVL34	WVL35	WVL36	WVL37	WVL38	WVL39	WVL40	WVL41
	WVL42	WVL43	WVL44	WVL45	WVL46	WVL47	WVL48	WVL49
	WVL50	WVL51	WVL52	WVL53	WVL54	WVL55	WVL56	WVL57
	WVL58	WVL59	WVL60	WVL61	WVL62	WVL63	WVL64	WVL65
	WVL66	WVL67	WVL68	WVL69	WVL70	WVL71	WVL153	WVL154
	WVL155	WVL156	WVL157	WVL158	WVL159	WVL160	WVL161	WVL162
	WVL163	WVL164	WVL165	WVL166	WVL167	WVL168	WVL169	WVL170
	WVL171	WVL172	WVL173	WVL175	WVL176	WVL177	WVL178	
	WVL179	WVL180	WVL181	WVL182	WVL183	WVL184	WVL185	WVL186
	WVL187	WVL188	WVL189	WVL190	WVL191	WVL192	WVL193	WVL194
	WVL195	WVL196	WVL197	WVL198	WVL199	WVL200	WVL201	WVL202
	WVL203	WVL204	WVL205	WVL206	WVL207	WVL208	WVL209	WVL210
	WVL211							
Volvo B9TL	VE1	VE2	VE3					

Rainham (Denver Industrial Estate, Ferry Lane, RM13 9DD) - BE

Streetlite	WS1	WS2	WS3	WS4	WS5	WS6	WS7	WS8
	WS9							
Dart	DP208							
Enviro 200	ED6	ED9	ED10	ED11	ED12	ED13	ED14	ED15
	ED16	ED17	ED18	ED19	ED20	ED21	ED22	ED23
	ED24	ED25	ED26	ED27	SE18	SE19	SE20	SE21
	SE22	SE23	SE24	SE25	SE26	SE27	SE28	SE29
	SE30	SE31	SE32	SE33	SE34	SE35	SE36	SE37
	SE38	SE39	SE40	SE41	SE42	SE43	SE44	SE45
	SE46	SE94	SE95	SE96	SE97	SE98	SE99	SE100

The 2012-13 Go-Ahead Bus Handbook

Joining the fleet during 2012 was a batch of nine Wrightbus Streetlite WF (Wheel Forward) buses. These are allocated to Rainham depot from where WS4, LJ12CGO, was working when pictured at Hainault.
Richard Godfrey

	SE101	SE102	SE103					
Volvo B7TL	PVL95	PVL96	PVL97	PVL209				
Volvo B9TL	WVL334	WVL335	WVL336	WVL337	WVL338	WVL339	WVL340	WVL341
	WVL342	WVL343	WVL344	WVL345	WVL346	WVL347	WVL348	WVL349
	WVL446							

Silvertown (Factory Road, E16 2EL) - SI

Optare Solo	OS1							
Enviro 200	SE104	SE105	SE106	SE107	SE108	SE109	SE110	SE111
	SE112	SE113	SE114	SE115	SE116	SE117	SE118	SE119
	SE120	SE121	SE122	SE123	SE124	SE125	SE126	SE127
	SE128	SE129	SE130	SE131	SE132	SE133	SE134	SE135
	SE136	SE137	SE138	SE139	SE140	SE141	SE142	SE143
	SE144	SE145	SE146	SE147	SE148	SE149	SE150	SE151
	SE152							
Volvo B9TL	VM1	WVL413	WVL414	WVL415	WVL416	WVL417	WVL418	WVL419
	WVL420	WVL421	WVL422	WVL423	WVL424	WVL425	WVL426	WVL427
	WVL428	WVL429	WVL430	WVL431	WVL432	WVL433	WVL434	
Scania OmniDekka	SO1	SO2	SO3	SO4	SO5	SOC1	SOC2	SOC3
	SOC4	SOC5	SOC6	SOC7	SOC8	SOC9		

Southwark (Unit 2, 5 Mandela Way, SE1 5SS) - MW

Citaro	MEC32	MEC37	MEC38	MEC40	MEC45	MEC48	MEC49	
Volvo B7TL	VWL27	VWL28	VWL29	VWL30	VWL31	VWL32	VWL33	VWL34
	VWL35	VWL36	VWL37	VWL38	VWL39	VWL40	VWL41	VWL42
	VWL43	VWL44	WVL271					
Enviro 400	E163	E164	E165	E166	E167	E168	E169	E170
	E171	E172	E173	E174	E175	E176	E177	E178
	E179	E180	E181	E182	E183	E184	E185	E186
	E187	E188	E189	E190	E191	E192	E193	E194
	E195	E196	E197	E198	E199	E200	E201	

Stockwell (Binfield Road, SW4 6ST) - SW

Dart	DP193	DP194	DP195	DP196	DP197	DP198	DP199	DP200
	DP201	DP202	DP203	DP204	DP205	DP209	LDP185	LDP187
	LDP197	LDP287	LDP288	LDP289	LDP290	LDP291		
Enviro 200	SE47	SE48	SE49	SE50	SE51	SE52	SE53	SE54

Enviro 400	E1	E2	E3	E4	E5	E6	E7	E8
	E9	E10	E11	E12	E13	E14	E15	E38
	E39	E57	E62	E63	E64	E65	E66	E67
	E68	E69	E70	E71	E72	E73	E74	E75
	E76	E77	E78	E79	E80	E81	E82	E83
	E84	E85	E86	E87	E88	E89	E90	E91
	E92	E93	E129	E130	E131	E132	E133	E134
	E135	E136	E137	E151	E152	E153	E154	E155
	E156	E157	E158	E159	E160	E161	E162	
Trident E400H	EH1	EH2	EH3	EH4	EH5			
VDL/Wrightbus	WHD1							
Volvo B5LH	WHY17	WHY18	WHY19	WHY20	WHY21	WHY22	WHY23	WHY24
	WHY25	WHY26	WHY27	WHY28	WHY29	WHY30	WHY31	
Volvo B7TL	PVL61	PVL93	PVL168	PVL201	PVL202	PVL203	PVL204	PVL205
	PVL206	PVL207	PVL214	PVL230	PVL231	PVL232	PVL233	PVL234
	PVL235	PVL236	PVL237	PVL238	WVL1	WVL2	WVL3	WVL4
	WVL5	WVL6	WVL7	WVL8	WVL9	WVL10	WVL11	WVL12
	WVL13	WVL105	WVL106	WVL107	WVL108	WVL109	WVL110	WVL111
	WVL112	WVL113	WVL114	WVL115	WVL116	WVL117	WVL118	WVL119
	WVL120	WVL121	WVL122	WVL123	WVL125	WVL126	WVL129	WVL130
	WVL131	WVL132	WVL133	WVL134	WVL135	WVL136	WVL137	WVL138
	WVL139	WVL140	WVL141	WVL142	WVL143	WVL144	WVL145	WVL146
	WVL147	WVL148	WVL149	WVL150	WVL151	WVL481	WVL482	WVL483
	WVL484	WVL485	WVL486	WVL487	WVL488	WVL489	WVL490	WVL491
	WVL492	WVL493	WVL494	WVL495				

Sutton (Bushey Road, SM1 1QJ) - A

Dart	LDP183							
Enviro 200	SE167	SE168	SE169	SE170	SE171	SE172	SE173	SE174
	SOE30	SOE31	SOE32	SOE33	SOE34	SOE35	SOE36	SOE37
	SOE38	SOE39	SOE40					
Trident 2	DOE1	DOE2	DOE3	DOE4	DOE5	DOE6	DOE7	DOE8
	DOE8	DOE10	DOE11	DOE12	DOE13	DOE14	DOE15	DOE16
	DOE17	DOE18	DOE19	DOE20	DOE21	DOE22	DOE23	DOE24
	DOE25	DOE26	DOE27	DOE28	DOE29	DOE30	DOE31	DOE32
	DOE33	DOE34	DOE35	DOE36	DOE37	DOE38	DOE39	DOE40
	DOE41	DOE42	DOE43	DOE44	DOE45	DOE46	DOE47	DOE48
	DOE49	DOE50	DOE51	DOE52	DOE53	DOE54		
Enviro 400	E58	E59	E60					
Volvo B7TL	PVL183	PVL218	PVL221	PVL222	PVL224	PVL226	PVL245	PVL263
	PVL265	PVL281	PVL282	PVL283	PVL284	PVL285	PVL286	PVL287
	PVL288	PVL289	PVL290	PVL291	PVL292	PVL293	PVL294	PVL295
	PVL296	PVL297						

Waterloo (Cornwall Road, SE1 8TE) - RA

MB Citaro O530	MEC1	MEC2	MEC3	MEC4	MEC5	MEC6	MEC7	MEC8
	MEC9	MEC10	MEC11	MEC12	MEC13	MEC14	MEC15	MEC16
	MEC17	MEC18	MEC19	MEC20	MEC21	MEC22	MEC23	MEC24
	MEC25	MEC26	MEC27	MEC28	MEC29	MEC30	MEC31	MEC33
	MEC34	MEC35	MEC36	MEC39	MEC41	MEC42	MEC43	MEC44
	MEC46	MEC47	MEC49	MEC50				

Wimbledon (Waterside Way, SW17 0HB) - PL

Dart	LDP186	LDP211	LDP212	LDP213	LDP214	LDP215	LDP216	LDP217
	LDP218	LDP219	LDP220	LDP221	LDP222	LDP223	LDP224	LDP225
	LDP226	LDP227	LDP263	LDP264	LDP265	LDP266	LDP267	LDP268
	LDP269	LDP270	LDP271	LDP272	LDP292	LDP293	LDP294	
Enviro 200	SE175	SE176	SE177	SE178	SE179	SE180	SE181	SE182
	SE183	SE184	SE185	SE186	SE187	SE188	SE189	SE190
	SE191	SE192	SE193					
Volvo B7TL	PVL220	PVL244						

unallocated/stored/refurbishing - u/w

remainder

METROBUS

Metrobus Ltd, Wheatstone Close, Crawley, RH10 9UA

Metrobus was formed in 1983 to operate the bus and coach services previously provided by Tillingbourne (Metropolitan) Ltd; the business consisted of six vehicles based at Green Street Green near Orpington, Kent. The opportunity to expand was soon realised and the company was to benefit from the London tendering system set up in 1985. Gaining London Transport contracts and commercial initiatives increased the fleet to 120 buses by 1997.

Expansion outside of London occurred in June 1997 with the acquisition of East Surrey Bus Services of South Godstone with a portfolio of mainly County Council tendered work in the East Grinstead and Edenbridge areas. At much the same time, the company set up a base in Lewes, East Sussex, to operate many of the services previously provided by Leisurelink of Newhaven. In September 1999, the company joined the Go-Ahead Group and steady progress continued both inside and outside of London.

The prestigious Gatwick Direct service started in May 2000 as a precursor to the proposed Fastway network of services planned for the Gatwick and Crawley areas from 2003; this now consists of three routes.

In March 2001, Arriva gave up the operation of bus services in Crawley and Metrobus stepped in with a replacement network. At the same time Surrey County Council had invited tenders for most of the work from the Arriva Merstham depot in East Surrey and Metrobus was successful with a bid for most of this work. Arriva's Bus interests in Horsham were also acquired in October 2009, requiring a further nineteen vehicles.

Further development within London came in late 2007 when the Orpington operation belonging to First London was taken over, with seven TfL services and thirty-five Dennis Darts being transferred.

| 101 | MB | YJ56WVF | Optare Solo M710 SE | | | Optare | | | N17F | 2006 | | |
| 102 | MB | YJ56WVG | Optare Solo M710 SE | | | Optare | | | N17F | 2006 | | |

135-147			TransBus Dart 8.9m			Marshall Capital			N25F	2002	FirstBus, 2007	
135	MB	LT02ZDE	139	MB	LT02ZDN	142	C	LT02ZDR	146	MB	LT02ZDW	
137	MB	LT02ZDG	140	MB	LT02ZDO	143	MB	LT02ZDS	147	MB	LT02ZDX	
138	MB	LT02ZDM	141	MB	LT02ZDP							

148-162			ADL Dart 4 8.9m			ADL Enviro 200			N26F	2011	
148	MB	YX60FTO	152	MB	YX60FTV	156	MB	YX60FUW	160	MB	YX60FVC
149	MB	YX60FTP	153	MB	YX60FTY	157	MB	YX60FUY	161	MB	YX60FVD
150	MB	YX60FTT	154	MB	YX60FTZ	158	MB	YX60FVA	162	MB	YX60FVE
151	MB	YX60FTU	155	MB	YX60FUV	159	MB	YX60FVB			

163-178			ADL Dart 4 8.9m			ADL Enviro 200			N26F	2011	
163	MB	YX61ENC	167	MB	YX61ENJ	171	MB	YX61ENN	175	MB	YX61ENT
164	MB	YX61ENE	168	MB	YX61ENK	172	MB	YX61ENO	176	MB	YX61ENU
165	MB	YX61ENF	169	MB	YX61ENL	173	MB	YX61ENP	177	MB	YX61ENV
166	MB	YX61ENH	170	MB	YX61ENM	174	MB	YX61ENR	178	MB	YX61ENW

Featuring an off-side central emergency exit is Enviro 200 174, YX61ENR. It is one of a batch of sixteen of the model supplied in 2011 for use on TfL tendered services. *Mark Doggett*

201-219   TransBus Dart 10.7m   TransBus Pointer   N36D*   2003   *210-6/9 are N33D

201	CY	SN03WKU	206	CY	SN03WLH	212	C	SN03WMC	216	C	SN03WMP
202	CY	SN03WKY	207	CY	SN03WLL	213	C	SN03WMF	217	CY	SN03WMT
203	CY	SN03WLA	210	C	SN03WLX	214	C	SN03WMG	218	CY	SN03WMV
204	CY	SN03WLE	211	C	SN03WLZ	215	C	SN03WMK	219	C	SN03WMY
205	CY	SN03WLF									

228-236   ADL Dart 4 9m   East Lancs Esteem   N24F   2006

228	MB	PO56JEU	231	MB	PO56JFF	233	MB	PO56JFJ	235	MB	PO56JFN
229	MB	PO56JFA	232	MB	PO56JFG	234	MB	PO56JFK	236	MB	PO56JFU
230	MB	PO56JFE									

241	CY	R741BMY	Dennis Dart SLF 10.2m	Plaxton Pointer	N32F	1998
244	CY	R744BMY	Dennis Dart SLF 10.2m	Plaxton Pointer	N35F	1998
247	CY	R747BMY	Dennis Dart SLF 10.2m	Plaxton Pointer	N35F	1998

251-256   ADL Dart 8.8m   ADL Mini Pointer   N23F   2004

251	MB	SN54GPV	253	MB	SN54GPY	255	MB	SN54GRF	256	MB	SN54GRK
252	MB	SN54GPX	254	MB	SN54GPZ						

257-268   ADL Dart 9m   East Lancs Esteem   N24F   2006

257	MB	PN06UYL	260	MB	PN06UYP	263	MB	PN06UYT	266	MB	PN06UYW
258	MB	PN06UYM	261	MB	PN06UYR	264	MB	PN06UYU	267	MB	PN06UYX
259	MB	PN06UYO	262	MB	PN06UYS	265	MB	PN06UYV	268	MB	PN06UYY

271-289   TransBus Dart 8.8m   TransBus Mini Pointer   N23F*   2003   *287-9 are N29F

271	MB	SN03YBA	276	MB	SN03YBK	281	MB	SN03YBY	286	MB	SN03YCK
272	MB	SN03YBB	277	MB	SN03YBR	282	MB	SN03YBZ	287	CY	SN03YCL
273	MB	SN03YBC	278	MB	SN03YBS	283	MB	SN03YCD	288	CY	SN03YCM
274	MB	SN03YBG	279	MB	SN03YBT	284	MB	SN03YCE	289	CY	SN03YCT
275	MB	SN03YBH	280	MB	SN03YBX	285	MB	SN03YCF			

310	CY	T310SMV	Dennis Dart SLF 10.2m	Alexander ALX200	N28F	1999
311	CY	T311SMV	Dennis Dart SLF 10.2m	Alexander ALX200	N32F	1999
320	CY	LX03OJP	TransBus Dart SLF 10.7m	TransBus Pointer	N37F	2003
321	CY	LX03OJN	TransBus Dart SLF 10.7m	TransBus Pointer	N37F	2003

Metrobus' own livery is shown on Mini Pointer Dart 344, X344YGU, the survivor from a batch supplied in 2000. It is seen in Horsham. *Dave Heath*

322-334
Dennis Dart SLF 10.7m   Plaxton Pointer 2   N31D   1999-2000

322	u	V322KMY	325	u	V325KMY	328	u	V328KMY	331 u V331KMY
323	u	V323KMY	326	u	V326KMY	329	u	V329KMY	334 C W334VGX
324	u	V324KMY	327	u	V327KMY	330	u	V330KMY	

344	CY	X344YGU	Dennis Dart SLF 8.8m	Plaxton Pointer MPD	N29F	2000

359-379
Dennis Dart SLF 11m   Caetano Nimbus   N38F*   2001   *seating varies

359	CY	Y359HMY	365	CY	Y365HMY	371	CY	Y371HMY	376	CY Y376HMY
361	CY	Y361HMY	366	CY	Y366HMY	372	CY	Y372HMY	377	CY Y377HMY
362	CY	Y362HMY	367	CY	Y367HMY	373	CY	Y373HMY	378	CY Y378HMY
363	CY	Y363HMY	368	CY	Y368HMY	374	CY	Y374HMY	379	CY Y379HMY
364	CY	Y364HMY	369	CY	Y369HMY					

390	CY	P380FPK	Dennis Dart SLF 10.7m	Plaxton Pointer	B39F	1997	Arriva S Counties, 2009
393	CY	P283FPK	Dennis Dart SLF 10.7m	Plaxton Pointer	B39F	1997	Arriva S Counties, 2009
394	CY	P274FPK	Dennis Dart SLF 10.7m	Plaxton Pointer	B39F	1997	Arriva S Counties, 2009
395	CY	P285FPK	Dennis Dart SLF 10.7m	Plaxton Pointer	B39F	1997	Arriva S Counties, 2009
396	CY	N232TPK	Dennis Dart SLF 10.2m	Plaxton Pointer	B35F	1996	Arriva S Counties, 2009
398	CY	P278FPK	Dennis Dart SLF 10.7m	Plaxton Pointer	B39F	1997	Arriva S Counties, 2009

431-447
Scania N94UD 10.6m   East Lancs OmniDekka 4.4m N45/27D*   2003   *447 N45/29D

431	C	YV03PZW	436	C	YV03PZF	440	C	YV03PZK	444	C YV03RCZ
432	C	YV03PZX	437	C	YV03PZG	441	C	YV03PZL	445	C YV03RAU
433	C	YV03PZY	438	C	YV03PZH	442	C	YV03PZM	446	C YV03RAX
434	C	YV03PZZ	439	C	YV03PZJ	443	C	YV03RCY	447	C YV03RBF
435	C	YV03PZE								

451-471
Scania N94UD 10.6m   East Lancs OmniDekka 4.4m N45/27D*   2003   *456/69-71 are N45/29D

451	C	YU52XVK	458	MB	YN03DFD	462	MB	YN03DFK	468	MB YN03DFY
455	C	YN03DFA	459	MB	YN03DFE	465	MB	YN03DFU	469	CY YV03RBU
456	C	YN03DFC	460	MB	YN03DFG	466	MB	YN03DFV	470	CY YV03RBX
457	MB	YU52XVR	461	MB	YN03DFJ	467	MB	YN03DFX	471	CY YN53USG

472-497 — Scania N94UD 10.6m — East Lancs OmniDekka 4.4m N45/29D* — 2003-05 — *480/1 are N45/27D

No.		Reg	No.		Reg	No.		Reg	No.		Reg
472	CY	YN53RYA	479	MB	YN53RYM	486	CY	YN53RYY	492	CY	YN53RZE
473	CY	YN53RYB	480	C	YN53RYP	487	CY	YN53RYZ	493	CY	YN53RZF
474	CY	YN53RYC	481	C	YN53RYR	488	CY	YN53RZA	494	CY	YN54AJU
475	CY	YN53RYD	482	CY	YN53RYT	489	CY	YN53RZB	495	CY	YN54AJV
476	CY	YN53RYF	483	CY	YN53RYV	490	CY	YN53RZC	496	CY	YN54AJX
477	CY	YN53RYH	484	CY	YN53RYW	491	CY	YN53RZD	497	CY	YN54AJY
478	CY	YN53RYK	485	CY	YN53RYX						

513	CY	YP52CTO	Scania OmniCity CN94 UB 12m	Scania	N42F	2002

514-530 — Scania OmniCity CN94 UB 12m — Scania — N32D — 2003

No.		Reg	No.		Reg	No.		Reg	No.		Reg
514	MB	YN53RXF	519	MB	YN53RXL	523	MB	YN53RXR	527	MB	YN53RXW
515	MB	YN53RXG	520	MB	YN53RXM	524	MB	YN53RXT	528	MB	YN53RXX
516	MB	YN53RXH	521	MB	YN53RXO	525	MB	YN53RXU	529	MB	YN53RXY
517	MB	YN53RXJ	522	MB	YN53RXP	526	MB	YN53RXV	530	MB	YN53RXZ
518	MB	YN53RXK									

531-540 — Scania OmniCity CN94 UB 12m — Scania — N37D — 2003

No.		Reg	No.		Reg	No.		Reg	No.		Reg
531	CY	YN03UWU	534	CY	YN03WPP	537	u	YN03WRG	539	u	YN03WRL
532	CY	YN03UWY	535	CY	YN03WPR	538	u	YN03WRJ	540	u	YN03WRP
533	CY	YN03UPM	536	u	YN03WRF						

546-558 — Scania OmniCity CN94 UB 12m — Scania — N37D* — 2005 — *552-8 N34D, 559/60 N36D

No.		Reg	No.		Reg	No.		Reg	No.		Reg
546	CY	YN05HCA	550	CY	YN05HCF	553	CY	YN55PWK	556	CY	YN55PWU
547	CY	YN05HCC	551	CY	YN05HCG	554	CY	YN55PWL	557	CY	YN55PWV
548	CY	YN05HCD	552	CY	YN55PWJ	555	CY	YN55PWO	558	CY	YN55PWX
549	CY	YN05HCE									

559-567 — Scania OmniCity CN230 UB 12m — Scania — N33D* — 2007-08 — *seating varies

No.		Reg	No.		Reg	No.		Reg	No.		Reg
559	CY	YN07LKF	562	C	YN58BNA	564	C	YN08OAW	566	C	YN08OAY
560	CY	YN07LKG	563	C	YN08OAV	565	C	YN08OAX	567	C	YN08OAZ
561	C	YN08OAS									

568-581 — Scania OmniCity CN230 UB 12m — Scania — N36D — 2009

No.		Reg	No.		Reg	No.		Reg	No.		Reg
568	CY	YT09BKD	572	CY	YT09BKJ	576	CY	YT09BKO	579	CY	YT09BKX
569	CY	YT09BKE	573	CY	YT09BKK	577	CY	YT09BKU	580	CY	YT09BKY
570	CY	YT09BKF	574	CY	YT09BKL	578	CY	YT09BKV	581	CY	YT09BKZ
571	CY	YT09BKG	575	CY	YT09BKN						

601-623 — Scania OmniTown N94 UB 10.6m — East Lancs Esteem — N29D — 2006

No.		Reg	No.		Reg	No.		Reg	No.		Reg
601	MB	YM55SWU	607	MB	YM55SXA	613	MB	YN06JXT	619	MB	YM55SXO
602	MB	YM55SWV	608	MB	YM55SXB	614	MB	YM55SXH	620	MB	YM55SXP
603	MB	YN06JXR	609	MB	YM55SXC	615	MB	YN06JXU	621	MB	YM55SXR
604	MB	YM55SWX	610	MB	YM55SXD	616	MB	YN06JXV	622	MB	YN06JXY
605	MB	YM55SWY	611	MB	YM55SXE	617	MB	YN06JXW	623	MB	YN06JXZ
606	MB	YN06JXS	612	MB	YM55SXF	618	MB	YN06JXX			

624-633 — Scania OmniCity N230 UB 10.9m — Scania — N33F — 2008

No.		Reg	No.		Reg	No.		Reg	No.		Reg
624	CY	YN08DFJ	627	CY	YN08DFO	630	CY	YN08DFV	632	CY	YN08DFY
625	CY	YN08DFK	628	CY	YN08DFP	631	CY	YN08DFX	633	CY	YN08DFZ
626	CY	YN08DFL	629	CY	YN08DFU						

701-705 — MAN 12.240 10.3m — East Lancs Esteem — N27D — 2007

No.		Reg	No.		Reg	No.		Reg	No.		Reg
701	MB	PN07KRK	703	MB	PN07KRU	704	MB	PN07KRV	705	MB	PN07KRX
702	MB	PN07KRO									

706	C	YX58DXB	MAN 14.240 10.8m	ADL Enviro 200	N34D	2009
707	C	YX58DXC	MAN 14.240 10.8m	ADL Enviro 200	N34D	2009
708	C	YX58DXD	MAN 14.240 10.8m	ADL Enviro 200	N34D	2009

709-723 — MAN 14.240 10.8m — MCV Evolution — N28D — 2009

No.		Reg	No.		Reg	No.		Reg	No.		Reg
709	C	AE09DHG	713	C	AE09DHP	717	C	AJ58WBG	721	C	AJ58WBK
710	C	AE09DHK	714	C	AJ58WBE	718	C	AE09DHU	722	C	AJ58WBF
711	C	AJ58WBD	715	C	AE09DHJ	719	C	AE09DHN	723	C	AE09DHV
712	C	AE09DHM	716	C	AE09DHO	720	C	AE09DHL			

Recent arrivals in Metrobus livery are six 10.8 metre Alexander Dennis Enviro 200s. All are allocated to Crawley with 736, SN12AAJ, seen passing through Roffey while operating service 98. *Mark Lyons*

725-730

						ADL Dart 4 10.2m		ADL Enviro 200		N29D	2007	Arriva S Counties, 2009
725	CY	GN07AVR	727	CY	GN07AVU	729	CY	GN07AVW	730	CY	GN07AUY
726	CY	GN07AVT	728	CY	GN07AVV						

731	MB	YX11CTE	ADL Dart 4 10.2m	ADL Enviro 200	N29D	2011
732	MB	YX11CTF	ADL Dart 4 10.2m	ADL Enviro 200	N29D	2011
733	MB	YX11CTK	ADL Dart 4 10.2m	ADL Enviro 200	N29D	2011

734-739

						ADL E20D 10.8m		ADL Enviro 200		N38F	2012	
734	CY	SN12AAE	736	CY	SN12AAJ	738	CY	SN12AAO	739	CY	SN12AAU
735	CY	SN12AAF	737	CY	SN12AAK						

870-899

						Scania OmniCity N230 UD 10.8m Optare Olympus				N45/23D	2009	
870	C	PN09EKR	878	C	PN09ELU	886	C	PN09ENC	893	C	PN09ENO
871	C	PN09EKT	879	C	PN09ELV	887	C	PN09ENE	894	C	PN59KFW
872	C	PN09EKU	880	C	PN09ELW	888	C	PN09ENF	895	C	PN59KFX
873	C	PN09EKV	881	C	PN09ELX	889	C	PN09ENH	896	C	PN59KFY
874	C	PN09EKW	882	C	PN09EMF	890	C	PN09ENK	897	C	PN59KFZ
875	C	PN09EKX	883	C	PN09EMK	891	C	PN09ENL	898	C	PN59KGA
876	C	PN09EKY	884	C	PN09EMV	892	C	PN09ENM	899	C	PN59KGE
877	C	PN09ELO	885	C	PN09EMX						

901-927

						Scania N94 UD 10.6m		East Lancs OmniDekka		N45/26D	2006	
901	MB	YN55PZC	908	MB	YN55PZL	915	MB	YN55PZW	922	C	YN06JYG
902	MB	YN55PZD	909	MB	YN55PZM	916	MB	YN55PZX	923	C	YN06JYH
903	MB	YN55PZE	910	MB	YN55PZO	917	C	YN06JYB	924	C	YN06JYJ
904	MB	YN55PZF	911	MB	YN55PZP	918	C	YN06JYC	925	C	YN06JYK
905	MB	YN55PZG	912	MB	YN55PZR	919	C	YN06JYD	926	C	YN06JYL
906	MB	YN55PZH	913	MB	YN55PZU	920	C	YN06JYE	927	C	YN06JYO
907	MB	YN55PZJ	914	MB	YN55PZV	921	C	YN06JYF			

928-946

						Scania N94 UD 10.6m		East Lancs OmniDekka		N45/26D	2006	
928	C	YN56FDA	933	MB	YN56FDG	938	MB	YN56FDO	943	MB	YN56FDY
929	C	YN56FDC	934	MB	YN56FDJ	939	MB	YN56FDP	944	MB	YN56FDZ
930	MB	YN56FDD	935	MB	YN56FDK	940	MB	YN56FDU	945	MB	YN56FEF
931	MB	YN56FDE	936	MB	YN56FDL	941	MB	YN56FDV	946	MB	YN56FEG
932	MB	YN56FDF	937	MB	YN56FDM	942	MB	YN56FDX			

The principal double-deck bus in the Metrobus fleet is the Scania OmniCity double-deck bus and the earlier variant, the OmniDekka bodied by East Lancs. Waiting time at North Greenwich is 938, YN56FDO, an OmniDekka. *Richard Godfrey*

947-952

Scania N230 UD 10.8m   East Lancs OmniDekka   N45/23D   2007

947	C	YN07EXF	949	C	YN07EXH	951	C	YN07EXM	952	C	YN07EXO
948	C	YN07EXG	950	C	YN07EXK						

953-978

Scania OmniCity N230 UD   Scania   N41/22D   2008-10   *953-4 are N41/31F

953	CY	YN08OBP	960	C	YT59DYC	967	C	YT59DYM	973	C	YT59DYW
954	CY	YN08OBR	961	C	YT59DYD	968	C	YT59DYO	974	MB	YR10BCE
955	C	YR58SNY	962	C	YT59DYF	969	C	YT59DYP	975	MB	YR10BCF
956	C	YR58SNZ	963	C	YT59DYG	970	C	YT59DYS	976	MB	YR10BCK
957	C	YP58UFV	964	C	YT59DYH	971	C	YT59DYU	977	MB	YR10BCO
958	C	YT59DYA	965	C	YT59DYN	972	C	YT59DYV	978	MB	YR10BCU
959	C	YT59DYB	966	C	YT59DYJ						

Ancillary vehicles:

7208	CYt	SN03WLP	TransBus Dart 10.7m	TransBus Pointer	TV	2003	
7209	CYt	SN03WLU	TransBus Dart 10.7m	TransBus Pointer	TV	2003	
7380	CYt	LK51LYJ	Dennis Dart SLF 10.2m	Marshall Capital	TV	2001	FirstBus, 2007
7381	CYt	LK51JYL	Dennis Dart SLF 10.2m	Marshall Capital	TV	2001	FirstBus, 2007
7382	CYt	LK51JYN	Dennis Dart SLF 10.2m	Marshall Capital	TV	2001	FirstBus, 2007
7764	CYt	M516VJO	Dennis Dart 9.8m	Marshall C37	TV	1995	Oxford Citybus, 2004
7767	CYt	M507VJO	Dennis Dart 9.8m	Marshall C37	TV	1995	Oxford Citybus, 2004

Depots and allocations:

Crawley (Wheatstone Close, RH10 9UA) - CY

Dart	201	202	203	204	205	206	207	217
	218	241	244	247	287	288	289	310
	311	320	321	344	359	361	362	363
	364	365	366	367	368	369	371	372
	373	374	375	376	377	378	379`	390
	393	394	395	396	398			
Enviro 200	725	726	727	728	729	730	734	735
	736	737	738	739				

Scania sd	513	531	532	533	534	535	546	547
	548	549	550	551	552	553	554	555
	556	557	558	559	560	568	569	570
	571	572	573	574	575	576	577	578
	579	580	581	624	625	626	627	628
	629	630	631	632	633			
Scania dd	469	470	471	472	473	474	475	476
	477	478	482	483	484	485	486	487
	488	489	490	491	492	493	494	495
	496	497	953	954				
Ancillary	*7208*	*7209*	*7380*	*7381*	*7382*	*7764*	*7767*	

Croydon (Beddington Lane) - C

Dart	142	210	211	212	213	214	215	216
	219	334						
MAN 12.240	706	707	708	709	710	711	712	713
	714	715	716	717	718	719	720	721
	722	723						
Scania sd	561	562	563	564	565	566	567	
Scania dd	431	432	433	434	435	436	437	438
	439	440	441	442	443	444	445	446
	447	451	455	456	480	481	870	871
	872	873	874	875	876	877	878	879
	880	881	882	883	884	885	886	887
	888	889	890	891	892	893	894	895
	896	897	898	899	917	918	919	920
	921	922	923	924	925	926	927	940
	943	947	948	949	950	951	952	928
	929	955	956	957	958	959	960	961
	962	963	964	965	966	967	968	969
	970	971	972	973				

Orpington (Farnborough Hill, Green Street Green) - MB

Solo	101	102						
Dart	135	137	138	139	140	141	143	146
	147	228	229	230	231	232	233	234
	235	236	251					
	252	253	254	255	256	257	258	259
	260	261	262	263	264	265	266	267
	268	271	272	273	274	275	276	277
	278	279	280	281	282	283	284	285
	286							
Enviro 200	148	149	150	151	152	153	154	155
	156	157	158	159	160	161	162	163
	164	165	166	167	168	169	170	171
	172	173	174	175	176	177	178	731
	732	733						
MAN 12.240	701	702	703	704	705			
Scania OmniCity	514	515	516	517	518	519	520	521
	522	523	524	525	526	527	528	529
	530							
Scania OmniTown	601	602	603	604	605	606	607	608
	609	610	611	612	613	614	615	616
	617	618	619	620	621	622	623	
Scania OmniDekka	457	458	459	460	461	462	465	466
	467	468	479	901	902	903	904	905
	906	907	908	909	910	911	912	913
	914	915	916	930	931	932	933	934
	935	936	937	938	939	940	941	942
	943	944	945	946	974	975	976	977
	978							

BRIGHTON & HOVE

Brighton & Hove Bus and Coach Company Ltd, 43 Conway Street, Hove, BN3 3LT

The company began life as Brighton, Hove and Preston United running regular horse bus services across the town in 1884 from the site of the current head office and garage in Conway Street, Hove. In 1916 these operations became a division of the privately owned Tilling Group that had already commenced bus operation in the towns.

The company was established as a separate legal entity within Tillings as Brighton, Hove & District Omnibus Company Ltd in 1935, with a change of ownership, when absorbed by the British Transport Commission in 1948 and the Transport Holding Company in 1962.

The state-owned National Bus Company took over in 1969 and Brighton, Hove & District Omnibus Company became dormant with its operations merged into the neighbouring Southdown bus company.

The dormant company began trading again in 1986 and was renamed Brighton & Hove Bus and Coach Company Ltd. Privatised through a management buy-out in 1987, it was acquired by Go-Ahead in 1993, which in turn was floated as a plc in 1994.

The Group has gone on to acquire other bus companies, including Brighton Transport Ltd in 1997 (whose origins can be traced back to the start of tram operations in Brighton in 1901), when it merged with Brighton & Hove.

Since then, the enlarged Brighton & Hove company has gone from strength to strength achieving up to 5% passenger growth year by year. Key initiatives such as real time information, a citywide flat fare and frequent Metro services have attracted many new customers, making the bus in Brighton an essential feature of city life.

In September 2005, the company acquired the neighbouring business interests of Stagecoach in the Lewes, Uckfield, Seaford and Eastbourne areas thus expanding its operations into East Sussex.

51-57			Scania OmniLink N230		Scania			N43F	2008		
51	CS	YN58BCE	53	CS	YN58BCK	55	CS	YN58BCU	57	CS	YN58BCY
52	CS	YN58BCF	54	CS	YN58BCO	56	LR	YN58BCV			

101-104			Mercedes-Benz Citaro O530G		Mercedes-Benz			AN49D	2002	Go-Ahead London, 2010
101	LR	BX02YZH	102	LR	BX02YZM	103	LR	BX02YZP	104	LR	BX02YZW

105-118			Mercedes-Benz Citaro O530G		Mercedes-Benz			AN49D	2004/07	Go-Ahead London, 2012
105	LR	BD57WDC	109	LR	BD57WDM	113	LR	BD57WDS	116	u	BX54EFD
106	LR	BD57WDE	110	LR	BD57WDN	114	LR	BD57WDT	117	u	BX54UCM
107	LR	BD57WDK	111	LR	BD57WDP	115	u	BX54EFC	118	u	BX54UCN
108	LR	BD57WDL	112	LR	BD57WDR						

207	CS	N207NNJ	Dennis Dart SLF 10.1m		Plaxton Pointer			N39F	1996	Brighton Blue Bus, 1997
209	CS	N209NNJ	Dennis Dart SLF 10.1m		Plaxton Pointer			N39F	1996	Brighton Blue Bus, 1997
210	CS	N210NNJ	Dennis Dart SLF 10.1m		Plaxton Pointer			N39F	1996	Brighton Blue Bus, 1997

The latest arrivals at Brighton & Hove are further Volvo B9TL buses with Wrightbus Gemini bodywork.
Most are lettered for route 1 as shown by 425, BF12KWZ, seen in Church Road, Hove. *Richard Godfrey*

216-236

Volvo B10BLE — Wright Renown — N46F — 1997-98

216	CS	R216HCD	223	u	R223HCD	228	CS	R228HCD	232	CS	R232HCD
217	CS	R217HCD	224	u	R224HCD	230	CS	R230HCD	233	CS	R233HCD
219	u	R219HCD	226	u	R226HCD	231	LR	R231HCD			

240-244

Dennis Dart SLF 8.8m — Plaxton Pointer MPD — N29F — 2000 — Metrobus, Crawley, 2008

240	WK	W791VMV	242	CS	W796VMV	243	LR	W798VMV	244	LR	W799VMV
241	WK	W792VMV							

245	LR	W339VGX	Dennis Dart SLF 8.8m	Plaxton Pointer 2	N29F	2000	Go-West Midlands, 2008
248	LR	T312SMV	Dennis Dart SLF 8.8m	Plaxton Pointer MPD	N29F	1999	Metrobus, Crawley, 2008
249	LR	T313SMV	Dennis Dart SLF 8.8m	Plaxton Pointer MPD	N29F	1999	Metrobus, Crawley, 2008
250	LR	GU52HWA	Dennis Dart SLF 10.7m	Plaxton Pointer 2	N38F	2002	Reading Buses, 2009
251	CS	GU52HWB	Dennis Dart SLF 10.7m	Plaxton Pointer 2	N38F	2002	Reading Buses, 2009

401-421

Volvo B9TL — Wrightbus Gemini 2 — N43/28F — 2011

401	CS	BJ11XHA	407	CS	BJ11XHG	412	CS	BJ11XHN	417	CS	BJ11XHT
402	CS	BJ11XHB	408	CS	BJ11XHH	413	CS	BJ11XHO	418	CS	BJ11XHU
403	CS	BJ11XHC	409	CS	BJ11XHK	414	CS	BJ11XHP	419	WK	BJ11XHV
404	CS	BJ11XHD	410	CS	BJ11XHL	415	CS	BJ11XHR	420	WK	BJ11XHW
405	CS	BJ11XHE	411	CS	BJ11XHM	416	CS	BJ11XHS	421	CS	BJ11XHX
406	CS	BJ11XHF									

422-439

Volvo B9TL — Wrightbus Gemini 2 — NC43/23F — 2012

422	WK	BF12KWX	427	WK	BF12KXD	432	WK	BF12KXE	436	WK	BF12KXO
423	WK	BF12KWY	428	WK	BF12KXC	433	WK	BF12KXL	437	WK	BF12KXM
424	WK	BF12KXB	429	WK	BF12KXH	434	WK	BF12KXK	438	WK	BF12KXR
425	WK	BF12KWZ	430	WK	BF12KXJ	435	WK	BF12KXN	439	WK	BF12KXS
426	WK	BF12KXA	431	WK	BF12KXG						

Brighton & Hove operates two Volvo Hybrid buses which carry lettering for route 7 along with a hybrid feature on the rear of their Wrightbus bodies. Buckingham Place is the location for this view of 441, BG61SXS. *Richard Godfrey*

440	CS	BK10MGV	Volvo B5LH			Wrightbus Gemini 2	NC43/23F	2010	Volvo demonstrator, 2011
441	CS	BG61SXS	Volvo B5LH			Wrightbus Gemini 2	NC43/23F	2012	Volvo demonstrator, 2012

442-452

Volvo B5LH — Wrightbus Gemini 2 — NC43/23F — 2012

442	-	BF62UXH	445	-	BF62UXL	448	-	BF62UXO	451	-	BF62UXS
443	-	BF62UXJ	446	-	BF62UXM	449	-	BF62UXP	452	-	BF62UXT
444	-	BF62UXK	447	-	BF62UXN	450	-	BF62UXR			

501	CS	YN08JAU	Scania K114 IB4	Irizar Century 12.35	C49FT	2008	
502	CS	HF08UHT	Scania K340 RB4	Irizar PB	C49FT	2008	Marchwood M'ways, 2009
503	CS	YR58RUH	Scania K340 RB4	Irizar PB	C49FT	2008	Buslines, Ashford, 2011
504	CS	YR58RUU	Scania K340 RB4	Irizar PB	C49FT	2008	Buslines, Ashford, 2011
505	CS	UK59UCL	Scania K340 RB4	Irizar PB	C49FT	2009	
509	CS	YN04ANU	Scania K114 IB4	Irizar Century 12.35	C49FT	2004	
510	u	YN05GZS	Scania K114 IB4	Irizar Century 12.35	C49FT	2005	
511	u	YN03WPX	Scania K114 IB4	Irizar Century 12.35	C49FT	2003	Excalibur, New Cross, 2007
550	CS	BF12KXP	Volvo B9TL	Wrightbus Gemini 2	NC43/23F	2012	
551	CS	BF12KXT	Volvo B9TL	Wrightbus Gemini 2	NC43/23F	2012	

601-618

Scania N94 UD 10.6m — East Lancs Cityzen — N47/32F* — 2003 — *617/8 are CO47/32F

601	LR	GX03SVF	606	CS	GX03SUF	611	WK	GX03SVA	615	LR	GX03SSU
602	LR	GX03SVG	607	CS	GX03SUH	612	WK	GX03SVC	616	LR	GX03SSV
603	LR	GX03SVJ	608	CS	GX03SUU	613	CS	GX03SVD	617	LR	GX03SSZ
604	LR	GX03SVK	609	CS	GX03SUV	614	WK	GX03SVE	618	LR	GX03STZ
605	CS	GX03SUA	610	CS	GX03SUY						

619-654

Scania OmniDekka N94 UD 10.6m East Lancs 4.4m — N47/32F — 2004-05

619	WK	YN04GJE	628	WK	YN04GKA	637	LR	YN54AOM	646	LR	YN54AOY
620	WK	YN04GJF	629	WK	YN04GKC	638	LR	YN54AOO	647	LR	YN05GZK
621	WK	YN04GJG	630	WK	YN04GKD	639	LR	YN54AOP	648	LR	YN05GZM
622	WK	YN04GJJ	631	WK	YN04GJX	640	LR	YN54AOR	649	LR	YN05GZH
623	WK	YN04GJK	632	WK	YN04GKE	641	LR	YN54AOT	650	LR	YN05GZJ
624	WK	YN04GJU	633	WK	YN04GKF	642	LR	YN54AOU	651	LR	YN05GZL
625	WK	YN04GJV	634	WK	YN04GKG	643	LR	YN54AOV	652	LR	YN05GZO
626	WK	YN04GJY	635	WK	YN04GKJ	644	LR	YN54AOW	653	LR	YN05GZP
627	WK	YN04GJZ	636	WK	YN04GKK	645	LR	YN54AOX	654	LR	YN05GZR

Open-top services are provided by converted double-decks have been a feature of English seaside resorts for many years. Four are operated by Brighton & Hove. However, seen on the Coastal service in spring 2012 was 918, YN56FFV, a Scania N94 UD. *Richard Godfrey*

655-670 Scania N94 UD 10.6m East Lancs OmniDekka N47/33F 2005-06

655	LR	YN55NFF	659	LR	YN55NFL	663	WK	YN55NFA	667	WK	YN06SZW
656	LR	YN55NFO	660	LR	YN55NFM	664	WK	YN55NFC	668	CS	YN06SZX
657	LR	YN55NFH	661	LR	YN55NFE	665	WK	YN55NFD	669	CS	YN06SZY
658	LR	YN55NFK	662	LR	YN55NFJ	666	WK	YN55NFG	670	LR	YN06SZZ

671-688 Scania N230 UD 10.6m East Lancs OmniDekka NC47/28F 2007

671	WK	YN07UOT	676	LR	YN57FYD	681	LR	YN57FYL	685	LR	YN57FYP
672	WK	YN07UOU	677	LR	YN57FYA	682	LR	YN57FYM	686	LR	YN57FYF
673	LR	YN07UOF	678	LR	YN57FYJ	683	LR	YN57FYE	687	LR	YN57FYG
674	LR	YN07UOG	679	LR	YN57FYB	684	LR	YN57FYO	688	LR	YN57FYH
675	LR	YN57FYC	680	LR	YN57FYK						

701-713 Scania OmniCity N230 UD Scania N45/31F 2009

701	CS	YP58UGA	705	CS	YP58UGE	708	CS	YP58UGH	711	CS	YP58UGL
702	CS	YP58UGB	706	CS	YP58UGF	709	CS	YP58UGJ	712	CS	YP58UGM
703	CS	YP58UGC	707	CS	YP58UGG	710	CS	YP58UGK	713	CS	YP58UGN
704	CS	YP58UGD									

714-731 Scania OmniCity N230 UD Scania N45/31F 2009

714	CS	YP09HWA	719	CS	YP09HWF	724	CS	YP09HWL	728	CS	YP09HWR
715	CS	YP09HWB	720	CS	YP09HWG	725	CS	YP09HWM	729	CS	YP09HWS
716	CS	YP09HWC	721	CS	YP09HWH	726	CS	YP09HWN	730	CS	YP09HWT
717	CS	YP09HWD	722	CS	YP09HWJ	727	CS	YP09HWO	731	CS	YP09HWU
718	CS	YP09HWE	723	CS	YP09HWK						

781	LR	R881HCD	Scania N113DRB	East Lancs Cityzen	O47/31F	1998
808	LR	T808RFG	Dennis Trident 10.5m	East Lancs Lolyne	O47/31F	1999
819	LR	T819RFG	Dennis Trident 10.5m	East Lancs Lolyne	CO47/31F	1999
820	LR	T820RFG	Dennis Trident 10.5m	East Lancs Lolyne	CO47/31F	1999

The Brighton & Hove fleet contains a couple of special event vehicles including Routemaster RML2317, CUV317C. Painted in Thomas Tilling livery it was seen working route 472 that links Brighton with East Grinstead on special event days. *Mark Bailey*

824-840
Dennis Trident 10.5m   East Lancs Lolyne   N47/31F   1999-2000

824	LR	W824NNJ	832	LR	W832NNJ	835	LR	W835NNJ	838	LR	W838NNJ
826	LR	W826NNJ	833	LR	W833NNJ	836	LR	W836NNJ	839	LR	W839NNJ
827	LR	W827NNJ	834	LR	W834NNJ	837	LR	W837NNJ	840	LR	W840NNJ
831	LR	W831NNJ									

841-864
Dennis Trident 10.5m   Plaxton President   N47/30F   2001

841	WK	Y871GCD	847	WK	Y847GCD	853	WK	Y853GCD	859	CS	Y859GCD
842	WK	Y868GCD	848	WK	Y848GCD	854	CS	Y854GCD	860	CS	Y869GCD
843	WK	Y843GCD	849	WK	Y849GCD	855	CS	Y865GCD	861	CS	Y861GCD
844	WK	Y844GCD	850	WK	Y866GCD	856	CS	Y856GCD	862	CS	Y862GCD
845	WK	Y845GCD	851	WK	Y851GCD	857	CS	Y857GCD	863	LR	Y863GCD
846	WK	Y846GCD	852	WK	Y852GCD	858	CS	Y858GCD	864	LR	Y864GCD

865-876
Dennis Trident 10.5m   Plaxton President   N47/31F   2002

865	LR	PK02RCZ	868	LR	PK02RDV	871	LR	PK02REU	874	LR	PK02RFF
866	LR	PK02RDO	869	LR	PK02RDX	872	LR	PK02REU	875	CS	PK02RFJ
867	LR	PK02RDU	870	LR	PK02RDY	873	LR	PK02RFE	876	CS	PK02RFL

881-887
Dennis Trident 10.5m   Alexander ALX400 4.2m   N51/26F   1999   Stagecoach, 2005

881	WK	T669KPU	883	WK	T671KPU	885	WK	T673KPU	887	WK	T677KPU
882	WK	T670KPU	884	WK	T672KPU	886	WK	T675KPU			

901-918
Scania OmniDekka N94UD 10.6m East Lancs 4.4m   N51/37F   2006

901	WK	YN56FFA	906	WK	YN56FFG	911	WK	YN56FFM	915	WK	YN56FFS
902	WK	YN56FFB	907	WK	YN56FFH	912	WK	YN56FFO	916	WK	YN56FFT
903	WK	YN56FFC	908	WK	YN56FFJ	913	WK	YN56FFP	917	WK	YN56FFU
904	WK	YN56FFD	909	WK	YN56FFK	914	WK	YN56FFR	918	WK	YN56FFV
905	WK	YN56FFE	910	WK	YN56FFL						

919	CS	YN06NYK	Scania N94 UD 10.6m	East Lancs OmniDekka	NC51/33F	2006
920	CS	YN06NYL	Scania N94 UD 10.6m	East Lancs OmniDekka	NC51/33F	2006

Special event vehicles:

6447	LR	HAP985	Bristol KSW6G	Eastern Coach Works	B32/28R	1953	
RML2317	LR	CUV317C	AEC Routemaster R2RH/3	Park Royal	B40/32R	1965	London Transport

The 2012-13 Go-Ahead Bus Handbook

Ancillary vehicles:

T1	WKt	R221HCD	Volvo B10BLE	Wright Renown	TV	1997	
T2	WKt	N202NNJ	Dennis Dart SLF 10.1m	Plaxton Pointer	TV	1996	Brighton Blue Bus, 1997
T3	WKt	R235HCD	Volvo B10BLE	Wright Renown	TV	1998	
T4	WKt	R236HCD	Volvo B10BLE	Wright Renown	TV	1998	
T5	WKt	R235HCD	Volvo B10BLE	Wright Renown	TV	1998	
T6	WKt	N216NNJ	Dennis Dart SLF 10.1m	Plaxton Pointer	TV	1996	Brighton Blue Bus, 1997

Web: www.buses.co.uk

Brighton (Lewes Road) - LR

Outstation: Uckfield

Scania sd	56							
Mercedes-Benz Citaro	101	102	103	104	105			
Dart	243	244	245	246	247	248	249	
	250	251						
Scania DD	601	602	603	604	605	615	616	617
	618	637	638	639	640	641	642	643
	644	645	646	647	648	649	650	651
	652	653	654	655	656	657	658	659
	660	661	662	670	673	674	675	676
	677	678	679	680	681	682	683	684
	685	686	687	688	781			
Trident	808	819	824	826	827	831	832	833
	834	835	836	837	838	839	840	863
	864	865	866	867	868	869	870	871
	872	873	874					
Heritage	6447	RML2317						

Brighton (Whitehawk Road) - WK

Outstations: Eastbourne and Newhaven

Dart	240	241						
Volvo B9TL	419	420	422	423	424	425	426	427
	428	429	430	431	432	433	434	435
	436	437	438	439				
Scania	611	612	614	619	620	621	622	623
	624	625	626	627	628	629	630	631
	632	633	634	635	636	663	664	665
	666	667	671	672	841	842	843	844
	845	846	847	848	849	850	851	852
	853	901	902	903	904	905	906	907
	908	909	910	911	912	913	914	915
	916	917	918					
Trident	881	882	883	884	885	886	887	

Hove (Conway Street) - CS

Outstation: Durrington

Solo	301							
Dart	207	209	210	242				
Volvo B10BLE	216	217	228	230	231	232	233	
Scania coach	501	502	503	504	505	509	510	511
Scania	606	607	608	609	610	613	668	668
	669	701	702	703	704	705	706	707
	708	709	710	711	712	713	714	715
	716	717	718	719	720	721	722	723
	724	725	726	727	728	729	730	731
	776	777	780	781	919	920		
Trident	854	855	856	857	858			
	859	860	861	862	875	876		
Volvo B9TL	401	402	403	404	405	406	407	408
	409	410	411	412	413	414	415	416
	417	418	421	550	551			
Volvo V5LH	440	441						

Unallocated/stored - u   Remainder

PLYMOUTH CITYBUS

Plymouth Citybus Ltd, Milehouse, Plymouth, Devon, PL3 4AA

The company began in 1892 as Plymouth Corporation Tramways Department, operating horse trams. In 1914, the Corporation acquired the Devonport & District Tramways Company. This resulted in a move to the current Milehouse site, which was originally opened in 1901 by the Devonport company. A further acquisition was the Plymouth, Stonehouse and Devonport Tramways Company in 1922.

The Corporation had been using the Milehouse site since 1914 when the three towns merged and when they bought out the Devonport and District Tramways Company and it was this company who first opened Milehouse depot when they formed in 1901.

Over the next three decades the horse tram established itself as the principal means of local public transport although an attempt had been made in 1880 by another company to establish a tram network hauled by steam locomotives, giving up after just one year because of "numerous complaints of excessive noise, black smoke, obnoxious smells and bad timekeeping".

Tram operation ended in 1945, and the arm's length Plymouth Citybus company was established in 1986. Council ownership continued until December 2009, when the company was wholly acquired by the Go-Ahead Group.

In addition to bus services throughout the area, the company also operates a number of coaches under the Citycoach brand, providing excursions and private hire. Plymouth Citybus now operates mainly a modern low floor single deck fleet, though some nineteen former London General Volvo B7 double decks operated by the company rejoined Go-Ahead with the Citybus acquisition.

1-12			Dennis Dart SLF			Plaxton Pointer		N39F	1996		
1	PL	N101UTT	4	PL	N104UTT	8	PL	N108UTT	10	PL	N110UTT
2	u	N102UTT	5	PL	N105UTT	9	PL	N109UTT	12	PL	N112UTT
3	PL	N103UTT	7	PL	N107UTT						

13-27			Dennis Dart SLF			Plaxton Pointer 2		N39F	1998-99		
13	PL	R113OFJ	17	PL	R117OFJ	21	PL	R121OFJ	25	PL	R125OFJ
14	PL	R114OFJ	18	PL	R118OFJ	22	PL	R122OFJ	26	PL	R126OFJ
15	PL	R115OFJ	19	PL	R119OFJ	23	PL	R123OFJ	27	PL	S127FTA
16	PL	R116OFJ	20	PL	R120OFJ	24	PL	R124OFJ			

28-40			Dennis Dart SLF			Plaxton Pointer SPD		N43F	1999		
28	w	T128EFJ	32	PL	T132EFJ	35	PL	T135EFJ	38	PL	T138EFJ
29	PL	T129EFJ	33	PL	T133EFJ	36	PL	T136EFJ	39	PL	T139EFJ
30	PL	T130EFJ	34	PL	T134EFJ	37	PL	T137EFJ	40	PL	T140EFJ
31	PL	T131EFJ									

Recent arrivals at Plymouth Citybus are ten Volvo B7RLEs with Wrightbus Eclipse bodies. Representing the batch is number 101 on page 1 and 105, WA12ACY, shown here. *Steve Rice*

41-48 — Dennis Dart SLF — Plaxton Pointer SPD — N41F — 2000-01

41	PL	X141CDV	43	PL	X143CFJ	45	PL	Y645NYD	47	PL	Y647NYD
42	PL	X142CDV	44	PL	Y644NYD	46	PL	Y646NYD	48	PL	Y648NYD

55-59 — Dennis Dart SLF 11.3m — Plaxton Pointer SPD — N41F — 2001

55	PL	WA51ACO	57	PL	WA51ACV	58	PL	WA51ACX	59	PL	WA51ACY
56	PL	WA51ACU									

60-71 — TransBus Dart 11.3m — TransBus Super Pointer — N41F — 2002-03

60	PL	WJ52GNY	63	PL	WJ52GOC	66	PL	WJ52GOK	69	PL	WA03BHY
61	PL	WJ52GNZ	64	PL	WJ52GOE	67	PL	WA03BHW	70	PL	WA03BHZ
62	PL	WJ52GOA	65	PL	WJ52GOH	68	PL	WA03BHX	71	PL	WA03BJE

72-79 — ADL Dart 10.7m — ADL Pointer — N37F — 2004

72	PL	WA54JVV	74	PL	WA54JVX	76	PL	WA54JVZ	78	PL	WA54JWD
73	PL	WA54JVW	75	PL	WA54JVY	77	PL	WA54JWC	79	PL	WA54JWE

80-94 — Mercedes-Benz Citaro O530 — Mercedes-Benz — N42F* — 2005-07 — *88-94 are N39F

80	PL	WJ55HLG	84	PL	WJ55HLN	88	PL	WA56OZM	92	PL	WA56OZS
81	PL	WJ55HLH	85	PL	WJ55HLO	89	PL	WA56OZO	93	PL	WA56OZT
82	PL	WJ55HLK	86	PL	WJ55HLP	90	PL	WA56OZP	94	PL	WA56OZU
83	PL	WJ55HLM	87	PL	WJ55HLR	91	PL	WA56OZR			

100-109 — Volvo B7RLE — Wrightbus Eclipse 2 — N36F — 2012

100	PL	WA12ACJ	103	PL	WA12ACV	106	PL	WA12ACZ	108	PL	WA12ADU
101	PL	WA12ACO	104	PL	WA12ACX	107	PL	WA12ADO	109	PL	WA12ADV
102	PL	WA12ACU	105	PL	WA12ACY						

133	PL	WA56HHO	ADL Dart 4 10.7m	ADL Enviro 200	N37F	2006
134	PL	WA56HHP	ADL Dart 4 10.7m	ADL Enviro 200	N37F	2006
135	PL	WA56HHN	ADL Dart 4 10.7m	ADL Enviro 200	N37F	2006

136-146 — ADL Dart 4 10.7m — ADL Enviro 200 — N38F — 2008

136	PL	WA08LDF	139	PL	WA08LDL	142	PL	WA08LDV	145	PL	WA08LEF
137	PL	WA08LDJ	140	PL	WA08LDN	143	PL	WA08LDX	146	PL	WA08LEJ
138	PL	WA08LDK	141	PL	WA08LDU	144	PL	WA08LDZ			

177	PL	H177GTT	Volvo Citybus B10M-50		East Lancs		BC48/30F	1991	
178	PL	H178GTT	Volvo Citybus B10M-50		East Lancs		BC48/30F	1991	

181-187

Volvo Citybus B10M-50 — Alexander RV — B47/37F — 1988-89 — Trent Buses, 1999-2000

181	PL	G615OTV	184	PL	F601GVO	186	PL	F603GVO	187	PL	F604GVO
182	PL	G621OTV	185	PL	F602GVO						

201	PL	X201CDV	Dennis Dart SLF	Plaxton Pointer MPD	N29F	2000	
202	PL	X202CDV	Dennis Dart SLF	Plaxton Pointer MPD	N29F	2000	
203	PL	X203CDV	Dennis Dart SLF	Plaxton Pointer MPD	N29F	2000	
204	PL	X204CDV	Dennis Dart SLF	Plaxton Pointer MPD	N29F	2000	
205	PL	WA03BJF	TransBus Dart 8.8m	TransBus Mini Pointer	N29F	2003	
214	u	R401FFC	Dennis Dart SLF	Wright Crusader	N30D	1998	Oxford Bus Company, 2010
215	u	R402FFC	Dennis Dart SLF	Wright Crusader	N30D	1998	Oxford Bus Company, 2010
216	u	R408FFC	Dennis Dart SLF	Wright Crusader	N30D	1998	Oxford Bus Company, 2010
311	PL	JSK264	Volvo B10M-62	Plaxton Première 350	C49FT	2000	
312	PL	JSK265	Volvo B10M-62	Plaxton Première 350	C53F	2000	
313	PL	Y313NYD	Volvo B10M-62	Plaxton Paragon	C49FT	2001	
314	PL	Y314NYD	Volvo B10M-62	Plaxton Paragon	C49FT	2001	
315	PL	WA03MGE	Volvo B12M	TransBus Paragon	C49FT	2003	
316	PL	WA03MGJ	Volvo B12M	TransBus Paragon	C49FT	2003	
317	PL	BX11GVP	Volvo B9R	Plaxton Panther	C49FT	2011	
318	PL	BX61DKV	Volvo B9R	Plaxton Panther	C49FT	2011	

401-419

Volvo B7TL 10.4m — East Lancs Vyking — N45/23D — 2002 — Go-Ahead London, 2010

401	PL	PN02XBX	406	PL	PN02XCJ	411	PL	PL51LGA	416	PL	PL51LGO
402	PL	PN02XCC	407	PL	PN02XCM	412	PL	PL51LGC	417	PL	PL51LGU
403	PL	PN02XCE	408	PL	PN02XCO	413	PL	PL51LGJ	418	PL	PL51LGW
404	PL	PN02XCG	409	PL	PN02XCP	414	PL	PL51LGK	419	PL	PL51LGX
405	PL	PN02XCH	410	PL	PL51LFE	415	PL	PL51LGN			

420-429

Volvo B7TL 10m — Plaxton President — N41/25D — 2000 — Go-Ahead London, 2011

420	PL	W509WGH	423	PL	X557EGK	426	PL	Y808TGH	428	PL	Y813TGH
421	PL	W511WGH	424	PL	X558EGK	427	PL	Y812TGH	429	PL	Y827TGH
422	PL	X556EGK	425	PL	Y828TGH						

Special event vehicle:

358	PL	MCO658	Leyland Titan PD2/12	Metro-Cammell	O30/26R	1956

Previous registrations:

JSK264	W311SDV		MCO658	MCO658, ADV935A
JSK265	W312SDV			

One of ten Volvo B7TLs with Plaxton President bodywork now with Plymouth Citybus is 428, Y813TGH.
Mark Bailey

Transferred from the London fleet to Plymouth shortly after the company was acquired by Go-Ahead were nineteen Volvo B7TLs with East Lancs Vyking bodywork. These formed part of a large order supplied to London General in 2002. An immaculate 418, PL51LGW, is seen working route 34. *Mark Bailey*

Allocations:

Plymouth (Milehouse) - PL

Dart	1	3	4	5	7	8	9	10
	12	13	14	15	16	17	18	19
	20	21	22	23	24	25	26	27
	28	29	30	31	32	33	34	35
	36	37	38	39	40	41	42	43
	44	45	46	47	48	55	56	57
	58	59	60	61	62	63	64	65
	66	67	68	69	70	71	72	73
	74	75	76	77	78	79	107	110
	112	116	117	119	120	121	122	123
	124	126	201	202	203	204	205	208
Dart 4/Enviro 200	133	134	135	136	137	138	139	140
	141	142	143	144	145	146		
Mercedes-Benz Citaro	80	81	82	83	84	85	86	87
	88	89	90	91	92	93	94	
Volvo B7RLE	100	101	102	103	104	105	106	107
	108	109						
Volvo B10M coach	311	312	313	314				
Volvo B12M coach	315	316						
Volvo B9R	317	318						
Volvo Citybus	177	178	181	184	185	186	187	
Volvo B7TL	401	402	403	404	405	406	407	408
	409	410	411	412	413	414	415	416
	417	418	419	420	421	422	423	424
	425	426	427	428	429			

Unallocated/stored - u

Remainder

GO SOUTH COAST

Wilts & Dorset - Damory Coaches - Tourist Coaches - Marchwood Motorways
Bell's Coaches - Kingston Coaches - Bluestar - Southern Vectis - Uni-Link - City Link
Wilts & Dorset Bus Co Ltd; Hants & Dorset Motor Services Ltd; Tourist Coaches Ltd;
Towngate House, Parkstone Road, Poole, BH15 2PR
Solent Blue Line Ltd, Barton Park, Eastleigh, SO50 6RR
Southern Vectis Omnibus Co Ltd, Nelson Road, Newport, PO31 1RD

The name Wilts & Dorset was first seen on the sides of buses in 1915, when a service commenced between Salisbury and Amesbury. Meanwhile on the South Coast, a company founded in 1916 as Bournemouth & District Motor Services changed its name to Hants & Dorset in 1920 as its network of routes expanded. The 1920s and 1930s were a period of development and growth, while the Second World War brought vastly increased traffic to the Wilts & Dorset fleet in particular, serving the many military establishments on Salisbury Plain. Both companies were nationalised in 1948, and from January 1969 became part of the National Bus Company. The name Wilts & Dorset disappeared in 1972 when the company was subsumed into Hants & Dorset.

In April 1983 Wilts & Dorset was reborn with an operating area now including Poole, Swanage, Lymington, Ringwood, Salisbury and Pewsey. Privatised in 1987, the company acquired five local coach operators: Damory, Tourist, Kingston, Bell's and Lever's during the 1990s. Wilts & Dorset became part of the Go-Ahead Group in August 2003.

Dodson & Campbell started a bus service between Cowes and Newport on the Isle of Wight in 1921 and traded as Vectis Bus Services from a year later (Vectis is the Roman name for the Isle of Wight). The Southern Railway purchased 50% of the share capital in 1929 and the company was named Southern Vectis in 1930. Also state owned from 1948 and part of the National Bus Company from 1969, Southern Vectis returned to private ownership following a management buy-out in 1986.

In May 1987 Southern Vectis started a small operation in Southampton with three cross-city routes branded as Solent Blue Line. Considerable expansion of the Solent Blue Line network came in October 1987 when the Hampshire Bus operations based in Southampton and Eastleigh were acquired together with Basil Williams' Hants & Sussex undertaking.

Wilts & Dorset, Southern Vectis, Bluestar, Marchwood, Damory, Tourist and refurbishment company Hants and Dorset Trim now form what is internally known as Go South Coast. The latest member to join the Go South Coast family is Marchwood Motorways, a coach operator based in Totton that had originally been founded by the Osborne family at Pooksgreen, near Marchwood, in 1955. In recent years Marchwood Motorways had also operated some bus routes under franchise to Solent Blue Line. Marchwood Motorways joined the Go-Ahead Group in October 2006.

Carrying Salisbury Reds livery is Mercedes-Benz Citaro 155, HF55JZC, in this view taken in the town.
Mark Bailey

The Go-Ahead Group has invested significantly in all of the undertakings; notable successes include the 'More' network in Poole & Bournemouth, the introduction of high specification Scania and Mercedes buses on the Isle of Wight and the Southampton-based Bluestar network, all producing sustained passenger growth.

507	IW	T165AUA	DAF SB220	Ikarus Citibus 481	N43F	1999	
508	BL	V710LWT	DAF SB220	Ikarus Citibus 481	N43F	1999	
589	DO	N976UPR	Volvo B10M-62	Plaxton Première 320	C53F	1996	Woodstones, K'minster, '02
596	IW	L728JWX	Volvo B10M-60	Plaxton Première 320	C53F	1993	Thamesdown, 1999
702	IW	CDL899	Bristol K5G	Eastern Coach Works	O30/26R	1939	Southern Vectis
1001	AL	YN54AFK	Scania N94UD	East Lancs OmniDekka	N51/39F	2004	Reading Buses, 2011
1002	AL	YN54AFX	Scania N94UD	East Lancs OmniDekka	N51/39F	2004	Reading Buses, 2011

1011-1022 Scania N94UD   East Lancs OmniDekka   N47/33F   2006   Reading Buses, 2011

1011	EH	YN06JWD	1014	AL	YN06JWJ	1017	AL	YN06JWU	1020	AL	YN06JWX
1012	EH	YN06JWE	1015	AL	YN06JWM	1018	AL	YN06JWV	1021	AL	YN06JWY
1013	EH	YN06JWG	1016	AL	YN06JWO	1019	AL	YN06JWW	1022	AL	YN06JWZ

1051-1055 Scania N94UD 10.6m   East Lancs OmniDekka   N45/29D   2003   Metrobus, 2010

| 1051 | IW | YU52XVL | 1053 | IW | YU52XVN | 1054 | IW | YN03DFL | 1055 | IW | YN03DFP |
| 1052 | IW | YU52XVM | | | | | | | | | |

| 1091 | EH | YN55NFP | Scania N94UD | | East Lancs OmniDekka | N45/31F | 2005 | Uni-Link, S'hampton, 2009 |

1101-1152 Scania OmniCity N230 UD   Scania   N45/31F*   2008-09   *1118-24/32-41 H45/29F

1101	IW	HW08AOP	1114	IW	HW58ATK	1127	EH	HF58KCC	1140	SA	HF09BJZ
1102	IW	HW08AOR	1115	IW	HW58ATN	1128	EH	HF58KCE	1141	SA	HF09BKA
1103	IW	HW08AOS	1116	IW	HW58ATO	1129	EH	HF58KCG	1142	IW	HW09BBU
1104	IW	HW08AOT	1117	IW	HW58ATU	1130	EH	HF58KCJ	1143	IW	HW09BBV
1105	IW	HW58ARU	1118	RI	HF58GYW	1131	EH	HF58KCK	1144	IW	HW09BBX
1106	IW	HW58ARX	1119	RI	HF58GYY	1132	SA	HF09BJE	1145	IW	HW09BBZ
1107	IW	HW58ARZ	1120	RI	HF58GYZ	1133	SA	HF09BJJ	1146	IW	HW09BCE
1108	IW	HW58ASO	1121	RI	HF58GZA	1134	SA	HF09BJK	1147	IW	HW09BCF
1109	IW	HW58ASU	1122	RI	HF58GZB	1135	SA	HF09BJO	1148	IW	HW09BCK
1110	IW	HW58ASV	1123	RI	HF58GZC	1136	SA	HF09BJU	1149	IW	HW09BCO
1111	IW	HW58ASX	1124	RI	HF58GZD	1137	SA	HF09BJV	1150	IW	HW09BCU
1112	IW	HW58ASZ	1125	EH	HF58GZP	1138	SA	HF09BJX	1151	IW	HW09BCV
1113	IW	HW58ATF	1126	EH	HF58KCA	1139	SA	HF09BJY	1152	IW	HW09BAA

Seen at Shanklin on the Isle of Wight is 1997 (previously 196), HW52EPV, a Volvo B7TL with Plaxton President bodywork. The livery adopted for the island's vehicles continues the green associated with Southern Vectis. Southern Vectis began life as a company called Dodson & Campbell Ltd in 1921 and two years later 1923 Dodson's became The Vectis Bus Company. The company had associations with Christopher Dodson, bus body builders in London resulting in Vectis buses of the period having Dodson bodywork. *Richard Godfrey*

1191-1199
Scania OmniCity N230 UD   Scania   N45/23D   2008

1191	UN	HF58GZE	1194	UN	HF58GZJ	1196	UN	HF58GZL	1198	UN	HF58GZN
1192	UN	HF58GZG	1195	UN	HF58GZK	1197	UN	HF58GZM	1199	UN	HF58GZO
1193	UN	HF58GZH									

1401	SW	HF09FVU	Scania OmniCity N230 UD	Optare Visionaire	CO45/23F	2009
1402	SW	HF09FVV	Scania OmniCity N230 UD	Optare Visionaire	CO45/23F	2009
1403	SW	HF09FVW	Scania OmniCity N230 UD	Optare Visionaire	CO45/23F	2009

1404-1412
Scania OmniCity N230 UD   Optare Olympus   CO45/23F*   2009   *1410-2 N45/23F

1404	SW	HF09FVX	1407	SW	HF59DMU	1409	SW	HF59DMX	1411	SW	HF09FVS
1405	SW	HF09FVY	1408	SW	HF59DMV	1410	SW	HF09FVR	1412	SW	HF09FVT
1406	SW	HF59DMO									

1501-1506
Scania N230 UD   ADL Enviro 400   N51/29F   2010

1501	PO	HF59FAA	1503	PO	HF59FAK	1505	PO	HF59FAO	1506	PO	HF59FAU
1502	PO	HF59FAJ	1504	PO	HF59FAM						

1654	SA	R154NPR	DAF DB250	Optare Spectra	N50/28F	1998
1655	SA	R155NPR	DAF DB250	Optare Spectra	N50/28F	1998
1656	SA	R156NPR	DAF DB250	Optare Spectra	N50/28F	1998

1658-1666
DAF DB250   Optare Spectra   N50/28F   1999-2000

1658	SA	T158ALJ	1661	RI	W161RFX	1663	LY	W163RFX	1665	LY	W165RFX
1659	SA	T159ALJ	1662	LY	W162RFX	1664	SA	W164RFX	1666	LY	W166RFX
1660	SA	T160ALJ									

1667-1675
DAF DB250   Optare Spectra   N50/27F   2001

1667	RI	Y167FEL	1670	LY	Y199FEL	1672	PO	Y172FEL	1674	PO	Y174FEL
1669	PO	Y169FEL	1671	BL	Y171FEL	1673	LY	Y173FEL	1675	PO	Y975FEL

1676-1685
DAF DB250   Optare Spectra   N50/26F   2002-03

1676	PO	HJ02WDK	1680	SA	HJ52VFW	1682	SA	HJ52VFY	1684	DP	HJ52VGA
1677	BL	HJ02WDL	1681	SA	HJ52VFX	1683	PO	HJ52VFZ	1685	DP	HF03AEG
1679	RI	HJ02WDN									

Bluestar started life under the Solent Blue Line name, as a subsidiary of Southern Vectis, in 1987 and now links Southampton with Winchester, Eastleigh, Romsey, Hedge End, Totton and the Hythe and Waterside area. Seen in the livery is 576, now renumbered 3307, SN03ECA, a TransBus Mini Pointer Dart. *Mark Bailey*

1742-1749

			Dennis Trident	9.9m			East Lancs Lolyne		N47/27F	1999	
1742	SA	T742JPO	1744	SA	T744JPO	1746	SA	T746JPO	1748	SA	T748JPO
1743	SA	T743JPO	1745	SA	T745JPO	1747	SA	T747JPO	1749	SA	T749JPO

1801-1808

			Volvo B7TL				East Lancs Vyking		N46/27F	2001	
1801	EH	HX51ZRA	1803	EH	HX51ZRD	1805	EH	HX51ZRF	1807	EH	HX51ZRJ
1802	EH	HX51ZRC	1804	EH	HX51ZRE	1806	EH	HX51ZRG	1808	EH	HX51ZRK
1809	PO	PL51LFG	Volvo B7TL 10.4m			East Lancs Vyking			N45/27F	2002	Go-Ahead London, 2012
1810	DO	PL51LFJ	Volvo B7TL 10.4m			East Lancs Vyking			N45/27F	2002	Go-Ahead London, 2012
1811	PO	PL51LGE	Volvo B7TL 10.4m			East Lancs Vyking			N45/27F	2002	Go-Ahead London, 2012

1821-1833

			Volvo B7TL				East Lancs Vyking		CO49/29F	2005	
1821	PO	HF54KXT	1825	PO	HF05GGE	1828	MB	HF05GGO	1831	LY	HF05GGV
1822	PO	HF54KXU	1826	LY	HF05GGJ	1829	MB	HF05GGP	1832	LY	HF05GGX
1823	PO	HF54KXV	1827	LY	HF05GGK	1830	LY	HF05GGU	1833	LY	HF05GGY
1824	PO	HF54KXW									
1851	EH	SN56AWX	Volvo B7TL			ADL Enviro 400			N47/34F	2006	Alexander-Dennis, 2007

1901-1928

			Volvo B7TL 10.4m			Plaxton President			N41/21D	2000	Go-Ahead London, '11-12
1901	PO	W501WGH	1907	s	W507WGH	1912	UN	USV115	1918	s	W518WGH
1902	u	W502WGH	1908	u	W508WGH	1913	UN	SBL364	1921	s	W521WGH
1903	u	W503WGH	1909	s	W399WGH	1915	s	W415WGH	1922	s	W522WGH
1904	PO	W504WGH	1910	UN	VJI3968	1916	s	W516WGH	1927	u	W997WGH
1905	u	W908WGH	1911	UN	YSU875	1917	s	W517WGH	1928	s	W498WGH
1906	s	W506WGH									

1939-1977

			Volvo B7TL 10m			Plaxton President			N41/21D	2001	Go-Ahead London, 2011
1939	s	Y739TGH	1943	s	Y743TGH	1951	IW	PL51LDK	1972	s	X572EGK
1940	s	Y704TGH	1946	s	Y746TGH	1952	IW	PL51LDN	1973	s	X573EGK
1941	s	Y741TGH	1947	s	Y747TGH	1955	s	PL51LDO	1974	s	X574EGK
1942	SA	Y742TGH	1949	s	Y748TGH	1959	s	X559EGK	1977	SA	X577EGK

1991-1997

			Volvo B7TL			Plaxton President			N51/28F	2002	
1991	IW	HW52EPK	1993	IW	HW52EPN	1995	IW	HW52EPP	1997	IW	HW52EPV
1992	IW	HW52EPL	1994	IW	HW52EPO	1996	IW	HW52EPU			

			Scania OmniCity N94 UB	Scania		N37D	2006	Uni-Link, S' hampton, 2009
2001	UN	YN06CGO						

2002-2012 Scania OmniCity N94 UB — Scania — N37D — 2008-11

2002	UN	HF58HTG	2005	UN	HF58HTL	2008	UN	HF58HTP	2011	UN	HF61FWL
2003	UN	HF58HTJ	2006	UN	HF58HTN	2009	UN	HF58HTT	2012	UN	HF61FWM
2004	UN	HF58HTK	2007	UN	HF58HTO	2010	UN	HF58HTU			

			Scania N230UB	Wrightbus Solar	N37D	2009
2101	PO	YT59SFJ				

2201-2238 Volvo B7RLE — Wrightbus Eclipse Urban — N40F — 2004

2201	PO	HF54HFO	2211	PO	HF54HGA	2221	PO	HF54HGO	2230	PO	HF54HHE
2202	PO	HF54HFP	2212	PO	HF54HGC	2222	PO	HF54HGP	2231	PO	HF54HHJ
2203	PO	HF54HFR	2213	PO	HF54HGD	2223	PO	HF54HGU	2232	PO	HF54HHK
2204	PO	HF54HFT	2214	PO	HF54HGE	2224	PO	HF54HGX	2233	PO	HF54HHL
2205	PO	HF54HFU	2215	PO	HF54HGG	2225	PO	HF54HGY	2234	PO	HF54HHM
2206	PO	HF54HFV	2216	PO	HF54HGJ	2226	PO	HF54HHA	2235	PO	HF05HXD
2207	PO	HF54HFW	2217	PO	HF54HGK	2227	PO	HF54HHB	2236	PO	HF05HXE
2208	PO	HF54HFX	2218	PO	HF54HGL	2228	PO	HF54HHC	2237	PO	HF05HXG
2209	PO	HF54HFY	2219	PO	HF54HGM	2229	PO	HF54HHD	2238	PO	HF05HXH
2210	PO	HF54HFZ	2220	PO	HF54HGN						

2251-2286 Volvo B7RLE — Wrightbus Eclipse 2 — N40F — 2012

2251	PO	HF12GVP	2260	PO	HF12GWA	2269	PO	HF12GWN	2278	-	HF12GXA
2252	PO	HF12GVR	2261	PO	HF12GWC	2270	PO	HF12GWU	2279	-	HF12GXB
2253	PO	HF12GVT	2262	PO	HF12GWD	2271	-	HF12GWP	2280	-	HF12GXC
2254	PO	HF12GVU	2263	PO	HF12GWE	2272	-	HF12GWU	2281	-	HF12GXD
2255	PO	HF12GVV	2264	PO	HF12GWG	2273	-	HF12GWV	2282	-	HF12GXE
2256	PO	HF12GVW	2265	PO	HF12GWJ	2274	-	HF12GWW	2283	-	HF12GXG
2257	PO	HF12GVX	2266	PO	HF12GWK	2275	-	HF12GWX	2284	-	HF12GXH
2258	PO	HF12GVY	2267	PO	HF12GWL	2276	-	HF12GWY	2285	-	HF12GXJ
2259	PO	HF12GVZ	2268	PO	HF12GWM	22771	-	HF12GWZ	2286	-	HF12GXK

2401-2428 Mercedes-Benz Citaro O530 — Mercedes-Benz — N39F — 2006

2401	EH	HF55JYX	2408	SA	HF55JZG	2415	EH	HF55JZP	2422	EH	HF06FTP
2402	EH	HF55JYY	2409	SA	HF55JZJ	2416	EH	HF55JZR	2423	EH	HF06FTT
2403	SA	HF55JYZ	2410	SA	HF55JZK	2417	PO	HF55JZT	2424	EH	HF06FTU
2404	SA	HF55JZA	2411	EH	HF55JZL	2418	PO	HF55JZU	2425	EH	HF06FTV
2405	SA	HF55JZC	2412	EH	HF55JZM	2419	EH	HF55JZV	2426	EH	HF06FTX
2406	SA	HF55JZD	2413	EH	HF55JZN	2420	MB	HF55JZW	2427	EH	HF06FTY
2407	SA	HF55JZE	2414	EH	HF55JZO	2421	EH	HF06FTO	2428	EH	HF06FTZ

2431-2440 Mercedes-Benz Citaro O530 — Mercedes-Benz — N39F — 2006

2431	MB	HX06EYZ	2434	MB	HX06EZC	2437	MB	HX06EZF	2439	MB	HX06EZH
2432	MB	HX06EZA	2435	MB	HX06EZD	2438	MB	HX06EZG	2440	MB	HX06EZJ
2433	MB	HX06EZB	2436	MB	HX06EZE						

2451-2457 Mercedes-Benz Citaro O530 — Mercedes-Benz — N39F — 2007

2451	MB	HW07CXR	2453	MB	HW07CXT	2455	MB	HW07CXV	2457	MB	HW07CXY
2452	MB	HW07CXS	2454	MB	HW07CXU	2456	MB	HW07CXX			

2601-2609 Optare Excel L1180 — Optare — N43F* — 2000 — *2609 is N42F

2601	RI	W601PLJ	2604	RI	W604PLJ	2606	PO	X606XFX	2608	PO	X608XFX
2602	PO	W602PLJ	2605	PO	X605XFX	2607	PO	X607XFX	2609	PO	X609WLJ

2610-2615 Optare Excel L1180 — Optare — N42F — 2002-03

2610	PO	HJ02WDE	2612	PO	HJ02WDG	2614	PO	HF03HJZ	2615	PO	HF03HKA
2611	PO	HJ02WDF	2613	PO	HF03HJY						

2901-2913 Mercedes-Benz Citaro O530G — Mercedes-Benz — AN49T — 2002 — Go-Ahead London, 2010>

2901	PO	BX02YYZ	2905	S	BX54UDN	2908	S	BX54UDU	2911	S	BX54UDZ
2902	S	BX54UDE	2906	S	BX54UDO	2909	S	BX54UDW	2912	S	BX54UEB
2903	S	BX54UDG	2907	S	BX54UDT	2910	S	BX54UDY	2913	S	BX54EFB
2904	S	BX54UDL									

3205-3213 Dennis Dart SLF 10.1m — Plaxton Pointer — N39F — 1996 — Brighton & Hove, 2011

3205	PO	N205NNJ	3208	PO	N208NNJ	3211	PO	N211NNJ	3213	PO	N213NNJ

3237	EH	P737RYL	Dennis Dart SLF 10m	Plaxton Pointer 2	N35F	1996	Go-Ahead London, 2011
3264	EH	R464LGH	Dennis Dart SLF 10m	Plaxton Pointer	N33F	1997	Go-Ahead London, 2011
3301	SA	HW52EPX	Dennis Dart SLF 8.8m	Plaxton MPD	N29F	2002	

The Scania OmniCity double-deck features highly in the Go South Coast fleet with twenty-eight now allocated to Southern Vectis work. Shanklin centre provides the background to this view of 1109, HW58ASU, which was heading for Newport when pictured last July. *Richard Godfrey*

3302-3313

TransBus Dart 8.8m   TransBus Mini Pointer   N29F   2003

3302	MB	SN03EBP	3305	MB	SN03EBX	3308	SA	SN03ECC	3311	SA	SN03LDK
3303	MB	SN03EBU	3306	MB	SN03EBZ	3309	SA	SN03ECD	3312	SA	SN03LDL
3304	MB	SN03EBV	3307	MB	SN03ECA	3310	SA	SN03LDJ	3313	SA	SN03LDU

3314-3327

ADL Dart 8.8m   ADL Mini Pointer   N27F   2004-05

3314	IW	HW54BTU	3318	SA	HW54BTZ	3322	IW	HW54BUH	3325	IW	HW54BUP
3315	IW	HW54BTV	3319	SA	HW54BUA	3323	IW	HW54BUJ	3326	IW	HW54BUU
3316	SA	HW54BTX	3320	SA	HW54BUE	3324	IW	HW54BUO	3327	SA	HW54BUV
3317	IW	HW54BTY	3321	IW	HW54BUF						

3328	IW	HW54DBZ	Dennis Dart SLF 8.8m	Plaxton Pointer MPD	N29F	2004	*Operated for IOW Council*
3329	IW	HW54DCE	Dennis Dart SLF 8.8m	Plaxton Pointer MPD	N29F	2004	*Operated for IOW Council*
3344	EH	HX51LPN	Dennis Dart SLF 10.7m	Caetano Nimbus	N29D	2001	
3351	EH	PE55WPP	Dennis Dart SLF 10.1m	East Lancs Myllennium	N29D	2006	
3352	EH	PE55WSU	Dennis Dart SLF 10.1m	East Lancs Myllennium	N29D	2006	
3361	IW	HW54DCF	Dennis Dart SLF 10m	Plaxton Pointer 2	N37F	2004	*Operated for IOW Council*
3362	IW	HW54DCO	Dennis Dart SLF 10m	Plaxton Pointer 2	N37F	2004	*Operated for IOW Council*
3363	IW	HW54DCU	Dennis Dart SLF 10m	Plaxton Pointer 2	N37F	2004	*Operated for IOW Council*
3401	EH	Y291HUA	DAF SB120	Wrightbus Cadet	N39F	2001	Go North East, 2011
3402	EH	Y292HUA	DAF SB120	Wrightbus Cadet	N39F	2001	Go North East, 2011

3403-3412

DAF SB120   Wrightbus Cadet 2   N39F   2002

3403	SA	YG52CDZ	3406	SA	YG52CEN	3409	EH	YG52CLX	3411	DP	YG52CME
3404	PO	YG52CEF	3407	EH	YG52CLO	3410	MB	YG52CLY	3412	EH	YG52CMF
3405	DP	YG52CEJ	3408	SA	YG52CLV						

3413	MB	NK04FOV	VDL SB120	Wrightbus Cadet	N39F	2004	Go North East, 2011
3414	MB	NK04FPA	VDL SB120	Wrightbus Cadet	N39F	2004	Go North East, 2011
3415	EH	YJ07JTX	VDL SB120	Wrightbus Cadet 2	N39F	2002	
3416	SA	YJ07JTY	VDL SB120	Wrightbus Cadet 2	N39F	2002	

3602-3622

Optare Solo M850   Optare   N30F   1998

3602	VC	R602NFX	3605	HE	R605NFX	3615	VC	R615NFX	3620	VC	R620NFX
3603	u	R603NFX	3609	EH	R609NFX	3618	VC	R618NFX	3621	VC	R620NFX
3604	u	R604NFX	3610	EH	R610NFX	3619	BL	R619NFX	3622	BL	R620NFX

3628	DS	S628JRU	Optare Solo M850		Optare	N30F	1998	
3631	IW	S631JRU	Optare Solo M850		Optare	N30F	1998	
3632	VC	S632JRU	Optare Solo M850		Optare	N30F	1998	

3633-2649 · Optare Solo M850 · Optare · N30F · 1999-2001

3633	EH	T633AJT	3637	DO	T637AJT	3641	PO	T641AJT	3646	BL	T646AJT
3634	MB	T634AJT	3638	IW	T638AJT	3642	RI	T642AJT	3647	BL	T647AJT
3635	DO	T635AJT	3639	SA	T639AJT	3644	VC	T644AJT	3648	PO	T648AJT
3636	BL	T636AJT	3640	IW	T640AJT	3645	BL	T645AJT	3649	VC	T649AJT

3652-3688 · Optare Solo M850 · Optare · N30F · 1999-2001

3652	SA	V653DFX	3661	FI	V661DFX	3671	SA	V671FEL	3681	LY	V681FEL
3653	SA	V652DFX	3662	LY	V662DFX	3672	SA	V672FEL	3682	LY	V682FEL
3654	BL	V654DFX	3663	SA	V663DFX	3673	SA	V673FEL	3683	PO	V683FEL
3655	LY	V655DFX	3664	SA	V665DFX	3674	PO	V674FEL	3684	PO	V684FEL
3656	DP	V656DFX	3665	SA	V664DFX	3675	LY	V675FEL	3685	HE	V685FEL
3657	DO	V657DFX	3666	SA	V966DFX	3676	BL	V676FEL	3686	FI	V686FEL
3658	SA	V658DFX	3667	SA	V667DFX	3677	PO	V677FEL	3687	FI	X687XJT
3659	DP	V659DFX	3669	MB	V669DFX	3679	LY	V679FEL	3688	FI	X688XJT
3660	MB	V660DFX	3670	DO	V670DFX	3680	FI	V680FEL			

3701-3704 · Optare Solo M850 · Optare · N25F · 2004 · Go North East, 2010

3701	RI	NK54DEU	3702	RI	NK54DFA	3703	PO	NK54DFC	3704	PO	NK54DFD

3705	DO	NT05NBM	Optare Solo	M880	Optare	N25F	2005	Britannia, Bournemouth '11
3706	DO	NT55JKJ	Optare Solo	M880	Optare	N25F	2005	Britannia, Bournemouth '11
3707	DO	MV07DWM	Optare Solo	M880	Optare	N25F	2007	Britannia, Bournemouth '11
3708	DO	MX07NSV	Optare Solo	M880	Optare	N25F	2007	Britannia, Bournemouth '11
3709	HE	MX57CAO	Optare Solo	M880	Optare	N25F	2008	Evans, Bromborough, 2011
3710	HE	MX57CAU	Optare Solo	M880	Optare	N25F	2008	Evans, Bromborough, 2011
3711	HE	MX57CAV	Optare Solo	M880	Optare	N25F	2008	Britannia, Bournemouth '11
3712	HE	MX08MYP	Optare Solo	M880	Optare	N25F	2008	Britannia, Bournemouth '11
3713	u	NM02DNUE	Optare Solo	M850	Optare	N29F	2002	
3714	BL	VU52UEE	Optare Solo	M850	Optare	N29F	2002	
3715	BL	VU52UEF	Optare Solo	M850	Optare	N29F	2002	
3716	DP	MX53FEF	Optare Solo	M850	Optare	N29F	2003	
3717	DO	YJ06FZP	Optare Solo	M920	Optare	N23F	2006	*Operated for Dorset CC*
3718	DO	YJ06FYU	Optare Solo	M920	Optare	N23F	2006	*Operated for Dorset CC*
3719	BL	YJ58PGO	Optare Solo	M880	Optare	N23F	2008	*Operated for Dorset CC*
3720	BL	YJ58PGY	Optare Solo	M880	Optare	N23F	2008	*Operated for Dorset CC*
3721	BL	YJ58PGV	Optare Solo	M880	Optare	N23F	2008	*Operated for Dorset CC*
3722	LY	YJ05XMR	Optare Solo	M880	Optare	N23F	2008	*Operated for Dorset CC*
3751	SA	GP02DPV	Optare Solo	M920	Optare	N30F	2002	Meteor Parking, 2010
3752	SA	VU02TTK	Optare Solo	M920	Optare	N29F	2002	Meteor Parking, 2010
3753	SA	VU52UES	Optare Solo	M920	Optare	N33F	2002	Meteor Parking, 2010
3754	SA	MX03YDD	Optare Solo	M920	Optare	N33F	2003	Meteor Parking, 2010

3755-3758 · Optare Solo M850 · Optare · N19F · 2006 · Meteor Parking, 2010

3755	SA	YJ06FYB	3756	SA	YJ06FYC	3757	SA	YJ06FYD	3758	SA	YJ06FYE

3759	HE	MX07JNV	Optare Solo M950		Optare	N33F	2007	
3760	DO	MX07NTC	Optare Solo M950		Optare	N33F	2007	
3761	DO	MX07NTD	Optare Solo M950		Optare	N33F	2007	
3762	HE	MX57CAA	Optare Solo M880		Optare	N33F	2008	Padarn, Llanberis, 2011
3763	HE	MX57CCU	Optare Solo M950		Optare	N33F	2008	
3764	BL	MX08MZF	Optare Solo M950		Optare	N33F	2008	
3765	BL	MX08MZJ	Optare Solo M950		Optare	N33F	2008	Holmeswood Cs, 2011
3771	BL	YJ54UWN	Optare Solo M950		Optare	N33F	2004	
3772	BL	YN53YGY	Optare Solo M950		Optare	N33F	2004	
3773	HE	PM04MKP	Optare Solo M950		Optare	N33F	2004	
3774	HE	YN04LWZ	Optare Solo M950		Optare	N33F	2004	
3775	BL	YJ56WUO	Optare Solo M950		Optare	N33F	2007	
3776	BL	MX57UPC	Optare Solo M950		Optare	N29F	2007	
3777	BL	MX57UPY	Optare Solo M950		Optare	N29F	2007	
3778	DO	CE52UXC	Optare Solo M950		Optare	N29F	2007	
3779	DS	CE52UXD	Optare Solo M950		Optare	N29F	2007	
3780	DO	YJ56WUL	Optare Solo M950		Optare	N29F	2007	
3781	DO	YJ56WUM	Optare Solo M950		Optare	N29F	2007	
3801	PO	BP09ONE	Optare Solo M960 SR		Optare	N30F	2009	*Operated for Poole Council*
3802	PO	PB09ONE	Optare Solo M960 SR		Optare	N30F	2009	*Operated for Poole Council*

Part of the 2012 intake comprises a further batch of thirty-six Volvo B7RLEs that carry the More fleetname and are used in Bournemouth and Poole. The dark blue More buses were introduced in 2004 as part of the Wilts & Dorset operation. Representing the new arrivals is 2259, HF12GYZ. *Richard Godfrey*

3803-3819

			Optare Solo M960 SR			Optare			N30F	On order		
3803	-	-		3808	-	-		3812	-	-		3816	-	-
3804	-	-		3809	-	-		3813	-	-		3817	-	-
3805	-	-		3810	-	-		3814	-	-		3818	-	-
3806	-	-		3811	-	-		3815	-	-		3819	-	-
3807	-	-											

4113	IW	N13WAL	DAF DB250		Northern Counties Palatine II	CO47/30F	1995	Wall's of Manchester, 1997

4136-4147

DAF DB250   Optare Spectra   BC45/28F   1995*   *4143 is B48/29F

4136	s	M136KRU	4139	s	M139KRU	4143	BL	M143KRU	4147	s	M147KRU
4138	s	M138KRU	4140	s	M140KRU						

4148	s	M17WAL	DAF DB250	Northern Counties Palatine II	CO47/30F	1995	Wall's of Manchester, 1997
4149	s	M18WAL	DAF DB250	Northern Counties Palatine II	CO47/30F	1995	Wall's of Manchester, 1997
4150	s	M19WAL	DAF DB250	Northern Counties Palatine II	CO47/30F	1995	Wall's of Manchester, 1997
4151	s	M20WAL	DAF DB250	Northern Counties Palatine II	CO47/30F	1995	Wall's of Manchester, 1997
4157	s	M645RCP	DAF DB250	Northern Counties Palatine	CO47/30F	1995	A Bus, Brislington, 1998
4637	IW	R737XRV	Volvo Olympian	Northern Counties Palatine	PO47/29F	1998	
4638	IW	R738XRV	Volvo Olympian	Northern Counties Palatine	PO47/29F	1998	
4639	IW	R739XRV	Volvo Olympian	Northern Counties Palatine	PO47/29F	1998	
4641	IW	R741XRV	Volvo Olympian	Northern Counties Palatine	PO47/29F	1998	
4642	IW	K742ODL	Leyland Olympian ON2R50C13Z5	Northern Counties	PO41/29F	1993	
4643	IW	K743ODL	Leyland Olympian ON2R50C13Z5	Northern Counties	PO41/29F	1993	
4706	DP	F706RDL	Leyland Olympian ONCL10/1RZ	Leyland	BC39/29F	1989	
4707	RI	F707RDL	Leyland Olympian ONCL10/1RZ	Leyland	BC39/29F	1989	
4710	BL	TIL6710	Leyland Olympian ONCL10/1RZ	Leyland	BC41/29F	1989	
4711	BL	TIL6711	Leyland Olympian ONCL10/1RZ	Leyland	BC41/29F	1989	
4712	DP	TIL6712	Leyland Olympian ONCL10/1RZ	Leyland	BC41/29F	1989	

4713-4727
Leyland Olympian ON2R50C13Z5 Leyland   B47/29F*   1989-90   *4713/21/3 are BC41/29F

4713	LY	TIL6713	4717	DS	TIL6717	4721	BL	G721WDL	4725	PO	TIL6725
4714	BL	TIL6714	4718	DP	TIL6718	4723	LY	TIL6723	4726	RI	TIL6726
4715	HE	TIL6715	4719	BL	TIL6719	4724	PO	TIL6724	4727	BL	TIL6727
4716	HE	TIL6716	4720	BL	TIL6720						

4728-4734 — Leyland Olympian ON2R50C13Z5 Leyland — B47/31F — 1991

4728	RI	H728DDL	4731	LY	H731DDL	4733	DP	H733DDL	4734	LY	H734DDL
4729	DP	H729DDL									

4735-4741 — Leyland Olympian ON2R50C13Z5 Northern Counties — B47/29F — 1993

4735	RI	K735ODL	4737	LY	K737ODL	4739	LY	K739ODL	4741	RI	K741ODL
4736	LY	K736ODL	4738	RI	K738ODL	4740	LY	K740ODL			

4744-4751 — Volvo Olympian YN2R50C18Z4 — Northern Counties — B48/29F* — 1995 — *4744/5 are BC41/39F

4744	DP	M744HDL	4746	SA	M746HDL	4749	SA	M749HDL	4751	SA	M751HDL
4745	SA	M745HDL	4748	DP	M748HDL	4750	SA	M750HDL			

4752-4759 — Volvo Olympian — Northern Counties Palatine — B48/29F* — 1998 — *4753/6 are BC41/29F

4752	SA	R752GDL	4754	SA	R754GDL	4756	SA	R756GDL	4758	SA	R758GDL
4753	SA	R753GDL	4755	SA	R755GDL	4757	SA	R757GDL	4759	SA	R759GDL

Fleet	Code	Reg	Chassis	Body	Seating	Year	Notes
4765	RI	M735BBP	Volvo Olympian YN2RC16Z5	East Lancs	B41/31F	1995	
4766	LY	M736BBP	Volvo Olympian YN2RV18Z4	East Lancs	B41/31F	1995	
4809	MB	N539LHG	Volvo Olympian YN2RV18Z4	Northern Counties	B47/27F	1996	Metrobus, 2004
4813	DS	N413JBL	Volvo Olympian YN2RV18Z4	Northern Counties	B47/27F	1996	Go-Ahead London, 200

4830-4845 — Volvo Olympian — East Lancs Pyoneer — B47/25D — 1997 — Metrobus, 2010

4830	VC	R830MFR	4834	VC	R834MFR	4837	VC	R837MFR	4841	VC	R841MFR
4831	VC	R831MFR	4835	VC	R835MFR	4838	VC	R838MFR	4843	VC	R843MFR
4832	VC	R832MFR	4836	VC	R836MFR	4839	VC	R839MFR	4845	VC	R845MFR
4833	u	R833MFR									

4862-4887 — Volvo Olympian — Northern Counties Palatine II B47/27D — 1998 — Go-Ahead London, 2010

4862	VC	R362LGH	4879	MB	R379LGH	4883	EH	R383LGH	4885	u	R385LGH
4868	VC	R368LGH	4882	EH	R382LGH	4884	u	R384LGH	4887	VC	R387LGH
4873	VC	R373LGH									

Fleet	Code	Reg	Chassis	Body	Seating	Year	Notes
5514	BL	M15WAL	DAF SB220	Ikarus CitiBus	B48F	1994	Wall's of Manchester, 1997
5515	BL	N15WAL	DAF SB220	Ikarus CitiBus	B49F	1995	Wall's of Manchester, 1997
5516	BL	N16WAL	DAF SB220	Ikarus CitiBus	B49F	1995	Wall's of Manchester, 1997
5602	DP	N602FJO	Volvo B10B	Plaxton Verde	B51F	1995	City of Oxford, 2006
5606	BL	N606FJO	Volvo B10B	Plaxton Verde	B51F	1995	City of Oxford, 2006
5616	BL	N416NRG	Volvo B10B	Plaxton Verde	B51F	1995	City of Oxford, 2006
5625	IW	K125BUD	Volvo B10B	Northern Counties Paladin	B47F	1993	Go-Ahead London, 2011
5526	RI	L526YDL	Volvo B10B	Alexander Strider	B51F	1994	
5527	DO	L527YDL	Volvo B10B	Alexander Strider	B51F	1994	
5528	DO	L528YDL	Volvo B10B	Alexander Strider	B51F	1994	
7002	FI	DAZ1563	Volvo B10M	Plaxton Première 320	C53F	1994	Stagecoach, 2011
7003	DO	FNZ7669	Volvo B10M	Plaxton Première 350	C53F	1994	
7004	DO	M304KOD	Volvo B10M-62	Plaxton Première 350	C49FT	1995	Plymouth Citybus, 2011
7005	VC	M305KOD	Volvo B10M	Plaxton Première 350	C53F	1995	
7006	BL	P41RCRD	Volvo B10M	Plaxton Première 350	C55F	1997	Marchwood, Totton, 2007
7007	VC	N307UTT	Volvo B10M	Plaxton Première 350	C53F	1997	Go-Ahead North East, 2011
7008	VC	P308CTT	Volvo B10M	Plaxton Première 350	C53F	1997	Plymouth Citybus, 2011
7009	VC	R309STA	Volvo B10M	Plaxton Première 350	C53F	1997	Go-Ahead North East, 2011
7010	VC	R807NUD	Volvo B10M-62	Plaxton Première 350	C53F	1997	City of Oxford, 2004
7011	VC	R811NUD	Volvo B10M-62	Plaxton Première 350	C53F	1997	City of Oxford, 2004
7012	VC	R812NUD	Volvo B10M-62	Plaxton Première 350	C53F	1997	City of Oxford, 2004
7013	VC	R813NUD	Volvo B10M-62	Plaxton Première 350	C53F	1997	City of Oxford, 2004
7014	DO	NLZ1822	Volvo B10M	Plaxton Première 350	C53F	1995	
7015	u	DIG5295	Volvo B10M	Plaxton Première 350	C53F	1992	
7016	u	N232HWX	Volvo B10M	Plaxton Première 350	C53F	1995	
7017	FI	OJI1875	Volvo B10M-62	Plaxton Première 350	C53F	1995	Woodstones, K'minster, '02
7018	FI	XAA299	Volvo B10M-62	Plaxton Première 320	C53F	1996	Bell, Winterslow, 1999
7019	FI	HJI2615	Volvo B10M-62	Plaxton Première 350	C57F	2000	Woodstones, K'minster, '02
7021	u	T518EUB	Volvo B10M	Plaxton Première 350	S70F	1999	Stagecoach, 2011
7022	DO	T600BCL	Volvo B10M	Plaxton Première 350	C46F	1999	
7023	DO	Y23OXF	Volvo B10M	Plaxton Excalibur	C53F	2000	Oxford City Bus, 2011
7024	BL	Y24OXF	Volvo B10M	Plaxton Excalibur	C53F	2000	Oxford City Bus, 2011
7025	DO	R435MEH	Volvo B10M-62	Plaxton Excalibur	C49FT	1996	Flights, Birmingham, 2002
7026	DO	R259DWL	Volvo B10M-62	Plaxton Excalibur	C49FT	1998	
7027	DO	R401DWL	Volvo B10M-62	Plaxton Excalibur	C49FT	1998	
7028	DS	UEL489	Volvo B10M-62	Plaxton Excalibur	C49FT	1996	City of Oxford, 2004
7029	VC	R809NUD	Volvo B10M-62	Plaxton Première 350	C53F	1997	City of Oxford, 2004
7030	VC	R810NUD	Volvo B10M-62	Plaxton Première 350	C53F	1997	City of Oxford, 2004

Pictured working on Southampton citylink services is Dennis Dart 3352, PE55WSU, which carries an East Lancs Myllennium body and is one of a pair that joined the fleet in 2006. *Steve Rice*

7031	VC	MV02ULK	Volvo B12M	Van Hool T9 Alizée	C53F	2002	Shearings, Wigan, 2011
7032	VC	MV02ULL	Volvo B12M	Van Hool T9 Alizée	C53F	2002	Shearings, Wigan, 2011
7033	DO	MV02ULM	Volvo B12M	Van Hool T9 Alizée	C53F	2002	Shearings, Wigan, 2011
7034	VC	MV02UMJ	Volvo B12M	Van Hool T9 Alizée	C53F	2002	Shearings, Wigan, 2011
7035	VC	MV02UMK	Volvo B12M	Van Hool T9 Alizée	C53F	2002	Shearings, Wigan, 2011
7036	VC	MV02UML	Volvo B12M	Van Hool T9 Alizée	C53F	2002	Shearings, Wigan, 2011
7037	VC	MV02UMM	Volvo B12M	Van Hool T9 Alizée	C53F	2002	Shearings, Wigan, 2011
7038	VC	MV02UMO	Volvo B12M	Van Hool T9 Alizée	C53F	2002	Shearings, Wigan, 2011
7039	VC	MV02UMR	Volvo B12M	Van Hool T9 Alizée	C53F	2002	Shearings, Wigan, 2011
7040	VC	MV02UMS	Volvo B12M	Van Hool T9 Alizée	C53F	2002	Shearings, Wigan, 2011
7041	VC	MV02UMT	Volvo B12M	Van Hool T9 Alizée	C53F	2002	Shearings, Wigan, 2011
7042	VC	MV02UMU	Volvo B12M	Van Hool T9 Alizée	C53F	2002	Shearings, Wigan, 2011
7043	VC	MV02UMW	Volvo B12M	Van Hool T9 Alizée	C53F	2002	Shearings, Wigan, 2011
7044	VC	MV02UMX	Volvo B12M	Van Hool T9 Alizée	C53F	2002	Shearings, Wigan, 2011
7051	SA	FJ61EVX	Volvo B9R	Caetano Levanté	C49FT	2011	
7060	VC	WKZ8697	Volvo B10M	Caetano Algarve	C53F		
7061	FI	AT02CJT	Volvo B7R	Jonckheere Modulo	C52F	2002	Turner, Bristol, 2006
7062	FI	BT02CJT	Volvo B7R	Jonckheere Modulo	C53F	2002	Turner, Bristol, 2006
7063	DO	WKZ8689	Volvo B10M	Jonckheere Mistral	C53F		
7070	VP	KP51UEX	Volvo B7R	Plaxton Panther	C53F	2002	
7071	BL	SFO5KWM	Volvo B7R	Plaxton Paragon	S70F	2005	
7079	DO	WX53WFP	Volvo B10M	Plaxton Paragon	C53F	2001	
7080	IW	VUV246	Volvo B10M-62	Plaxton Paragon	C49FT	2001	?
7081	VP	LIL2665	Volvo B10M-62	Plaxton Paragon	C49FT	2001	Go North East, 2010
7083	VP	LIL3748	Volvo B10M-62	Plaxton Paragon	C49FT	2001	Go North East, 2010
7084	VP	WKZ8689	Volvo B10M-62	Plaxton Paragon	C49FT	2001	Go North East, 2010
7085	IW	WKZ8679	Volvo B10M-62	Plaxton Paragon	C49FT	2001	Go North East, 2011
7086	IW	GSK962	Volvo B12M	Plaxton Paragon	C53F	2002	Go North East, 2011
7088	FI	NJ53AAE	Volvo B12M	Plaxton Paragon	C53F	2003	Go North East, 2011
7089	FI	NJ53AAF	Volvo B12M	Plaxton Paragon	C53F	2003	Go North East, 2011
7090	IW	GX02ATF	Volvo B12M	Plaxton Paragon	C53F	2002	
7091	IW	WV52AKY	Volvo B12M	Plaxton Paragon	C53F	2003	First, 2011

7092	IW	WV52FAO	Volvo B12M	Plaxton Paragon	C53F	2003	First, 2011
7093	IW	WV52HTT	Volvo B12M	Plaxton Paragon	C53F	2003	First , 2011
7094	BL	GU52WSY	Volvo B12M	Plaxton Paragon Expressliner	C53F	2002	Stagecoach, 2011
7095	BL	GU52WTG	Volvo B12M	Plaxton Paragon Expressliner	C53F	2002	Stagecoach, 2011
7096	BL	PX03KCN	Volvo B12M	Plaxton Paragon Expressliner	C53F	2003	Stagecoach, 2011
7097	BL	PX03KCU	Volvo B12M	Plaxton Paragon Expressliner	C53F	2003	Stagecoach, 2011
7098	BL	VU03VVX	Volvo B12M	Plaxton Paragon Expressliner	C53F	2003	Stagecoach, 2011
7099	BL	VU03VVY	Volvo B12M	Plaxton Paragon Expressliner	C53F	2003	Stagecoach, 2011

7101-7105
Scania K340 EB4 — Irizar PB — C49FT — 2008

7101	IW	HF08UHS	7103	IW	HF08UHU	7104	FI	HF08UHV	7105	FI	HF08UHW

7131	SA	YN07EWS	Scania K340 EB4	Caetano Levanté	C49FT	2007	
7132	SA	YN07EWT	Scania K340 EB4	Caetano Levanté	C49FT	2007	

7174-7180
Scania K340 EB4 — Irizar PB — C49FT — 2008 — Clarkes of London, 2012

7174	BL	YN04GHD	7176	FI	YN04GHG	7178	BL	YN04GHJ	7180	VP	XDL872
7175	VP	WDL691	7177	FI	YN04GHH	7179	FI	YN04GHK			

7201	u	701GOO	DAF SB3000	Plaxton Première 350	C53F	1996	
7202	BL	N45FWU	DAF SB3000	Plaxton Première 350	C53F	1996	
7203	BL	LIL3748	DAF SB3000	Plaxton Première 350	C57F	1996	Armchair, Brentford, 1999
7214	u	R214NFX	DAF SB3000	Plaxton Première 320	C53F	1998	
7215	HE	R215NFX	DAF SB3000	Plaxton Première 320	C53F	1998	
7216	FI	T216REL	DAF SB3000	Plaxton Prestige	C49FT	1999	
7217	FI	T217REL	DAF SB3000	Plaxton Prestige	C49FT	1999	
7218	SA	T218REL	DAF SB3000	Plaxton Prestige	C49FT	1999	
7220	u	T110AUA	DAF SB3000	Ikarus Blue Danube 350	C55F	1997	Marchwood, Totton, 2007
7222	DO	P886RWW	DAF SB3000	Ikarus Blue Danube	C49FT	1997	Marchwood, Totton, 2007
7223	BL	P887RWW	DAF SB3000	Ikarus Blue Danube	C49FT	1997	Marchwood, Totton, 2007
7224	IW	P124RWR	DAF SB3000	Ikarus Blue Danube	C55F	1997	Marchwood, Totton, 2007
7225	DO	P125RWR	DAF SB3000	Ikarus Blue Danube 350	C55F	1997	Marchwood, Totton, 2007
7226	DO	P126RWR	DAF SB3000	Ikarus Blue Danube 350	C55F	1997	Marchwood, Totton, 2007
7227	u	R63GNW	DAF SB3000	Ikarus Blue Danube	C53F	1998	Marchwood, Totton, 2007
7242	u	R929JYG	Bova Futura FHD10.340	Bova	C41F	1998	
7261	VC	K408XFX	DAF MB230	Van Hool Alizée	C51FT	1993	First Lowland, 2000
7262	MB	TJI9462	DAF MB230	Van Hool Alizée	C57F	1993	First Lowland, 2001
7263	FI	SIB5373	DAF MB230	Van Hool Alizée	C51F	1994	Hallmark, Luton, 2001
7264	FI	SIL7914	DAF MB230	Van Hool Alizée	C49FT	1995	Wilson, Bonnyrigg, 2000
7265	VC	K529RJX	DAF MB230	Van Hool Alizée	C53F	1993	Wootten, Northampton, '00
7271	MB	381VHX	DAF SB3000	Van Hool Alizée HE	C49FT	1996	Wood, Barnsley, 2000
7272	EH	HSV342	DAF SB3000	Van Hool Alizée HE	C49FT	1996	Couplands, Wyre, 1999
7273	FI	YMW843	DAF SB3000	Van Hool Alizée HE	C53F	1997	Berkley, H Hempstead, '01
7274	PO	M574RCP	DAF SB3000	Van Hool Alizée HE	C55F	1994	North Kent Express, 2002
7275	u	1045MM	DAF SB3000	Van Hool Alizée HE	C51FT	1995	Marchwood, Totton, 2007
7276	PO	M746RCP	DAF SB3000	Van Hool Alizée HE	C55F	1994	North Kent Express, 2002
7277	BL	M577RCP	DAF SB3000	Van Hool Alizée HE	C55F	1994	North Kent Express, 2002
7278	EH	M826RCP	DAF SB2700	Van Hool Alizée HE	C57FT	1994	Marchwood, Totton, 2007
7280	BL	M580RCP	DAF SB3000	Van Hool Alizée HE	C55F	1994	North Kent Express, 2002
7281	BL	WIL2574	DAF SB3000	Van Hool T9 Alizée	C51F	2000	Marchwood, Totton, 2007
7282	HE	W182CDN	DAF SB3000	Van Hool T9 Alizée	C51FT	2000	Marchwood, Totton, 2007
7284	FI	MJI7514	DAF SB3000	Van Hool T9 Alizée	C51F	2000	
7285	VP	YJ03PPF	DAF SB4000	Van Hool T9 Alizée	C49FT	2003	
7286	VP	YJ03PPK	DAF SB4000	Van Hool T9 Alizée	C51F	2003	Marchwood, Totton, 2007
7287	BL	YJ03PPU	DAF SB4000	Van Hool T9 Alizée	C49FT	2003	Marchwood, Totton, 2007
7288	BL	YJ03PPV	DAF SB4000	Van Hool T9 Alizée	C49FT	2003	Marchwood, Totton, 2007
7289	FI	YJ03PPX	DAF SB4000	Van Hool T9 Alizée	C49FT	2003	Marchwood, Totton, 2007
7301	VP	ODL447	Dennis R	Caetano Enigma	C49FT	2004	
7302	VP	VDL744	Dennis R	Caetano Enigma	C49FT	2004	
7311	BL	KP51UEO	Dennis R	Plaxton Panther	C49FT	2001	
7312	BL	KP51UES	Dennis R	Plaxton Panther	C49FT	2001	
7313	BL	KP51UFA	Dennis R	Plaxton Panther	C49FT	2001	
7314	BL	KT51BXH	Dennis R	Plaxton Panther	C49FT	2001	
7315	BL	YR02ZKV	Dennis R	Plaxton Panther	C49FT	2002	
7316	BL	YR02ZKW	Dennis R	Plaxton Panther	C49FT	2002	
7317	BL	YR02ZKX	Dennis R	Plaxton Panther	C49FT	2002	
7318	VC	YR02ZKY	Dennis R	Plaxton Panther	C49FT	2002	
7325	HE	N443WUX	Dennis Javelin 12m	Plaxton Première 320	C49FT	1996	
7326	FI	NXI5358	Dennis Javelin 12m	Plaxton Première 320	C49FT	1996	
7327	u	UJI2507	Dennis Javelin 12m	Plaxton Première 320	C53F	1998	Stort Valley, Stansted, 2000

Tourist Group started as a trading name of Southern Coach Hire, which covers a group of bus and coach operators all of which are subsidiaries of Wilts & Dorset. The name continues on vehicles allocated to Figheldean depot. Showing the livery now used is 7215, R215NFX. *Mark Bailey*

7329	FI	RJI6155	Dennis Javelin 12m	Plaxton Première 320	C49FT	1996	
7330	FI	LSV749	Dennis Javelin 12m	Plaxton Première 320	C49FT	1996	
7351	VC	F783AFX	Dennis Javelin 12m	Plaxton Première 320	C49FT	1996	
7360	u	S610VAY	Dennis Javelin 12m	Marcopolo	C49FT	1998	
7361	u	S611VAY	Dennis Javelin 12m	Marcopolo	C49FT	1998	
7381	HE	HBZ4674	Dennis Javelin 12m	Duple 320	C49FT	1988	
7382	HE	LIL9974	Dennis Javelin 12m	Duple 320	C49FT	1988	
7383	u	M993ROS	Dennis Javelin 12m	UVG Urbanstar	S70F	1993	
7391	BL	ONZ1208	Dennis Javelin 12m	Caetano Algarve	C49FT	1993	
7401	VP	LX03KPA	Mercedes-Benz Touro 1836RL	Mercedes-Benz	C49FT	2003	
7402	VP	BU03LXX	Mercedes-Benz Touro 1836RL	Mercedes-Benz	C49FT	2003	Hemmings, 2006
7411	VP	N411WJL	Mercedes-Benz 711D	Autobus Classique Nouvelle	C24F	1995	Bell, Winterslow, 1999
7431	u	TDL856	Setra S415 HD	Setra	C49FT	2004	
7452	FI	XAM152	Mercedes-Benz Atego 1190L	Ferqui/Optare Solera	C35F	2000	
7454	FI	W254KDO	Mercedes-Benz Vario O814	Autobus Nouvelle 2	C29F	2000	Benson, Seaton, 2002
7501	FI	YN05ATV	Irisbus EuroRider 397E.12.35	Beulas Stergo e	C53F	2005	Pullmanor, Herne Hill, 2008
7502	FI	YN05ATY	Irisbus EuroRider 397E.12.35	Beulas Stergo e	C53F	2005	Pullmanor, Herne Hill, 2008
7503	u	YN05AUC	Irisbus EuroRider 397E.12.35	Beulas Stergo e	C53F	2005	Pullmanor, Herne Hill, 2008
7504	BL	YN05AUK	Irisbus EuroRider 397E.12.35	Beulas Stergo e	C53F	2005	Pullmanor, Herne Hill, 2008
7602	HE	S602KUT	Toyota Coaster BB50R	Caetano Optimo IV	C21F	1998	Marchwood, Totton, 2007
7603	VC	934BDL	Toyota Coaster BB50R	Caetano Optimo IV	C18F	1995	Marchwood, Totton, 2007
7604	VC	M845LFP	Toyota Coaster HZB50R	Caetano Optimo III	C18F	1995	Marchwood, Totton, 2007
7605	VC	L396YAM	Toyota Coaster HZB50R	Caetano Optimo III	C21F	1994	Bell, Winterslow, 1999
7636	VP	V736OOF	Toyota Coaster BB50R	Caetano Optimo IV	C18F	2000	
7766	u	T866JBC	MAN 18.310	Marcopolo Continental 340	C49FT	1999	
7767	u	T867JBC	MAN 18.310	Marcopolo Continental 340	C49FT	1999	
7768	u	T868JBC	MAN 18.310	Marcopolo Continental 340	C49FT	1999	
7769	u	T869JBC	MAN 18.310	Marcopolo Continental 340	C49FT	1999	
7846	VC	XDL872	MAN 11.190	Caetano Algarve II	C35F	1995	Marchwood, Totton, 2007
7943	DO	NG56HGO	Ford Transit	Ford Tourneo	M17	2006	

7952	BL	EX06AYD	Ford Tourneo	Ford	M8	2006	
7971	IW	V671RNP	Renault Master	Renault	M17	1998	Wightrollers, 2011
7991	DO	X319YEL	LDV Convoy	LDV	M16	2003	
7992	DS	BT03FHZ	LDV Convoy	LDV	M16	2003	
7993	FI	WA03CTK	LDV Convoy	LDV	M16	2003	
7994	BL	HX03UBP	LDV Pilot	LDV	M8	2003	
7995	BL	RE56OUU	Mercedes-Benz Vito	Mercedes-Benz	M8	2006	
8101	FI	HF08TKX	Scania N230UD	East Lancs Olympus	NC51/35F	2008	
8102	BL	HF08TKY	Scania N230UD	East Lancs Olympus	NC51/35F	2008	
8201	FI	YJ05PXM	VDL Bus DB250	East Lancs Lowlander	N51/30F	2005	Marchwood, Totton, 2007
8202	FI	YJ05PXN	VDL Bus DB250	East Lancs Lowlander	N51/30F	2005	Marchwood, Totton, 2007
8232	VC	W232CDN	DAF DB250	Optare Spectra	N47/28F	2000	Marchwood, Totton, 2007
9217	BL	K17FTG	Volvo B10M-60	Plaxton Excalibur	C53F	1993	

Previous registrations:

1045MM	L526LHD	R387LGH	R387LGH ,197CLT
381VHX	N89FWU	R401DWL	R8OXF, MIL9575
5184MM	BU03LXX	R435MEH	A5FTG, VUV246
701GOO	N61FWU	R807NUD	R1OXF
934BDL	GX02ATF	R809NUD	R7OXF, ODL447
F783AFX	F910UPR	R810NUD	R5OXF
GSK962	NA52RNE	R811NUD	R4OXF, XXI8502
GP02DPV	A15GPS	R812NUD	R3OXF
HJI2615	V37KWO	R813NUD	R2OXF
HSV342	N68FWU	SBL364	W481WGH
HBZ4674	F698PAY	SIB5373	L526EHD
K125BUD	K8KLL	SIL7914	K547RJX
K408XFX	K537RJX, MJI7514	SJI8751	W254KDO
KT51BXH	Y5HMC	S603KUT	934BDL
LSV749	R130XWF	TDL856	PG04HOF
LIL2665	Y871MFT	TIL6710	F710SDL
LIL3748	Y873MFT	TIL6711	F711SDL
LIL9974	F631SAY	TIL6712	F712SDL
MIL9575	WV52AKY	TIL6713	G713WDL
MJI7514	W184CDN	TIL6714	G714WDL
M599VNN	M6REL, WKZ8697	TIL6715	G715WDL
M694BTU	KSK982, WKZ8689	TIL6716	G716WDL
M846LFP	XDL872	TIL6717	G717WDL
M933ROS	CX47AA	TIL6718	G718WDL
MV07DVM	T10BHN	TIL6719	G719WDL
NBZ2184	WV52FAO	TIL6720	G720WDL
NCZ6561	W232CDN	TIL6723	G723XDL
NLJ1822	?	TIL6724	G724XDL
NXI5358	R126XWF	TIL6725	G725XDL
N307UTT	N307UTT, JSK261	TIL6726	G726XDL
N983FWU	LIL3748	TIL6727	G727XDL
NJ53AEE	574CPT	TJI9462	K535RJX
NJ53AAF	524FUP	UEL489	R402DWL, R9OXF
NM02DNU	ON02STX	UJI2507	R127XWF
NT05NBM	T27BXG	USV115	W478WGH
NT55JXJ	T28BXG	VJI3968	W474WGH
ODL447	FG03KLL	VDL744	FJ53VDM
OJI1875	XEL24	VUV246	Y867GCD
ONZ1208	P995DNR	WDL691	YN04GHF
P308CTT	P308CTT, JSK262	WIL2574	W181CDN
PM04MKP	K3SLT	WKZ8689	Y874MFT
RJI6155	R129XWF	WKZ8697	Y875MFT
R41RCR	GSK962	XAA299	A11XEL, N255THO
R94LHO	YSU975	XAM152	T35RJL
R259DWL	R10OXF	XDL892	YN04GHV
R309STA	R309STA, JSK263	XXI8502	WU52HTT
R379LGH	R379LGH ,VLT149	YMW843	P890PWW
R384LGH	R384RGH ,WLT284	YSU875	W477WGH

Depots and allocations:

Alton - Marchwood - AL

Scania OmniDekka	1001	1002	1014	1015	1016	1017	1018	1019
	1020	1021	1022					

Blandford (Pimperme) - Damory - BL

Ford	7952							
LDV	7994							
MB Vito	7995							
Optare Solo	3619	3622	3636	3645	3646	3647	3654	3676
	3714	3715	3719	3720	3721	3764	3765	3771
	3772	3775	3776	3777				
DAF SB220	508	5514	5515	5516				
Volvo B10B	5606	5616						
DAF coach	7202	7203	7223	7277	7280	7281	7287	7288
Dennis coach	7311	7312	7313	7314	7315	7316	7317	7391
Iveco coach	7504							
Scania coach	7174	7178						
Volvo Coach	7006	7024	7071	7096	9217			
DAF DB250	1671	1677	4143					
Olympian	4710	4711	4714	4719	4720	4721	4727	
Scania CN230 UD	8102							

Dorchester - Damory - DO

Ford Transit	7943							
LDV	7991							
Volvo B10B	5627	5628						
Optare Solo	3635	3637	3657	3670	3705	3706	3707	3708
	3717	3718	3760	3761	3778	3780	3781	
DAF Coach	7222	7225	7226					
Volvo Coach	7003	7004	7014	7022	7023	7025	702	7027
	7033	7063	7079	7094	7095	7097	7098	
Volvo B7TL	1810							

Poole - Damory - DP

Optare Solo	3656	3659	3716				
DAF SB120	3405	3411					
Volvo B10B	5602						
DAF DB250	1684	1685					
Olympian	4706	4712	4718	4729	4733	4744	4748

Dorchester (Swanage) - Damory - DS

LDV	7992	
Optare Solo	3628	3779
Volvo B10M	7028	
Olympian	4717	4813

Eastleigh (Barton Park) - Solent Blue Line - EH

Optare Solo	3609	3610	3633					
Dart	3237	3264	3344	3351	3352			
DAF SB3000	7272	7278						
SB120	3401	3402	3407	3409	3412	3415		
Citaro	2401	2402	2411	2412	2413	2414	2415	2416
	2419	2421	2422	2423	2424	2425	2426	2427
	2428							
Olympian	4882	4883						
Scania OmniCity	1011	1012	1013	1091	1125	1126	1127	1128
	1129	1130	1131					
Volco B7TL	1801	1802	1803	1804	1805	1806	1807	1808
	1851							

Figheldean - Tourist - FI

LDV	7993						
Mercedes-Benz	7452	7454					
Optare Solo	3661	3680	3686	3687	3688		
Scania coach	7104	7105	7176	7177	7179		
DAF/VDL coach	7216	7217	7263	7264	7273	7284	7289
Dennis coach	7326	7329	7330				
Volvo B10M	7017	7018	7019				
Volvo B12M	7088	7089					
Volvo B7R	7061	7062					
Iveco coach	7501	7502					
DAF DB250	8201	8202					
Scania DD	8101						

Hensbridge - Tourist - HE

Toyota Coaster	7602						
Optare Solo	3605	3685	3709	3710	3711	3712	3759	3762
	3763	3773	3774				
DAF/VDL coach	7215	7282					
Dennis coach	7325	7381	7382				
Volvo B12M	7099						
Olympian	4715	4716					

Newport (Nelson Road) - Southern Vectis - IW

Outstation - Ryde

Renault Master	7971						
Optare Solo	3631	3638	3640				
Dart	3314	3315	3317	3321	3322	3323	3324	3325
	3326	3361	3362	3363			
DAF SB220	507						
Volvo B10B	5625						
DAF/VDL coach	7224						
Volvo B10M	596	7080	7085				
Volvo B12M	7086	7093					
Bristol K	702						
DAF DB250	4113						
Olympian	4637	4638	4639	4641	4642	4643		
Scania OmniCity DD	1051	1052	1053	1054	1055	1101	1102	1103
	1104	1105	1106	1107	1108	1109	1110	1111
	1112	1113	1114	1115	1116	1117	1142	1143
	1144	1145	1146	1147	1148	1149	1150	1151
	1152						
Volvo B7TL	1951	1952	1991	1992	1993	1994	1995	1996
	1997						

Lymington (Station Road) - Wilts & Dorset - LY

Optare Solo	3655	3662	3675	3679	3681	3682	3722	
Olympian	4713	4723	4731	4734	4736	4737	4739	4740
	4766						
DAF DB250	1662	1663	1665	1666	1670	1673		
Volvo B7TL	1826	1827	1830	1831	1832	1833		

Totton (Salisbury Road) - Marchwood - MB

Optare Solo	3634	3660	3669				
DAF SB120	3410	3413	3414				
Dart	3302	3303	3304	3305	3306	3307		
DAF coach	7262	7271					
Citaro	2420	2431	2432	2433	2434	2435	2436	2438
	2439	2440	2451	2452	2453	2454	2455	2456
	2457						
Olympian	4809	4879					
Volvo B7TL	1828	1829					

The perfect location for a 'Breezer' is Sandown Bay where open-top Volvo Olympian 4638, R738XRV is seen. This is one of four examples of the model with Northern Counties Palatine bodywork new in 1998, now converted to partial open-top. *Richard Godfrey*

Poole (Kingland Road) - Wilts & Dorset - PO

Outstation: Bournemouth

Optare Solo	3641	3648	3674	3677	3683	3684	3703	3704
	3801	3802						
Dart	3205	3208	3211	3213				
DAF SB120	3404							
Excel	2602	2605	606	2607	268	2609	2610	2611
	2612	2613	2614	2615				
DAF coach	7274	7276						
Scania K230	2101							
Volvo B7RLE	2201	2202	2203	2204	2205	2206	2207	2208
	2209	2210	2211	2212	2213	2214	2215	2216
	2217	2218	2219	2220	2221	2222	2223	2224
	2225	2226	2227	2228	2229	2230	2231	2232
	2233	2234	2235	2236	2237	2238	2251	2252
	2253	2254	2255	2256	2257	2258	2259	2260
	2261	2262	2263	2264	2265	2266	2267	2270
Mercedes-Benz Citaro	2417	2418						
Olympian	4724	4725						
Volvo B7TL	1811	1821	1822	1823	1824	1825	1901	1904
DAF DB250	1669	1672	1674	1675	1676	1683		
Scania CN230	1501	1502	1503	1504	1505	1506		
Citaro artic	2901							

Ringwood (West Street) - Wilts & Dorset - RI

Optare Solo	3642	3701	3702				
Excel	2601	2604					
Volvo B10B	5626						
Olympian	4707	4726	4728	4735	4738	4741	4765
DAF DB250	1661	1667	1679				
Scania CN230	1118	1119	1120	1121	1122	1123	1124

Salisbury (Castle Street) - Wilts & Dorset - SA

Outstations - Amesbury; Bower Chalke; Devizes; Downton; Hindon; Pewsey; Porton; Ringwood; Romsey; Shaftesbury; Swallow Cliffe; Warminster and Yeovil

Optare Solo	3639	3652	3653	3658	3663	3664	3665	3666
	3667	3671	3672	3673	3751	3752	3753	3754
	3755	3756	3757	3758				
Dart	3301	3308	3309	3310	3311	3312	3313	3316
	3318	3319	3320	3327				
SB120	3403	3406	3408	3416				
Mercedes-Benz Citaro	2403	2404	2405	2406	2407	2408	2409	2410
Volvo B9R	7051							
Scania coach	7131	7132						
DAF/VDL coach	7218							
Olympian	4745	4746	4749	4750	4751	4752	4753	4754
	4755	4756	4757	4758	4759			
DAF DB250	1654	1655	1656	1658	1659	1660	1664	1680
	1681	1682						
Trident	1742	1743	1744	1745	1746	1747	1748	1749
Volvo B7TL	1842	1977						
Scania CN230 UD	1132	1133	1134	1135	1136	1137	1138	1139
	1140	1141						

Southern Vectis Schools - VC

Mercedes	7411							
Optare Solo	3602	3615	3618	3620	2621	3632	3644	3649
Toyota Coaster	7603	7605	7606					
Dart	3328	3329						
DAF coach	7261	7265						
Dennis coach	7318	7351						
MAN coach	7846							
Volvo B10M	7005	7007	7008	7009	7010	7011	7012	7013
	7029	7030	7060					
Volvo B12M	7031	7032	7034	7035	7036	7037	7038	7039
	7040	7041	7042	7043	7044			
DAF DB250	8232							
Olympian	4830	4831	4832	4834	4835	4836	4837	4838
	4839	4841	4843	4845	4862	4868	4873	4887

Southern Vectis - VP

DAF coach	7285	7286		
Toyota Coaster	7636			
Dennis Coach	7301	7302		
Mercedes Touro	7401	7402		
Scania coach	7101	7103	7175	7180
Volvo B10M	7070	7081	7083	7084
Volvo B12M	7090	7091	7092	

Swanage (Kings Road West) - Wilts & Dorset - SW

Scania CN230	1401	1402	1403	1404	1405	1406	1407	1408
	1409	1410	1411	1412				

Uni-link - UN

Scania OmniCity	2001	2002	2003	2004	2005	2006	2007	2008
	2009	2010	2011	2012				
Scania CN230	1191	1192	1193	1194	1195	1196	1197	1198
	1199							
Volvo B7TL	1910	1911	1912	1913				

Unallocated/stored - u; Special event pool - s

Remainder

Vehicle index

Reg	Operator	Reg	Operator	Reg	Operator
340GUP	North East	AJ58WBG	Metrobus	BD57WDP	Brighton & Hove
381VHX	South Coast	AJ58WBK	Metrobus	BD57WDR	Brighton & Hove
574CPT	North East	AN61BUS	Anglian	BD57WDS	Brighton & Hove
701GOO	South Coast	AN61LAN	Anglian	BD57WDT	Brighton & Hove
934BDL	South Coast	AO02LVC	Anglian	BF09OXF	Oxford
1045MM	South Coast	AO52LJF	Anglian	BF10OXF	Oxford
AA08OXF	Oxford	AO57EZM	Anglian	BF12KWX	Brighton & Hove
AB07OXF	Oxford	AO57EZM	Anglian	BF12KWY	Brighton & Hove
AD57BDY	Anglian	AO57EZM	Anglian	BF12KWZ	Brighton & Hove
AD57EXA	Anglian	AO57EZM	Anglian	BF12KXA	Brighton & Hove
AE05EUX	Oxford	AT02CJT	South Coast	BF12KXB	Brighton & Hove
AE05EUZ	Oxford	AU04JKN	Anglian	BF12KXC	Brighton & Hove
AE06HCA	London	AU07KMK	Anglian	BF12KXD	Brighton & Hove
AE06HCC	London	AU07KMM	Anglian	BF12KXE	Brighton & Hove
AE06HCD	London	AU08DKL	Anglian	BF12KXG	Brighton & Hove
AE06HCF	London	AU08DKN	Anglian	BF12KXH	Brighton & Hove
AE06HCG	London	AU08GLY	Anglian	BF12KXJ	Brighton & Hove
AE06HCH	London	AU11EPE	Anglian	BF12KXK	Brighton & Hove
AE06HCJ	London	AU11EPF	Anglian	BF12KXL	Brighton & Hove
AE06HCK	London	AU11ESG	Anglian	BF12KXM	Brighton & Hove
AE08DKX	Oxford	AU54ENY	Anglian	BF12KXN	Brighton & Hove
AE08DKY	Oxford	AU54EOA	Anglian	BF12KXO	Brighton & Hove
AE08DLD	Oxford	AU58AKK	Anglian	BF12KXP	Brighton & Hove
AE09DHG	Metrobus	AU58AKN	Anglian	BF12KXR	Brighton & Hove
AE09DHJ	Metrobus	AU58AUV	Anglian	BF12KXS	Brighton & Hove
AE09DHK	Metrobus	AU61AVK	Anglian	BF12KXT	Brighton & Hove
AE09DHL	Metrobus	BB07OXF	Oxford	BF53OXF	Oxford
AE09DHM	Metrobus	BB08OXF	Oxford	BF55OXF	Oxford
AE09DHN	Metrobus	BD09ZPR	London	BF57OXF	Oxford
AE09DHO	Metrobus	BD09ZPS	London	BF61OXF	Oxford
AE09DHP	Metrobus	BD09ZPT	London	BF62UXH	Brighton & Hove
AE09DHU	Metrobus	BD09ZPU	London	BF62UXJ	Brighton & Hove
AE09DHV	Metrobus	BD09ZPV	London	BF62UXK	Brighton & Hove
AE56OUF	Oxford	BD09ZPW	London	BF62UXL	Brighton & Hove
AE56OUH	London	BD09ZPX	London	BF62UXM	Brighton & Hove
AE56OUJ	London	BD09ZPY	London	BF62UXN	Brighton & Hove
AE56OUK	London	BD09ZPZ	London	BF62UXO	Brighton & Hove
AE56OUL	London	BD09ZRA	London	BF62UXP	Brighton & Hove
AE56OUM	London	BD09ZRC	London	BF62UXR	Brighton & Hove
AE56OUN	London	BD09ZRE	London	BF62UXS	Brighton & Hove
AE56OUO	London	BD09ZRF	London	BF62UXT	Brighton & Hove
AE56OUP	London	BD09ZRG	London	BG09JJK	London
AE56OUS	London	BD09ZRJ	London	BG09JJL	London
AE57LYH	Oxford	BD09ZRK	London	BG09JJU	London
AE57LYJ	Oxford	BD09ZVS	London	BG09JJV	London
AE57LYK	Oxford	BD09ZVT	London	BG09JJX	London
AE57LYO	Oxford	BD09ZVU	London	BG09JJY	London
AE57LYP	Oxford	BD09ZVV	London	BG09JJZ	London
AE57LYR	Oxford	BD09ZVW	London	BG09JKE	London
AE57LYS	Oxford	BD09ZVX	London	BG09JKF	London
AE59AWH	Oxford	BD09ZVY	London	BG09JKJ	London
AE59AWJ	Oxford	BD09ZVZ	London	BG59FXA	London
AE59AWM	Oxford	BD09ZWA	London	BG59FXB	London
AE61EWO	Oxford	BD09ZWB	London	BG59FXC	London
AE61EWP	Oxford	BD09ZWC	London	BG59FXD	London
AE61EWR	Oxford	BD09ZWE	London	BG59FXE	London
AF09OXF	Oxford	BD09ZWF	London	BG59FXF	London
AF10OXF	Oxford	BD09ZWG	London	BG59FXH	London
AF53EUV	Oxford	BD09ZWH	London	BG61SXS	Brighton & Hove
AF53GCX	Oxford	BD57UYK	Konectbus	BJ10VUN	North East
AF53GCY	Oxford	BD57UYL	Konectbus	BJ10VUO	North East
AF53GCZ	Oxford	BD57WCY	Konectbus	BJ10VUP	North East
AF53OXF	Oxford	BD57WCZ	Konectbus	BJ10VUR	North East
AF55OXF	Oxford	BD57WDA	Konectbus	BJ10VUS	North East
AF57OXF	Oxford	BD57WDC	Brighton & Hove	BJ10VUT	North East
AF61OXF	Oxford	BD57WDE	Brighton & Hove	BJ10VUU	North East
AJ58PZS	Oxford	BD57WDK	Brighton & Hove	BJ10VUV	North East
AJ58WBD	Metrobus	BD57WDL	Brighton & Hove	BJ10VUW	North East
AJ58WBE	Metrobus	BD57WDM	Brighton & Hove	BJ11XGZ	London
AJ58WBF	Metrobus	BD57WDN	Brighton & Hove	BJ11XHA	Brighton & Hove

BJ11XHB	Brighton & Hove	BX02YZM	Brighton & Hove	DF09OXF	Oxford
BJ11XHC	Brighton & Hove	BX02YZP	Brighton & Hove	DF10OXF	Oxford
BJ11XHD	Brighton & Hove	BX02YZW	Brighton & Hove	DF53OXF	Oxford
BJ11XHE	Brighton & Hove	BX04AZU	London	DF55OXF	Oxford
BJ11XHF	Brighton & Hove	BX04AZV	London	DF57OXF	Oxford
BJ11XHG	Brighton & Hove	BX04AZW	London	DF61OXF	Oxford
BJ11XHH	Brighton & Hove	BX04AZZ	London	DIG5295	South Coast
BJ11XHK	Brighton & Hove	BX04BAA	London	EB07OXF	Oxford
BJ11XHL	Brighton & Hove	BX04BAU	London	EE08OXF	Oxford
BJ11XHM	Brighton & Hove	BX04BAV	London	EF09OXF	Oxford
BJ11XHN	Brighton & Hove	BX04BBE	London	EF10OXF	Oxford
BJ11XHO	Brighton & Hove	BX04BBF	London	EF53OXF	Oxford
BJ11XHP	Brighton & Hove	BX04BBJ	London	EF55OXF	Oxford
BJ11XHR	Brighton & Hove	BX04BKJ	London	EF57OXF	Oxford
BJ11XHS	Brighton & Hove	BX04BKK	London	EF61OXF	Oxford
BJ11XHT	Brighton & Hove	BX04BKL	London	EJ02KYY	Hedingham
BJ11XHU	Brighton & Hove	BX04BXL	London	EU03BZK	Hedingham
BJ11XHV	Brighton & Hove	BX04BXM	London	EU04BVF	Hedingham
BJ11XHW	Brighton & Hove	BX04BXN	London	EU04BVF	London
BJ11XHX	Brighton & Hove	BX04BXP	London	EU05AUR	Hedingham
BK10MGV	Brighton & Hove	BX11GVP		EU05AUT	Hedingham
BL57OXJ	North East	BX54EFB	South Coast	EU05CLJ	Hedingham
BL57OXK	North East	BX54EFC	Brighton & Hove	EU06KCX	Hedingham
BL57OXP	North East	BX54EFD	Brighton & Hove	EU07GVY	Hedingham
BL61ACX	London	BX54UCM	Brighton & Hove	EU10AOX	Hedingham
BL61ACY	London	BX54UCN	Brighton & Hove	EU53MVZ	Hedingham
BL61ACZ	London	BX54UCP	North East	EU53PXY	London
BL61ADO	London	BX54UCR	North East	EU53PXZ	London
BL61ADU	London	BX54UCU	North East	EU53PYA	London
BL61ADV	London	BX54UCV	North East	EU53PYB	London
BL61ADX	London	BX54UCW	North East	EU53PYD	London
BL61ADY	London	BX54UCZ	North East	EU53PYF	London
BP09ONE	South Coast	BX54UDB	North East	EU53PYG	London
BP57UYE	North East	BX54UDD	North East	EU53PYH	London
BP57UYF	North East	BX54UDE	South Coast	EU53PYJ	London
BP57UYG	North East	BX54UDG	South Coast	EU53PYL	London
BP57UYH	North East	BX54UDK	Konectbus	EU53PYO	London
BP57UYJ	North East	BX54UDL	South Coast	EU53PYP	London
BP57UYK	North East	BX54UDN	South Coast	EU55BWC	Hedingham
BP57UYL	North East	BX54UDO	South Coast	EU56FLM	Hedingham
BT02CJT	South Coast	BX54UDT	South Coast	EU56FLN	Hedingham
BT03FHZ	South Coast	BX54UDU	South Coast	EU56FLP	Hedingham
BT04BUS	London	BX54UDV	Konectbus	EU56FLR	Hedingham
BT09GOH	London	BX54UDW	South Coast	EU58JCJ	Hedingham
BT09GOJ	London	BX54UDY	South Coast	EU59AFF	Hedingham
BT09GOK	London	BX54UDZ	South Coast	EU59AFJ	Hedingham
BT09GOP	London	BX54UEA	Konectbus	EU59AYM	Hedingham
BT09GOU	London	BX54UEB	South Coast	EU59AYP	Hedingham
BT09GOX	London	BX55FYH	Chambers	EX02RYR	Hedingham
BT09GPE	London	BX55FYJ	Chambers	EX06AYD	South Coast
BT09GPF	London	BX61DKV	Plymouth	EY57FZE	Hedingham
BT09GPJ	London	C1WYC	Oxford	F601GVO	Plymouth
BU03LXX	South Coast	C2WYC	Oxford	F602GVO	Plymouth
BV10WVD	London	C3WYC	Oxford	F603GVO	Plymouth
BV10WVE	London	CB07OXF	Oxford	F604GVO	Plymouth
BV10WVF	London	CB51BUS	Oxford	F706RDL	South Coast
BV10WVG	London	CB53BUS	Oxford	F707RDL	South Coast
BV10WVH	London	CB54BUS	Oxford	F783AFX	South Coast
BV10WVJ	London	CC08OXF	Oxford	FB07OXF	Oxford
BV10WVK	London	CDL899	South Coast	FF08OXF	Oxford
BV10WVL	London	CE52UXC	South Coast	FF09OXF	Oxford
BV10WWA	London	CE52UXD	South Coast	FF10OXF	Oxford
BV10WWC	London	CF09OXF	Oxford	FF55OXF	Oxford
BV10WWD	London	CF10OXF	Oxford	FF57OXF	Oxford
BV10WWF	London	CF53OXF	Oxford	FF61OXF	Oxford
BV10WWO	London	CF55OXF	Oxford	FJ08KLF	North East
BV10WWP	London	CF57OXF	Oxford	FJ08KLS	North East
BV10WWR	London	CF61OXF	Oxford	FJ08KLU	North East
BV55UCT	London	CU6860	North East	FJ08KLX	North East
BV55UCU	London	CUV305C	London	FJ08KLZ	North East
BV55UCW	London	CUV317C	Brighton & Hove	FJ08KMU	North East
BV55UCX	London	CUV318C	London	FJ08KMV	North East
BV55UCY	London	DAZ1563	South Coast	FJ08KNV	North East
BX02YYZ	South Coast	DB07OXF	Oxford	FJ08KNW	North East
BX02YZH	Brighton & Hove	DD08OXF	Oxford	FJ54ZDC	London

Reg	Location	Reg	Location	Reg	Location
FJ54ZDP	London	H734DDL	South Coast	HF12GWE	South Coast
FJ54ZDR	London	HAP985	Brighton & Hove	HF12GWG	South Coast
FJ54ZDT	London	HB07OXF	Oxford	HF12GWJ	South Coast
FJ54ZDU	London	HB11OXF	Oxford	HF12GWK	South Coast
FJ54ZDV	London	HBZ4674	South Coast	HF12GWL	South Coast
FJ54ZDW	London	HC11OXF	Oxford	HF12GWM	South Coast
FJ54ZDX	London	HD11OXF	Oxford	HF12GWN	South Coast
FJ54ZDY	London	HE11OXF	Oxford	HF12GWO	South Coast
FJ54ZDZ	London	HF03AEG	South Coast	HF12GWP	South Coast
FJ54ZFA	London	HF03HJY	South Coast	HF12GWU	South Coast
FJ54ZTV	London	HF03HJZ	South Coast	HF12GWV	South Coast
FJ54ZTW	London	HF03HKA	South Coast	HF12GWW	South Coast
FJ54ZTX	London	HF05GGE	South Coast	HF12GWX	South Coast
FJ54ZTY	London	HF05GGJ	South Coast	HF12GWY	South Coast
FJ54ZTZ	London	HF05GGK	South Coast	HF12GWZ	South Coast
FJ54ZUA	London	HF05GGO	South Coast	HF12GXA	South Coast
FJ54ZUC	London	HF05GGP	South Coast	HF12GXB	South Coast
FJ54ZUD	London	HF05GGU	South Coast	HF12GXC	South Coast
FJ54ZVA	London	HF05GGV	South Coast	HF12GXD	South Coast
FJ54ZVB	London	HF05GGX	South Coast	HF12GXE	South Coast
FJ61EVX	South Coast	HF05GGY	South Coast	HF12GXG	South Coast
FNZ7669	South Coast	HF05HXD	South Coast	HF12GXH	South Coast
G530VBB	Oxford	HF05HXE	South Coast	HF12GXJ	South Coast
G534VBB	Oxford	HF05HXG	South Coast	HF12GXK	South Coast
G615OTV	Plymouth	HF05HXH	South Coast	HF54HFO	South Coast
G621OTV	Plymouth	HF06FTO	South Coast	HF54HFP	South Coast
G721WDL	South Coast	HF06FTP	South Coast	HF54HFR	South Coast
GB07OXF	Oxford	HF06FTT	South Coast	HF54HFT	South Coast
GF09OXF	Oxford	HF06FTU	South Coast	HF54HFU	South Coast
GF10OXF	Oxford	HF06FTV	South Coast	HF54HFV	South Coast
GF55OXF	Oxford	HF06FTX	South Coast	HF54HFW	South Coast
GF57OXF	Oxford	HF06FTY	South Coast	HF54HFX	South Coast
GF61OXF	Oxford	HF06FTZ	South Coast	HF54HFY	South Coast
GG08OXF	Oxford	HF06FUA	North East	HF54HFZ	South Coast
GN07AUY	Metrobus	HF06FUB	North East	HF54HGA	South Coast
GN07AVR	Metrobus	HF08TKX	South Coast	HF54HGC	South Coast
GN07AVT	Metrobus	HF08TKY	South Coast	HF54HGD	South Coast
GN07AVU	Metrobus	HF08UHS	South Coast	HF54HGE	South Coast
GN07AVV	Metrobus	HF08UHT	Brighton & Hove	HF54HGG	South Coast
GN07AVW	Metrobus	HF08UHU	South Coast	HF54HGJ	South Coast
GP02DPV	South Coast	HF08UHV	South Coast	HF54HGK	South Coast
GSK962	South Coast	HF08UHW	South Coast	HF54HGL	South Coast
GU52HWA	Brighton & Hove	HF09BJE	South Coast	HF54HGM	South Coast
GU52HWB	Brighton & Hove	HF09BJJ	South Coast	HF54HGN	South Coast
GU52WSY	South Coast	HF09BJK	South Coast	HF54HGO	South Coast
GU52WTG	South Coast	HF09BJO	South Coast	HF54HGP	South Coast
GX02ATF	South Coast	HF09BJU	South Coast	HF54HGU	South Coast
GX03SSU	Brighton & Hove	HF09BJV	South Coast	HF54HGX	South Coast
GX03SSV	Brighton & Hove	HF09BJX	South Coast	HF54HGY	South Coast
GX03SSZ	Brighton & Hove	HF09BJY	South Coast	HF54HHA	South Coast
GX03STZ	Brighton & Hove	HF09BJZ	South Coast	HF54HHB	South Coast
GX03SUA	Brighton & Hove	HF09BKA	South Coast	HF54HHC	South Coast
GX03SUF	Brighton & Hove	HF09FVR	South Coast	HF54HHD	South Coast
GX03SUH	Brighton & Hove	HF09FVS	South Coast	HF54HHE	South Coast
GX03SUU	Brighton & Hove	HF09FVT	South Coast	HF54HHJ	South Coast
GX03SUV	Brighton & Hove	HF09FVU	South Coast	HF54HHK	South Coast
GX03SUY	Brighton & Hove	HF09FVV	South Coast	HF54HHL	South Coast
GX03SVA	Brighton & Hove	HF09FVW	South Coast	HF54HHM	South Coast
GX03SVC	Brighton & Hove	HF09FVX	South Coast	HF54KXT	South Coast
GX03SVD	Brighton & Hove	HF09FVY	South Coast	HF54KXU	South Coast
GX03SVE	Brighton & Hove	HF09OXF	Oxford	HF54KXV	South Coast
GX03SVF	Brighton & Hove	HF10OXF	Oxford	HF54KXW	South Coast
GX03SVG	Brighton & Hove	HF11OXF	Oxford	HF55JYX	South Coast
GX03SVJ	Brighton & Hove	HF12GVP	South Coast	HF55JYY	South Coast
GX03SVK	Brighton & Hove	HF12GVR	South Coast	HF55JYZ	South Coast
H160HJN	Hedingham	HF12GVT	South Coast	HF55JZA	South Coast
H177GTT	Plymouth	HF12GVU	South Coast	HF55JZC	South Coast
H178GTT	Plymouth	HF12GVV	South Coast	HF55JZD	South Coast
H554GKX	Oxford	HF12GVW	South Coast	HF55JZE	South Coast
H556GKX	Oxford	HF12GVX	South Coast	HF55JZG	South Coast
H563GKX	Oxford	HF12GVY	South Coast	HF55JZJ	South Coast
H728DDL	South Coast	HF12GVZ	South Coast	HF55JZK	South Coast
H729DDL	South Coast	HF12GWA	South Coast	HF55JZL	South Coast
H731DDL	South Coast	HF12GWC	South Coast	HF55JZM	South Coast
H733DDL	South Coast	HF12GWD	South Coast	HF55JZN	South Coast

HF55JZO	South Coast	HR11OXF	Oxford	HX06EZJ	South Coast
HF55JZP	South Coast	HS11OXF	Oxford	HX51LPN	South Coast
HF55JZR	South Coast	HSV342	South Coast	HX51ZRA	South Coast
HF55JZT	South Coast	HW07CXR	South Coast	HX51ZRC	South Coast
HF55JZU	South Coast	HW07CXS	South Coast	HX51ZRD	South Coast
HF55JZV	South Coast	HW07CXT	South Coast	HX51ZRE	South Coast
HF55JZW	South Coast	HW07CXU	South Coast	HX51ZRF	South Coast
HF55OXF	Oxford	HW07CXV	South Coast	HX51ZRG	South Coast
HF57OXF	Oxford	HW07CXX	South Coast	HX51ZRJ	South Coast
HF58GYW	South Coast	HW07CXY	South Coast	HX51ZRK	South Coast
HF58GYY	South Coast	HW08AOP	South Coast	HY11BRD	Oxford
HF58GYZ	South Coast	HW08AOR	South Coast	HY11OXF	Oxford
HF58GZA	South Coast	HW08AOS	South Coast	J1OXF	Oxford
HF58GZB	South Coast	HW08AOT	South Coast	J127LHC	Anglian
HF58GZC	South Coast	HW09BAA	South Coast	J838TSC	Hedingham
HF58GZD	South Coast	HW09BBU	South Coast	JB07OXF	Oxford
HF58GZE	South Coast	HW09BBV	South Coast	JCN822	North East
HF58GZG	South Coast	HW09BBX	South Coast	JF09OXF	Oxford
HF58GZH	South Coast	HW09BBZ	South Coast	JF10OXF	Oxford
HF58GZJ	South Coast	HW09BCE	South Coast	JF55OXF	Oxford
HF58GZK	South Coast	HW09BCF	South Coast	JF57OXF	Oxford
HF58GZL	South Coast	HW09BCK	South Coast	JF61OXF	Oxford
HF58GZM	South Coast	HW09BCO	South Coast	JJ08OXF	Oxford
HF58GZN	South Coast	HW09BCU	South Coast	JJD472D	London
HF58GZO	South Coast	HW09BCV	South Coast	JJD520D	London
HF58GZP	South Coast	HW52EPK	South Coast	JSK264	Plymouth
HF58HTG	South Coast	HW52EPL	South Coast	JSK265	Plymouth
HF58HTJ	South Coast	HW52EPN	South Coast	K1OXF	Oxford
HF58HTK	South Coast	HW52EPO	South Coast	K2VOY	North East
HF58HTL	South Coast	HW52EPP	South Coast	K3VOY	North East
HF58HTN	South Coast	HW52EPU	South Coast	K17FTG	South Coast
HF58HTO	South Coast	HW52EPV	South Coast	K107JWJ	Hedingham
HF58HTP	South Coast	HW52EPX	South Coast	K119BUD	Oxford
HF58HTT	South Coast	HW54BTU	South Coast	K120BUD	Oxford
HF58HTU	South Coast	HW54BTV	South Coast	K125BUD	South Coast
HF58KCA	South Coast	HW54BTX	South Coast	K198EVW	Hedingham
HF58KCC	South Coast	HW54BTY	South Coast	K357DWJ	Hedingham
HF58KCE	South Coast	HW54BTZ	South Coast	K408XFX	South Coast
HF58KCG	South Coast	HW54BUA	South Coast	K508ESS	Hedingham
HF58KCJ	South Coast	HW54BUE	South Coast	K510ESS	Hedingham
HF58KCK	South Coast	HW54BUF	South Coast	K518ESS	Hedingham
HF59DMO	South Coast	HW54BUH	South Coast	K529RJX	South Coast
HF59DMU	South Coast	HW54BUJ	South Coast	K735ODL	South Coast
HF59DMV	South Coast	HW54BUO	South Coast	K736ODL	South Coast
HF59DMX	South Coast	HW54BUP	South Coast	K737ODL	South Coast
HF59FAA	South Coast	HW54BUU	South Coast	K738ODL	South Coast
HF59FAJ	South Coast	HW54BUV	South Coast	K739ODL	South Coast
HF59FAK	South Coast	HW54DBZ	South Coast	K740ODL	South Coast
HF59FAM	South Coast	HW54DCE	South Coast	K741ODL	South Coast
HF59FAO	South Coast	HW54DCF	South Coast	K742ODL	South Coast
HF59FAU	South Coast	HW54DCO	South Coast	K743ODL	South Coast
HF61FWL	South Coast	HW54DCU	South Coast	KB07OXF	Oxford
HF61FWM	South Coast	HW58ARU	South Coast	KF09OXF	Oxford
HF61OXF	Oxford	HW58ARX	South Coast	KF10OXF	Oxford
HG11OXF	Oxford	HW58ARZ	South Coast	KF55OXF	Oxford
HH08OXF	Oxford	HW58ASO	South Coast	KF57OXF	Oxford
HH11OXF	Oxford	HW58ASU	South Coast	KF61OXF	Oxford
HJ02WDE	South Coast	HW58ASV	South Coast	KP51UEO	South Coast
HJ02WDF	South Coast	HW58ASX	South Coast	KP51UES	South Coast
HJ02WDG	South Coast	HW58ASZ	South Coast	KP51UEX	South Coast
HJ02WDK	South Coast	HW58ATF	South Coast	KP51UFA	South Coast
HJ02WDL	South Coast	HW58ATK	South Coast	KT51BXH	South Coast
HJ02WDN	South Coast	HW58ATN	South Coast	L1OXF	Oxford
HJ11OXF	Oxford	HW58ATO	South Coast	L108HHV	Hedingham
HJ52VFW	South Coast	HW58ATU	South Coast	L109LHL	Hedingham
HJ52VFX	South Coast	HX03UBP	South Coast	L207RNO	Hedingham
HJ52VFY	South Coast	HX06EYZ	South Coast	L208RNO	Hedingham
HJ52VFZ	South Coast	HX06EZA	South Coast	L396YAM	South Coast
HJ52VGA	South Coast	HX06EZB	South Coast	L526YDL	South Coast
HJI2615	South Coast	HX06EZC	South Coast	L527YDL	South Coast
HK11OXF	Oxford	HX06EZD	South Coast	L528YDL	South Coast
HL11OXF	Oxford	HX06EZE	South Coast	L728JWX	South Coast
HM11OXF	Oxford	HX06EZF	South Coast	LB02YWX	London
HN11OXF	Oxford	HX06EZG	South Coast	LB02YWY	London
HP11OXF	Oxford	HX06EZH	South Coast	LB02YWZ	London

LB02YXA	London	LF52ZPO	London			LIL9974	South Coast
LB02YXC	London	LF52ZPP	London			LJ12CGF	London
LB02YXD	London	LF52ZPR	London			LJ12CGG	London
LB02YXE	London	LF52ZPS	London			LJ12CGK	London
LB02YXF	London	LF52ZPU	London			LJ12CGO	London
LB02YXG	London	LF52ZPV	London			LJ12CGU	London
LB02YXH	London	LF52ZPW	London			LJ12CGV	London
LB02YXJ	London	LF52ZPY	London			LJ12CGX	London
LB02YXK	London	LF52ZPZ	London			LJ12CGY	London
LB02YXL	London	LF52ZRA	London			LJ12CGZ	London
LB02YXM	London	LF52ZRC	London			LJ12CHC	London
LB02YXN	London	LF52ZRD	London			LJ12CHD	London
LF10OXF	Oxford	LF52ZRE	London			LJ12CHF	London
LF52TGN	London	LF52ZRG	London			LJ12CHG	London
LF52TGO	London	LF52ZRJ	London			LJ12CHH	London
LF52TGU	London	LF52ZRK	London			LJ12CHK	London
LF52TGV	London	LF52ZRL	London			LJ61GVP	London
LF52TGX	London	LF52ZRN	London			LJ61GVT	London
LF52TGY	London	LF52ZRO	London			LJ61GVW	London
LF52TGZ	London	LF52ZRP	London			LJ61GVX	London
LF52THG	London	LF52ZRR	London			LJ61GVY	London
LF52THK	London	LF52ZRT	London			LJ61GVZ	London
LF52THN	London	LF52ZRU	London			LJ61GWA	London
LF52THU	London	LF52ZRV	London			LJ61GWC	London
LF52THV	London	LF52ZRX	London			LJ61GXE	London
LF52THX	London	LF52ZRY	London			LJ61GXF	London
LF52THZ	London	LF52ZRZ	London			LJ61GXG	London
LF52TJO	London	LF52ZSD	London			LJ61GXH	London
LF52TJU	London	LF52ZSO	London			LJ61GXK	London
LF52TJV	London	LF52ZSP	London			LJ61GXL	London
LF52TJX	London	LF52ZSR	London			LJ61GXM	London
LF52TJY	London	LF52ZST	London			LJ61GXN	London
LF52TKA	London	LF52ZTG	London			LJ61GXO	London
LF52TKC	London	LF52ZTH	London			LJ61GXP	London
LF52TKD	London	LF52ZTJ	London			LJ61NUM	London
LF52TKE	London	LF52ZTK	London			LJ61NUO	London
LF52TKJ	London	LF52ZTL	London			LJ61NUP	London
LF52TKK	London	LF52ZTM	London			LJ61NUU	London
LF52TKN	London	LF52ZTN	London			LJ61NUV	London
LF52TKO	London	LF52ZTO	London			LJ61NUW	London
LF52TKT	London	LF52ZTP	London			LJ61NUX	London
LF52ZLZ	London	LF52ZTR	London			LJ61NUY	London
LF52ZMO	London	LF56OXF	Oxford			LJ61NVA	London
LF52ZMU	London	LF57OXF	Oxford			LJ61NVB	London
LF52ZND	London	LF61OXF	Oxford			LJ61NVC	London
LF52ZNE	London	LG02KGP	London			LJ61NVD	London
LF52ZNG	London	LG02KGU	London			LJ61NVE	London
LF52ZNH	London	LG02KGV	London			LJ61NVF	London
LF52ZNJ	London	LG02KGX	London			LJ61NVG	London
LF52ZNK	London	LG02KGY	London			LJ61NVH	London
LF52ZNL	London	LG02KGZ	London			LJ61NVK	London
LF52ZNM	London	LG02KHA	London			LJ61NVL	London
LF52ZNN	London	LG02KHE	London			LJ61NVM	London
LF52ZNO	London	LG02KHF	London			LJ61NVN	London
LF52ZNP	London	LG02KHH	London			LJ61NVP	London
LF52ZNR	London	LG02KHJ	London			LJ61NVR	London
LF52ZNS	London	LG02KHK	London			LJ61NVS	London
LF52ZNT	London	LG02KHL	London			LJ61NVZ	London
LF52ZNU	London	LG02KHM	London			LJ61NWA	London
LF52ZNV	London	LG02KHO	London			LJ61NWB	London
LF52ZNW	London	LG02KHP	London			LJ61NWC	London
LF52ZNX	London	LG02KHR	London			LJ61NWD	London
LF52ZNY	London	LG02KHT	London			LJ61NWE	London
LF52ZNZ	London	LG02KHU	London			LJ61NWF	London
LF52ZPB	London	LG02KHV	London			LJ61NWG	London
LF52ZPC	London	LG02KHW	London			LJ61NWH	London
LF52ZPD	London	LG02KHX	London			LJ61NWL	London
LF52ZPE	London	LG02KHY	London			LJ61NWM	London
LF52ZPG	London	LG02KHZ	London			LJ61NWN	London
LF52ZPH	London	LG02KJA	London			LJ61NWO	London
LF52ZPJ	London	LG02KJE	London			LJ61NWR	London
LF52ZPK	London	LG02KJF	London			LJ61NWU	London
LF52ZPL	London	LIL2665	South Coast			LJ61NWV	London
LF52ZPM	London	LIL3748	South Coast			LJ61NWW	London
LF52ZPN	London	LIL3748	South Coast			LJ61NWX	London

LJ61NWZ	London	LX03ECV	London	LX05FBY	London
LJ61NXA	London	LX03ECW	London	LX05FBZ	London
LJ61NXB	London	LX03ECY	London	LX05FCA	London
LJ61NXC	London	LX03EDR	London	LX05FCC	London
LJ61NXD	London	LX03EDU	London	LX05FCD	London
LJ61NXE	London	LX03EDV	London	LX05FCE	London
LJ61NXF	London	LX03EEA	London	LX05FCF	London
LK03NHF	London	LX03EEB	London	LX06DYS	London
LK03NHG	London	LX03EEF	London	LX06DYT	London
LK03NHP	London	LX03EEG	London	LX06DYU	London
LK03NHT	London	LX03EEH	London	LX06DYV	London
LK03NHV	London	LX03EEJ	London	LX06DYW	London
LK03NHX	London	LX03EEM	London	LX06DYY	London
LK03NHY	London	LX03EXU	London	LX06DZA	London
LK03NHZ	London	LX03EXV	London	LX06DZB	London
LK03NJE	London	LX03EXW	London	LX06DZC	London
LK03NJF	London	LX03EXZ	London	LX06DZE	London
LK03NJJ	London	LX03KPA	South Coast	LX06DZF	London
LK03NJN	London	LX03OJN	Metrobus	LX06DZG	London
LK03NJV	London	LX03OJP	Metrobus	LX06DZH	London
LK03NJX	London	LX05EXZ	London	LX06DZJ	London
LK03NJY	London	LX05EYA	London	LX06DZK	London
LK03NJZ	London	LX05EYM	London	LX06DZL	London
LK03NKA	London	LX05EYO	London	LX06DZM	London
LK08FLH	London	LX05EYP	London	LX06DZN	London
LK08FLJ	London	LX05EYR	London	LX06DZO	London
LK08FLL	London	LX05EYS	London	LX06DZP	London
LK08FLM	London	LX05EYT	London	LX06DZR	London
LK08FLN	London	LX05EYU	London	LX06DZS	London
LK08FLP	London	LX05EYV	London	LX06DZT	London
LK08FLR	London	LX05EYW	London	LX06DZU	London
LK51JYL	Metrobus	LX05EYY	London	LX06DZV	London
LK51JYN	Metrobus	LX05EYZ	London	LX06DZW	London
LK51LYJ	Metrobus	LX05EZA	London	LX06DZY	London
LK59FDE	London	LX05EZB	London	LX06DZZ	London
LK59FDF	London	LX05EZC	London	LX06EAA	London
LK59FDG	London	LX05EZD	London	LX06EAC	London
LK59FDJ	London	LX05EZE	London	LX06EAF	London
LK59FDL	London	LX05EZF	London	LX06EAG	London
LK59FDM	London	LX05EZG	London	LX06EAJ	London
LK59FDN	London	LX05EZH	London	LX06EAK	London
LK59FDO	London	LX05EZJ	London	LX06EAL	London
LK59FDP	London	LX05EZK	London	LX06EAM	London
LK59FDU	London	LX05EZL	London	LX06EAO	London
LK59FDV	London	LX05EZM	London	LX06EAP	London
LK59FDX	London	LX05EZN	London	LX06EAW	London
LK59FDY	London	LX05EZO	London	LX06EAY	London
LK59FDZ	London	LX05EZP	London	LX06EBA	London
LK59FEF	London	LX05EZR	London	LX06EBC	London
LK59FEG	London	LX05EZS	London	LX06EBD	London
LK59FEH	London	LX05EZT	London	LX06EBE	London
LK59FEJ	London	LX05EZU	London	LX06EBG	London
LK59FEM	London	LX05EZV	London	LX06EBJ	London
LK59FEO	London	LX05EZW	London	LX06EBK	London
LK59FEP	London	LX05EZZ	London	LX06EBL	London
LK59FET	London	LX05FAA	London	LX06EBM	London
LK59FEU	London	LX05FAF	London	LX06EBN	London
LN51GKD	London	LX05FAJ	London	LX06EBO	London
LN51GKE	London	LX05FAK	London	LX06EBP	London
LN51GKG	London	LX05FAM	London	LX06EBU	London
LN51GOJ	London	LX05FAO	London	LX06EBV	London
LN51GOK	London	LX05FAU	London	LX06EBZ	London
LSV749	South Coast	LX05FBA	London	LX06ECA	London
LT02NUK	London	LX05FBB	London	LX06ECC	London
LT02ZDE	Metrobus	LX05FBC	London	LX06ECD	London
LT02ZDG	Metrobus	LX05FBD	London	LX06ECE	London
LT02ZDM	Metrobus	LX05FBE	London	LX06ECF	London
LT02ZDN	Metrobus	LX05FBF	London	LX06ECJ	London
LT02ZDO	Metrobus	LX05FBJ	London	LX06ECN	London
LT02ZDP	Metrobus	LX05FBK	London	LX06ECT	London
LT02ZDR	Metrobus	LX05FBL	London	LX06ECV	London
LT02ZDS	Metrobus	LX05FBN	London	LX06EYT	London
LT02ZDW	Metrobus	LX05FBO	London	LX06EYU	London
LT02ZDX	Metrobus	LX05FBU	London	LX06EYV	London
LT52WXJ	London	LX05FBV	London	LX06EYW	London

LX06EYY	London	LX08EBV	London	LX09FAJ	London
LX06EYZ	London	LX08EBZ	London	LX09FAK	London
LX06EZA	London	LX08ECA	London	LX09FAM	London
LX06EZB	London	LX08ECC	London	LX09FAO	London
LX06EZC	London	LX08ECD	London	LX09FAU	London
LX06EZD	London	LX08ECE	London	LX09FBA	London
LX06EZE	London	LX08ECF	London	LX09FBB	London
LX06EZF	London	LX08ECJ	London	LX09FBC	London
LX06EZG	London	LX08ECN	London	LX09FBD	London
LX06EZH	London	LX08ECT	London	LX09FBE	London
LX06EZJ	London	LX08ECV	London	LX09FBF	London
LX06EZK	London	LX08ECW	London	LX09FBG	London
LX06EZL	London	LX08ECY	London	LX09FBJ	London
LX06EZM	London	LX09AXC	London	LX09FBK	London
LX06EZN	London	LX09AXU	London	LX09FBN	London
LX06EZO	London	LX09AXV	London	LX09FBO	London
LX06EZP	London	LX09AXW	London	LX09FBU	London
LX06EZR	London	LX09AXY	London	LX09FBV	London
LX06EZS	London	LX09AXZ	London	LX09FBY	London
LX06EZT	London	LX09AYA	London	LX09FBZ	London
LX06EZU	London	LX09AYB	London	LX09FCA	London
LX06EZV	London	LX09AYC	London	LX09FCC	London
LX06EZW	London	LX09AYD	London	LX09FCD	London
LX06EZZ	London	LX09AYE	London	LX09FCE	London
LX06FAA	London	LX09AYF	London	LX10AUP	London
LX06FAF	London	LX09AYG	London	LX10AUR	London
LX06FAJ	London	LX09AYH	London	LX10AUT	London
LX06FAK	London	LX09AYJ	London	LX10AUU	London
LX06FAM	London	LX09AYK	London	LX10AUV	London
LX06FAO	London	LX09AYL	London	LX10AUW	London
LX06FAU	London	LX09AYM	London	LX10AUY	London
LX06FBA	London	LX09AYN	London	LX10AVB	London
LX06FBB	London	LX09AYO	London	LX10AVC	London
LX06FBC	London	LX09AYP	London	LX10AVD	London
LX06FBD	London	LX09AYS	London	LX11CVL	London
LX06FBE	London	LX09AYT	London	LX11CVM	London
LX06FKL	London	LX09AYU	London	LX11CVN	London
LX06FKM	London	LX09AYV	London	LX11CVO	London
LX06FKN	London	LX09AYW	London	LX11CVP	London
LX06FKO	London	LX09AYY	London	LX11CVR	London
LX07BXH	London	LX09AYZ	London	LX11CVS	London
LX07BXJ	London	LX09AZA	London	LX11CVT	London
LX07BXK	London	LX09AZB	London	LX11CVU	London
LX07BXL	London	LX09AZD	London	LX11CVV	London
LX07BXM	London	LX09AZF	London	LX11CVW	London
LX07BXN	London	LX09AZG	London	LX11CVY	London
LX07BXO	London	LX09AZJ	London	LX11CVZ	London
LX07BXP	London	LX09AZL	London	LX11CWA	London
LX07BXR	London	LX09AZN	London	LX11CWC	London
LX07BXS	London	LX09AZO	London	LX11CWD	London
LX07BXU	London	LX09AZP	London	LX11CWE	London
LX07BXV	London	LX09AZR	London	LX11CWG	London
LX07BXW	London	LX09AZT	London	LX11CWJ	London
LX07BXY	London	LX09BXG	London	LX11CWK	London
LX07BYA	London	LX09BXH	London	LX11CWL	London
LX07BYB	London	LX09BXJ	London	LX11CWM	London
LX07BYC	London	LX09BXK	London	LX11CWN	London
LX07BYD	London	LX09BXL	London	LX11CWO	London
LX07BYF	London	LX09BXM	London	LX11CWP	London
LX07BYG	London	LX09BXO	London	LX11CWR	London
LX07BYH	London	LX09BXP	London	LX11CWT	London
LX07BYJ	London	LX09BXR	London	LX11CWU	London
LX07BYK	London	LX09BXS	London	LX11CWV	London
LX07BYL	London	LX09EVB	London	LX11CWW	London
LX07BYM	London	LX09EVC	London	LX11CWY	London
LX07BYN	London	LX09EVD	London	LX11CWZ	London
LX07BYO	London	LX09EVF	London	LX11CXA	London
LX07BYP	London	LX09EVG	London	LX11CXB	London
LX07BYR	London	LX09EVH	London	LX11CXC	London
LX07BYS	London	LX09EVJ	London	LX11CXD	London
LX07BYT	London	LX09EZU	London	LX11DVA	London
LX07BYU	London	LX09EZV	London	LX11DVB	London
LX07BZH	London	LX09EZW	London	LX11DVC	London
LX08EBP	London	LX09EZZ	London	LX11DVF	London
LX08EBU	London	LX09FAF	London	LX11DVG	London

LX11DVH	London	LX54HAE	London	LX58CXA	London
LX11FHV	London	LX54HAO	London	LX58CXB	London
LX11FHW	London	LX54HAU	London	LX58CXC	London
LX11FHY	London	LX54HBA	London	LX58CXD	London
LX11FHZ	London	LX54HBB	London	LX58CXE	London
LX11FJA	London	LX55EAC	London	LX58CXF	London
LX11FJC	London	LX55EAE	London	LX58CXG	London
LX11FJD	London	LX55EAF	London	LX58CXH	London
LX11FJE	London	LX55EAG	London	LX58CXJ	London
LX11FJF	London	LX55EAJ	London	LX58CXK	London
LX11FJJ	London	LX56ETD	London	LX58CXL	London
LX11FJK	London	LX56ETE	London	LX58CXN	London
LX11FJN	London	LX56ETF	London	LX58CXO	London
LX11FJO	London	LX56ETJ	London	LX58CXP	London
LX53AYM	London	LX56ETK	London	LX58CXR	London
LX53AYN	London	LX56ETL	London	LX58CXS	London
LX53AYO	London	LX56ETO	London	LX58CXT	London
LX53AYP	London	LX56ETR	London	LX58CXU	London
LX53AYT	London	LX56ETT	London	LX58CXV	London
LX53AYU	London	LX56ETU	London	LX58CXW	London
LX53AYV	London	LX56ETV	London	LX58CXY	London
LX53AYW	London	LX56ETY	London	LX58CXZ	London
LX53AYY	London	LX56ETZ	London	LX58CYA	London
LX53AYZ	London	LX56EUA	London	LX58CYC	London
LX53AZA	London	LX56EUB	London	LX58CYE	London
LX53AZB	London	LX56EUC	London	LX58CYF	London
LX53AZC	London	LX56EUD	London	LX58CYG	London
LX53AZD	London	LX57CHV	London	LX58DDJ	London
LX53AZF	London	LX57CHY	London	LX58DDK	London
LX53AZG	London	LX57CHZ	London	LX58DDL	London
LX53AZJ	London	LX57CJE	London	LX58DDN	London
LX53AZL	London	LX57CJF	London	LX58DDO	London
LX53AZN	London	LX57CJJ	London	LX59CYA	London
LX53AZO	London	LX57CJO	London	LX59CYC	London
LX53AZP	London	LX57CJU	London	LX59CYE	London
LX53AZR	London	LX57CJV	London	LX59CYF	London
LX53AZT	London	LX57CJY	London	LX59CYG	London
LX53AZU	London	LX57CJZ	London	LX59CYH	London
LX53AZV	London	LX57CKA	London	LX59CYJ	London
LX53BAA	London	LX57CKC	London	LX59CYK	London
LX53BAO	London	LX57CKD	London	LX59CYL	London
LX53BBZ	London	LX57CKE	London	LX59CYO	London
LX53BDO	London	LX57CKF	London	LX59CYP	London
LX53BDY	London	LX57CKG	London	LX59CYS	London
LX53BEY	London	LX57CKJ	London	LX59CYT	London
LX53BFK	London	LX57CKK	London	LX59CYU	London
LX53BGE	London	LX57CKL	London	LX59CYV	London
LX53BJK	London	LX57CKN	London	LX59CYW	London
LX53BJO	London	LX57CKO	London	LX59CYY	London
LX53BJU	London	LX57CKP	London	LX59CYZ	London
LX54GYV	London	LX57CKU	London	LX59CZA	London
LX54GYW	London	LX57CKV	London	LX59CZB	London
LX54GYY	London	LX57CKY	London	LX59CZC	London
LX54GYZ	London	LX57CLF	London	LX59CZD	London
LX54GZB	London	LX57CLJ	London	LX59CZF	London
LX54GZC	London	LX57CLN	London	LX59CZG	London
LX54GZD	London	LX57CLO	London	LX59CZH	London
LX54GZE	London	LX57CLV	London	LX59CZJ	London
LX54GZF	London	LX57CLY	London	LX59CZK	London
LX54GZG	London	LX57CLZ	London	LX59CZL	London
LX54GZH	London	LX58CWG	London	LX59CZM	London
LX54GZK	London	LX58CWJ	London	LX59CZN	London
LX54GZL	London	LX58CWK	London	LX59CZO	London
LX54GZM	London	LX58CWL	London	LX59CZP	London
LX54GZN	London	LX58CWM	London	LX59CZR	London
LX54GZO	London	LX58CWN	London	LX59CZS	London
LX54GZP	London	LX58CWO	London	LX59CZT	London
LX54GZR	London	LX58CWP	London	LX59CZU	London
LX54GZT	London	LX58CWR	London	LX59CZV	London
LX54GZU	London	LX58CWT	London	LX59CZW	London
LX54GZV	London	LX58CWU	London	LX59CZY	London
LX54GZW	London	LX58CWV	London	LX59CZZ	London
LX54GZY	London	LX58CWW	London	LX59DAA	London
LX54GZZ	London	LX58CWY	London	LX59DAO	London
LX54HAA	London	LX58CWZ	London	LX59DAU	London

LX59DBO	London	LX61GWM	London	MV02ULM	South Coast
LX59DBU	London	LX61GWN	London	MV02UMJ	South Coast
LX59DBV	London	LX61GWO	London	MV02UMK	South Coast
LX59DBY	London	LX61GWP	London	MV02UML	South Coast
LX59DBZ	London	LX61GWU	London	MV02UMM	South Coast
LX59DCE	London	LX61GWV	London	MV02UMO	South Coast
LX59DCF	London	LX61GWW	London	MV02UMR	South Coast
LX59DCO	London	LX61GWX	London	MV02UMS	South Coast
LX59DCU	London	LX61GWY	London	MV02UMT	South Coast
LX59DCV	London	LX61GWZ	London	MV02UMU	South Coast
LX59DCY	London	LX61GXA	London	MV02UMW	South Coast
LX59DCZ	London	LX61GXB	London	MV02UMX	South Coast
LX59DDA	London	LX61GXC	London	MV07DWM	South Coast
LX59DDE	London	LX61GXD	London	MX03YDD	South Coast
LX59DDF	London	M1OXF	Oxford	MX07JNV	South Coast
LX59DDJ	London	M15WAL	South Coast	MX07NSV	South Coast
LX59DDK	London	M17WAL	South Coast	MX07NTC	South Coast
LX59DDL	London	M18WAL	South Coast	MX07NTD	South Coast
LX59DDN	London	M19WAL	South Coast	MX08MYP	South Coast
LX59DDO	London	M20WAL	South Coast	MX08MYV	Oxford
LX59DDU	London	M136KRU	South Coast	MX08MYY	Oxford
LX59DDV	London	M138KRU	South Coast	MX08MZF	South Coast
LX59DDY	London	M139KRU	South Coast	MX08MZJ	South Coast
LX59DDZ	London	M140KRU	South Coast	MX09HHW	London
LX59DEU	London	M143KRU	South Coast	MX53FDM	Anglian
LX59DFA	London	M144UKN	Hedingham	MX53FDO	Anglian
LX59DFC	London	M146UKN	Hedingham	MX53FDP	Anglian
LX59DFD	London	M147KRU	South Coast	MX53FEF	South Coast
LX59DFE	London	M210VEV	Hedingham	MX57CAA	South Coast
LX59DFF	London	M211WHJ	Hedingham	MX57CAO	South Coast
LX59DFG	London	M212WHJ	Hedingham	MX57CAU	South Coast
LX59DFJ	London	M261KWK	Hedingham	MX57CAV	South Coast
LX59DFK	London	M262KWK	Hedingham	MX57CCU	South Coast
LX60DVY	London	M273UKN	Hedingham	MX57UPC	South Coast
LX60DVZ	London	M276UKN	Hedingham	MX57UPY	South Coast
LX60DWA	London	M282UKN	Hedingham	MX58AAF	Oxford
LX60DWC	London	M294UKN	Hedingham	MX58AAJ	Oxford
LX60DWD	London	M304KOD	South Coast	MX58AAN	Oxford
LX60DWE	London	M305KOD	South Coast	MX58KYV	Anglian
LX60DWF	London	M441CVG	Hedingham	MX58XDB	Anglian
LX60DWG	London	M507VJO	Metrobus	MX60BWH	Anglian
LX60DWJ	London	M516VJO	Metrobus	MX60BWJ	Anglian
LX60DWK	London	M571XKY	Hedingham	MX60BWK	Anglian
LX60DWL	London	M574RCP	South Coast	MX60GXA	Anglian
LX60DWM	London	M577RCP	South Coast	N1OXF	Oxford
LX60DWN	London	M580RCP	South Coast	N13WAL	South Coast
LX60DWO	London	M604TTV	Hedingham	N15WAL	South Coast
LX60DWP	London	M645RCP	South Coast	N16WAL	South Coast
LX60DWU	London	M655KVU	Chambers	N45FWU	South Coast
LX60DWV	London	M735BBP	South Coast	N101UTT	Plymouth
LX60DWW	London	M736BBP	South Coast	N102UTT	Plymouth
LX60DWY	London	M744HDL	South Coast	N103UTT	Plymouth
LX60DWZ	London	M745HDL	South Coast	N104UTT	Plymouth
LX60DXA	London	M746HDL	South Coast	N105UTT	Plymouth
LX60DXB	London	M746RCP	South Coast	N107UTT	Plymouth
LX60DXC	London	M748HDL	South Coast	N108UTT	Plymouth
LX60DXD	London	M749HDL	South Coast	N109UTT	Plymouth
LX60DXE	London	M750HDL	South Coast	N110UTT	Plymouth
LX60DXF	London	M751HDL	South Coast	N112UTT	Plymouth
LX60DXG	London	M826RCP	South Coast	N202NNJ	Brighton & Hove
LX60DXH	London	M845LFP	South Coast	N205NNJ	South Coast
LX60DXJ	London	M988NAA	Hedingham	N207NNJ	Brighton & Hove
LX60DXK	London	M993ROS	South Coast	N208NNJ	South Coast
LX60DXM	London	MA52OXF	Oxford	N209NNJ	Brighton & Hove
LX60DXO	London	MB52OXF	Oxford	N210NNJ	Brighton & Hove
LX60DXP	London	MC52OXF	Oxford	N211NNJ	South Coast
LX60DXR	London	MCO658	Plymouth	N213NNJ	South Coast
LX60DXS	London	ME52OXF	Oxford	N216NNJ	Brighton & Hove
LX60DXT	London	MF10OXF	Oxford	N232HWX	South Coast
LX61GWD	London	MF52OXF	Oxford	N232TPK	Metrobus
LX61GWE	London	MF56OXF	Oxford	N241EWC	Hedingham
LX61GWF	London	MF61OXF	Oxford	N307UTT	South Coast
LX61GWG	London	MJI7514	South Coast	N411WJL	South Coast
LX61GWK	London	MV02ULK	South Coast	N413JBL	South Coast
LX61GWL	London	MV02ULL	South Coast	N416NRG	South Coast

Reg	Location	Reg	Location	Reg	Location
N427JBV	Hedingham	NK06JXD	North East	NK11BHE	North East
N443WUX	South Coast	NK06JXE	North East	NK11BHF	North East
N465PAP	Chambers	NK07KPG	North East	NK11BHJ	North East
N529LHG	Chambers	NK07KPJ	North East	NK11BHL	North East
N531LHG	Chambers	NK07KPL	North East	NK11FXB	North East
N532LHG	Chambers	NK07KPN	North East	NK11FXC	North East
N539LHG	South Coast	NK07KPO	North East	NK11FXD	North East
N540LHG	Hedingham	NK07KPP	North East	NK11FXE	North East
N602FJO	South Coast	NK07KPR	North East	NK11FXF	North East
N606FJO	South Coast	NK07KPT	North East	NK11FXG	North East
N664THO	Hedingham	NK07KPU	North East	NK11FXH	North East
N760RCU	North East	NK08CFP	North East	NK11GWX	North East
N976UPR	South Coast	NK08CFU	North East	NK11GWY	North East
NA02NVL	North East	NK08CFV	North East	NK11HBB	North East
NA52AWF	North East	NK08CFX	North East	NK11HBC	North East
NA52AWG	North East	NK08CFZ	North East	NK11HDN	North East
NA52AWH	North East	NK08CGE	North East	NK11HDO	North East
NA52AWJ	North East	NK08CGF	North East	NK11HJC	North East
NA52AWM	North East	NK08CGG	North East	NK11HJE	North East
NA52AWN	North East	NK08CGO	North East	NK11HJF	North East
NA52AWO	North East	NK08CGU	North East	NK11HJG	North East
NA52AWP	North East	NK08CGV	North East	NK11HJP	North East
NA52AWR	North East	NK08CGX	North East	NK11HJT	North East
NA52AWU	North East	NK08CGY	North East	NK11HJV	North East
NA52AWV	North East	NK08CGZ	North East	NK11HJX	North East
NA52AWW	North East	NK08CHC	North East	NK12GCO	North East
NA52AWX	North East	NK08CHD	North East	NK12GCU	North East
NA52AWY	North East	NK08CHF	North East	NK12GCV	North East
NA52AWZ	North East	NK08CHG	North East	NK12GCX	North East
NA52AXB	North East	NK08CHH	North East	NK12GCY	North East
NA52AXC	North East	NK08CHJ	North East	NK12GCZ	North East
NA52AXD	North East	NK08CHL	North East	NK12GDA	North East
NA52AXF	North East	NK08CHN	North East	NK12GDE	North East
NA52AXG	North East	NK08CHO	North East	NK12GDF	North East
NA52AXH	North East	NK08CHV	North East	NK12GDJ	North East
NA52AXJ	North East	NK08CHX	North East	NK12GDO	North East
NA52AXK	North East	NK08CHY	North East	NK12GDU	North East
NA52AXM	North East	NK08MXY	North East	NK12GDX	North East
NA52AXN	North East	NK08MXZ	North East	NK12HCD	North East
NA52AXO	North East	NK08MYA	North East	NK12HCE	North East
NA52BUU	North East	NK08MYB	North East	NK12HCF	North East
NA52BUV	North East	NK08MYC	North East	NK51MJU	North East
NA52BUW	North East	NK08MYD	North East	NK51MJV	North East
NA52BVB	North East	NK08MYF	North East	NK51MJX	North East
NA52BVC	North East	NK08MYG	North East	NK51MJY	North East
NA52BVD	North East	NK08MZV	North East	NK51MKA	North East
NA52BVE	North East	NK08MZW	North East	NK51MKC	North East
NA52BVF	North East	NK09FUP	North East	NK51MKD	North East
NA52BVG	North East	NK09FUT	North East	NK51MKE	North East
NA52BVH	North East	NK09FUU	North East	NK51MKF	North East
NA52BVJ	North East	NK09FUV	North East	NK51MKG	North East
NA52RMZ	North East	NK09FUW	North East	NK51MKJ	North East
NG56HGO	South Coast	NK09FUY	North East	NK51MKL	North East
NJ07GJO	North East	NK09FVA	North East	NK51MKM	North East
NJ53AAE	South Coast	NK09FVB	North East	NK51MKN	North East
NJ53AAF	South Coast	NK09FVC	North East	NK51MKO	North East
NK04FOP	North East	NK09FVD	North East	NK51MKP	North East
NK04FOT	North East	NK09FVE	North East	NK51OKW	North East
NK04FOU	North East	NK09FVF	North East	NK51OKX	North East
NK04FOV	South Coast	NK09FVG	North East	NK51OLB	North East
NK04FPA	South Coast	NK09FVH	North East	NK51OLC	North East
NK04FPC	North East	NK09FVJ	North East	NK51OLE	North East
NK04FPD	North East	NK09FVL	North East	NK51OLG	North East
NK04FPE	North East	NK10GNY	North East	NK51OLH	North East
NK04ZKY	North East	NK10GNZ	North East	NK51OLJ	North East
NK04ZKZ	North East	NK10GOA	North East	NK51OLM	North East
NK04ZLE	North East	NK10GOC	North East	NK51OLN	North East
NK04ZNC	North East	NK10GOE	North East	NK51OLO	North East
NK04ZND	North East	NK10GOH	North East	NK51OLP	North East
NK04ZNE	North East	NK10GOJ	North East	NK51OLR	North East
NK05GZO	North East	NK10GOP	North East	NK51OLT	North East
NK05GZP	North East	NK10GOU	North East	NK51OLU	North East
NK05GZR	North East	NK11BGZ	North East	NK51OLV	North East
NK06JXB	North East	NK11BHA	North East	NK51UCN	North East
NK06JXC	North East	NK11BHD	North East	NK51UCO	North East

The 2012-13 Go-Ahead Bus Handbook

NK51UCP	North East	NK54NVM	North East	NK61FEV	North East
NK51UCR	North East	NK54NVN	North East	NK61FEX	North East
NK51UCS	North East	NK54NVO	North East	NK61FJO	North East
NK51UCT	North East	NK54NVP	North East	NK61FJP	North East
NK51UCU	North East	NK54NVT	North East	NK61FMD	North East
NK53TKD	North East	NK54NVU	North East	NK62CBV	North East
NK53TKE	North East	NK54NVV	North East	NK62CBV	North East
NK53TKF	North East	NK54NVW	North East	NK62CCY	North East
NK53TKN	North East	NK54NVX	North East	NK62CEN	North East
NK53TKO	North East	NK54NVY	North East	NK62CFN	North East
NK53TKT	North East	NK54NVZ	North East	NK62CJE	North East
NK53TKU	North East	NK54NWA	North East	NK62CJJ	North East
NK53TKV	North East	NK54NWB	North East	NK62CKC	North East
NK53TKX	North East	NK54PHV	North East	NK62CLZ	North East
NK53TKY	North East	NK55OLG	North East	NK62CME	North East
NK53TKZ	North East	NK55OLH	North East	NK62CXL	North East
NK53TLF	North East	NK55OLJ	North East	NK62CYC	North East
NK53TLJ	North East	NK55OLM	North East	NK62CYE	North East
NK53TLN	North East	NK55OLN	North East	NK62CYF	North East
NK53TLO	North East	NK55RUV	North East	NK62CZA	North East
NK53TLU	North East	NK55RUW	North East	NL02ZRX	North East
NK53TLV	North East	NK56KHB	North East	NL52WVM	North East
NK53TLX	North East	NK56KHC	North East	NL52WVN	North East
NK53TLY	North East	NK56KHD	North East	NL52WVO	North East
NK53TMO	North East	NK56KHE	North East	NL52WVP	North East
NK53TMU	North East	NK56KHF	North East	NL52WVR	North East
NK53TMV	North East	NK56KHG	North East	NL52WVS	North East
NK53TMX	North East	NK56KHH	North East	NL52WVT	North East
NK53TMY	North East	NK56KHJ	North East	NL52WVU	North East
NK53TMZ	North East	NK56KHL	North East	NL52WVV	North East
NK53UNT	North East	NK56KHM	North East	NL52WVW	North East
NK53UNU	North East	NK56KHO	North East	NL52WVX	North East
NK53UNV	North East	NK56KHP	North East	NLZ1822	South Coast
NK53UNW	North East	NK56KHR	North East	NM02DNUE	South Coast
NK53UNX	North East	NK56KHT	North East	NML604E	London
NK53UNY	North East	NK56KHU	North East	NT05NBM	South Coast
NK53UNZ	North East	NK56KHV	North East	NT55JKJ	South Coast
NK53UOA	North East	NK56KHW	North East	NXI5358	South Coast
NK53UOB	North East	NK56KHX	North East	OA02OXF	Oxford
NK53UOC	North East	NK56KHY	North East	OB02OXF	Oxford
NK54DEU	South Coast	NK56KHZ	North East	OC02OXF	Oxford
NK54DFA	South Coast	NK56KJA	North East	OD02OXF	Oxford
NK54DFC	South Coast	NK56KJE	North East	ODL447	South Coast
NK54DFD	South Coast	NK56KJF	North East	OE02OXF	Oxford
NK54NKT	North East	NK56KJJ	North East	OF02OXF	Oxford
NK54NKU	North East	NK56KJN	North East	OF09OXF	Oxford
NK54NKW	North East	NK56KJO	North East	OF10OXF	Oxford
NK54NKX	North East	NK56KJU	North East	OF56OXF	Oxford
NK54NKZ	North East	NK56KJV	North East	OF61OXF	Oxford
NK54NLC	North East	NK56KJX	North East	OJI1875	South Coast
NK54NLD	North East	NK56KJY	North East	ONZ1208	South Coast
NK54NTX	North East	NK56KJZ	North East	OP07ARE	London
NK54NTY	North East	NK56KKA	North East	OU04FMV	Oxford
NK54NUA	North East	NK56KKB	North East	OU08HGM	Oxford
NK54NUB	North East	NK56KKC	North East	OU08HGN	Oxford
NK54NUH	North East	NK56KKE	North East	OU08HGO	Oxford
NK54NUJ	North East	NK56KKF	North East	OU54PGZ	Oxford
NK54NUM	North East	NK56KKG	North East	OU57FGV	Oxford
NK54NUO	North East	NK56KKH	North East	OU57FGX	Oxford
NK54NUP	North East	NK56KKJ	North East	OU57FGZ	Oxford
NK54NUU	North East	NK56KKL	North East	OU57FHA	Oxford
NK54NUV	North East	NK58DVW	North East	OU57FKB	Oxford
NK54NUW	North East	NK58DVX	North East	P1OXF	Oxford
NK54NUX	North East	NK58DVY	North East	P41RCRD	South Coast
NK54NUY	North East	NK58DVZ	North East	P104OLX	Hedingham
NK54NVA	North East	NK58DWA	North East	P124RWR	South Coast
NK54NVB	North East	NK58DWC	North East	P125RWR	South Coast
NK54NVC	North East	NK58DWD	North East	P126RWR	South Coast
NK54NVD	North East	NK58DWE	North East	P274FPK	Metrobus
NK54NVE	North East	NK61DBX	North East	P278FPK	Metrobus
NK54NVF	North East	NK61DBY	North East	P283FPK	Metrobus
NK54NVG	North East	NK61DBZ	North East	P285FPK	Metrobus
NK54NVH	North East	NK61EFY	North East	P308CTT	South Coast
NK54NVJ	North East	NK61EGY	North East	P320AFT	North East
NK54NVL	North East	NK61FEU	North East	P321AFT	North East

P322AFT	North East	PJ02RDO	London	PJ53SOH	London		
P323AFT	North East	PJ02RDU	London	PJ53SOU	London		
P324AFT	North East	PJ02RDV	London	PJ53SPU	London		
P325AFT	North East	PJ02RDX	London	PJ53SPV	London		
P380FPK	Metrobus	PJ02RDY	London	PJ53SPX	London		
P395AAA	Hedingham	PJ02RDZ	London	PJ53SPZ	London		
P475MBY	Chambers	PJ02REU	London	PJ53SRO	London		
P476SWC	Anglian	PJ02RFE	London	PJ53SRU	London		
P478SWC	Anglian	PJ02RFF	London	PK02RCZ	Brighton & Hove		
P484MBY	Chambers	PJ02RFK	London	PK02RDO	Brighton & Hove		
P488MBY	Chambers	PJ02RFL	London	PK02RDU	Brighton & Hove		
P489MBY	Hedingham	PJ02RFN	London	PK02RDV	Brighton & Hove		
P494MBY	Hedingham	PJ02RFO	London	PK02RDX	Brighton & Hove		
P515UUG	Chambers	PJ02RFX	London	PK02RDY	Brighton & Hove		
P530CLJ	Hedingham	PJ02RFY	London	PK02RDZ	Brighton & Hove		
P549WGT	Chambers	PJ02RFZ	London	PK02REU	Brighton & Hove		
P602CAY	Hedingham	PJ02RGO	London	PK02RFE	Brighton & Hove		
P605CAY	Hedingham	PJ02RGU	London	PK02RFF	Brighton & Hove		
P606CAY	Hedingham	PJ02RGV	London	PK02RFJ	Brighton & Hove		
P608CAY	Hedingham	PJ02RHE	Hedingham	PK02RFL	Brighton & Hove		
P612CAY	Hedingham	PJ02TVN	London	PL03AGZ	London		
P737RYL	South Coast	PJ02TVO	London	PL51LDK	South Coast		
P886RWW	South Coast	PJ02TVP	London	PL51LDN	South Coast		
P887RWW	South Coast	PJ02TVT	London	PL51LDO	South Coast		
P901RYO	Chambers	PJ02TVU	London	PL51LFE	Plymouth		
P902RYO	Chambers	PJ52LVP	London	PL51LFG	South Coast		
P910RYO	Chambers	PJ52LVR	London	PL51LFJ	South Coast		
PB09ONE	South Coast	PJ52LVS	London	PL51LGA	Plymouth		
PE55WPP	South Coast	PJ52LVT	London	PL51LGC	Plymouth		
PE55WSU	South Coast	PJ52LVU	London	PL51LGE	South Coast		
PF06ENL	Oxford	PJ52LVV	London	PL51LGJ	Plymouth		
PF06ENM	Oxford	PJ52LVW	London	PL51LGK	Plymouth		
PF06ENN	Oxford	PJ52LVX	London	PL51LGN	Plymouth		
PF06ENO	Oxford	PJ52LVY	London	PL51LGO	Plymouth		
PF10OXF	Oxford	PJ52LVZ	London	PL51LGU	Plymouth		
PF52WPT	London	PJ52LWA	London	PL51LGW	Plymouth		
PF52WPU	London	PJ52LWC	London	PL51LGX	Plymouth		
PF52WPV	London	PJ52LWD	London	PM04MKP	South Coast		
PF52WPW	London	PJ52LWE	London	PN02XBL	London		
PF52WPX	London	PJ52LWF	London	PN02XBM	London		
PF52WPY	London	PJ52LWG	London	PN02XBO	London		
PF52WPZ	London	PJ52LWH	London	PN02XBW	London		
PF52WRA	London	PJ52LWK	London	PN02XBX	Plymouth		
PF52WRC	London	PJ52LWL	London	PN02XBZ	Oxford		
PF52WRD	London	PJ52LWM	London	PN02XCA	Oxford		
PF52WRE	London	PJ52LWN	London	PN02XCC	Plymouth		
PF52WRG	London	PJ52LWO	London	PN02XCE	Plymouth		
PF56OXF	Oxford	PJ52LWP	London	PN02XCF	North East		
PF61OXF	Oxford	PJ52LWR	London	PN02XCG	Plymouth		
PJ02PYU	North East	PJ52LWS	London	PN02XCH	Plymouth		
PJ02PYV	North East	PJ52LWT	London	PN02XCJ	Plymouth		
PJ02PYW	North East	PJ52LWU	London	PN02XCK	Oxford		
PJ02PYX	North East	PJ52LWV	London	PN02XCL	North East		
PJ02PYY	North East	PJ52LWW	London	PN02XCM	Plymouth		
PJ02PYZ	North East	PJ52LWX	London	PN02XCO	Plymouth		
PJ02PZA	North East	PJ53NKG	London	PN02XCP	Plymouth		
PJ02PZB	North East	PJ53NKH	London	PN02XCS	Oxford		
PJ02PZC	North East	PJ53NKK	London	PN02XCT	Oxford		
PJ02PZD	North East	PJ53NKL	London	PN06UYL	Metrobus		
PJ02PZE	North East	PJ53NKM	London	PN06UYM	Metrobus		
PJ02PZF	North East	PJ53NKN	London	PN06UYO	Metrobus		
PJ02PZG	North East	PJ53NKO	London	PN06UYP	Metrobus		
PJ02PZH	North East	PJ53NKP	London	PN06UYR	Metrobus		
PJ02PZK	North East	PJ53NKR	London	PN06UYS	Metrobus		
PJ02PZL	North East	PJ53NKS	London	PN06UYT	Metrobus		
PJ02RBO	London	PJ53NKT	London	PN06UYU	Metrobus		
PJ02RBV	London	PJ53NKW	London	PN06UYV	Metrobus		
PJ02RBZ	Chambers	PJ53NKX	London	PN06UYW	Metrobus		
PJ02RCF	London	PJ53NKZ	London	PN06UYX	Metrobus		
PJ02RCO	London	PJ53NLA	London	PN06UYY	Metrobus		
PJ02RCU	London	PJ53NLC	London	PN07KRK	Metrobus		
PJ02RCV	London	PJ53NLD	London	PN07KRO	Metrobus		
PJ02RCX	London	PJ53NLE	London	PN07KRU	Metrobus		
PJ02RCY	London	PJ53NLF	London	PN07KRV	Metrobus		
PJ02RCZ	London	PJ53SOF	London	PN07KRX	Metrobus		

Reg	Operator	Reg	Operator	Reg	Operator
PN09EKR	Metrobus	R227HCD	Hedingham	R620NFX	South Coast
PN09EKT	Metrobus	R228HCD	Brighton & Hove	R626MNU	Hedingham
PN09EKU	Metrobus	R229HCD	Hedingham	R629MNU	Hedingham
PN09EKV	Metrobus	R230HCD	Brighton & Hove	R63GNW	South Coast
PN09EKW	Metrobus	R231HCD	Brighton & Hove	R643MNU	Hedingham
PN09EKX	Metrobus	R232HCD	Brighton & Hove	R702DNH	Hedingham
PN09EKY	Metrobus	R233HCD	Brighton & Hove	R737XRV	South Coast
PN09ELO	Metrobus	R235HCD	Brighton & Hove	R738XRV	South Coast
PN09ELU	Metrobus	R235HCD	Brighton & Hove	R739XRV	South Coast
PN09ELV	Metrobus	R236HCD	Brighton & Hove	R741BMY	Metrobus
PN09ELW	Metrobus	R255LGH	North East	R741XRV	South Coast
PN09ELX	Metrobus	R257LGH	North East	R744BMY	Metrobus
PN09EMF	Metrobus	R259DWL	South Coast	R747BMY	Metrobus
PN09EMK	Metrobus	R259LGH	Hedingham	R752GDL	South Coast
PN09EMV	Metrobus	R262LGH	North East	R753GDL	South Coast
PN09EMX	Metrobus	R264LGH	North East	R754GDL	South Coast
PN09ENC	Metrobus	R267LGH	Oxford	R755GDL	South Coast
PN09ENE	Metrobus	R270LGH	Oxford	R756GDL	South Coast
PN09ENF	Metrobus	R273LGH	Chambers	R757GDL	South Coast
PN09ENH	Metrobus	R274LGH	North East	R758GDL	South Coast
PN09ENK	Metrobus	R276LGH	North East	R759GDL	South Coast
PN09ENL	Metrobus	R279LGH	Oxford	R807NUD	South Coast
PN09ENM	Metrobus	R279LHG	Hedingham	R809NUD	South Coast
PN09ENO	Metrobus	R280LGH	Oxford	R810NUD	South Coast
PN59KFW	Metrobus	R281LGH	North East	R811NUD	South Coast
PN59KFX	Metrobus	R282LGH	North East	R812NUD	South Coast
PN59KFY	Metrobus	R283LGH	North East	R813NUD	South Coast
PN59KFZ	Metrobus	R284LGH	North East	R830MFR	South Coast
PN59KGA	Metrobus	R285LGH	North East	R831MFR	South Coast
PN59KGE	Metrobus	R286LGH	North East	R832MFR	South Coast
PO56JEU	Metrobus	R309STA	South Coast	R833MFR	South Coast
PO56JFA	Metrobus	R355LGH	North East	R834MFR	South Coast
PO56JFE	Metrobus	R362LGH	South Coast	R835MFR	South Coast
PO56JFF	Metrobus	R368LGH	South Coast	R836MFR	South Coast
PO56JFG	Metrobus	R370LGH	London	R837MFR	South Coast
PO56JFJ	Metrobus	R371LGH	London	R837PRG	North East
PO56JFK	Metrobus	R373LGH	South Coast	R838MFR	South Coast
PO56JFN	Metrobus	R379LGH	South Coast	R838PRG	North East
PO56JFU	Metrobus	R382LGH	South Coast	R839MFR	South Coast
PX03KCN	South Coast	R383LGH	South Coast	R839PRG	North East
PX03KCU	South Coast	R384LGH	South Coast	R841MFR	South Coast
R1OXF	Oxford	R385LGH	South Coast	R841PRG	North East
R43LHK	Chambers	R387LGH	South Coast	R842PRG	North East
R49LHK	Chambers	R390LGH	North East	R843MFR	South Coast
R81EMB	Anglian	R391LGH	North East	R843PRG	North East
R82EMB	Anglian	R395LGH	North East	R844PRG	North East
R112NTA	Chambers	R396LGH	North East	R845MFR	South Coast
R113OFJ	Plymouth	R397LGH	North East	R845PRG	North East
R114OFJ	Plymouth	R398LGH	North East	R846PRG	North East
R115OFJ	Plymouth	R399LGH	North East	R847PRG	North East
R116OFJ	Plymouth	R401DWL	South Coast	R848PRG	North East
R117OFJ	Plymouth	R401FFC	Plymouth	R849PRG	North East
R118OFJ	Plymouth	R402FFC	Plymouth	R851PRG	North East
R119OFJ	Plymouth	R408FFC	Plymouth	R852PRG	North East
R120OFJ	Plymouth	R435MEH	South Coast	R853PRG	North East
R121OFJ	Plymouth	R453FWT	Hedingham	R854PRG	North East
R122OFJ	Plymouth	R464LGH	South Coast	R855PRG	North East
R123OFJ	Plymouth	R552LGH	Chambers	R856PRG	North East
R124OFJ	Plymouth	R553LGH	North East	R881HCD	Brighton & Hove
R125OFJ	Plymouth	R554LGH	North East	R929JYG	South Coast
R126OFJ	Plymouth	R556LGH	North East	R935FNG	Hedingham
R154NPR	South Coast	R557LGH	North East	R941YOV	Chambers
R155NPR	South Coast	R558LGH	North East	R971FNW	North East
R156NPR	South Coast	R559LGH	North East	R972FNW	North East
R214NFX	South Coast	R602NFX	South Coast	R975FNW	North East
R215NFX	South Coast	R603NFX	South Coast	R976FNW	Oxford
R216HCD	Brighton & Hove	R604NFX	South Coast	R978KAR	Chambers
R217HCD	Brighton & Hove	R605NFX	South Coast	R979FNW	North East
R218HCD	Oxford	R609NFX	South Coast	R982FNW	North East
R219HCD	Brighton & Hove	R610NFX	South Coast	R983FNW	North East
R221HCD	Brighton & Hove	R615NFX	South Coast	R987KAR	Chambers
R223HCD	Brighton & Hove	R618NFX	South Coast	R989KAR	Chambers
R224HCD	Brighton & Hove	R619NFX	South Coast	RE56OUU	South Coast
R225HCD	Oxford	R620NFX	South Coast	RF10OXF	Oxford
R226HCD	Brighton & Hove	R620NFX	South Coast	RF56OXF	Oxford

Reg	Operator	Reg	Operator	Reg	Operator
RF61OXF	Oxford	SK07DWJ	London	SN03YBY	Metrobus
RGV284N	Hedingham	SK07DWK	London	SN03YBZ	Metrobus
RJI6155	South Coast	SK07DWL	London	SN03YCD	Metrobus
RX07BNF	Oxford	SK07DWM	London	SN03YCE	Metrobus
RX60DLY	Oxford	SK07DWO	London	SN03YCF	Metrobus
RX60DLZ	Oxford	SK07DWP	London	SN03YCK	Metrobus
RX60DME	Oxford	SK07DWU	London	SN03YCL	Metrobus
RX60DMF	Oxford	SK07DWV	London	SN03YCM	Metrobus
RX60FKF	Oxford	SK07DWW	London	SN03YCT	Metrobus
S127FTA	Plymouth	SK07DWX	London	SN06BNA	London
S127RLE	Hedingham	SK07DWY	London	SN06BNB	London
S131RLE	Chambers	SK07DWZ	London	SN06BND	London
S169UAL	Hedingham	SK07DXA	London	SN06BNE	London
S218YOO	Chambers	SK07DXB	London	SN06BNF	London
S233RLH	Chambers	SK07DZM	London	SN06BNJ	London
S290TVW	Hedingham	SK07DZN	London	SN06BNK	London
S291TVW	Hedingham	SK07DZO	London	SN06BNL	London
S300XHK	Hedingham	SK52MLU	London	SN06BNO	London
S358ONL	North East	SK52MLV	London	SN06BNU	London
S359ONL	North East	SK52MLX	London	SN06BNV	London
S360ONL	North East	SK52MLY	London	SN06BNX	London
S361ONL	North East	SK52MLZ	London	SN06BNY	London
S372ONL	North East	SK52MMA	London	SN06BNZ	London
S373ONL	North East	SK52MME	London	SN06BOF	London
S376MVP	Hedingham	SK52MMU	London	SN10CCV	Hedingham
S590KJF	North East	SK52MMV	London	SN10CCX	Oxford
S602KUT	South Coast	SK52MMX	London	SN10CCY	Oxford
S610VAY	South Coast	SK52MOA	London	SN10CCZ	Oxford
S611VAY	South Coast	SK52MOF	London	SN10CEX	Konectbus
S628JRU	South Coast	SK52MOU	London	SN10CFD	Konectbus
S631JRU	South Coast	SK52MOV	London	SN10CFE	Konectbus
S632JRU	South Coast	SK52MPE	London	SN10CFF	Konectbus
S783RNE	North East	SK52MPF	London	SN10CFG	Konectbus
S811FVK	North East	SK52MPO	London	SN11BTY	London
S812FVK	North East	SN03EBP	South Coast	SN11BTZ	London
S813FVK	North East	SN03EBU	South Coast	SN11BUA	London
S814FVK	North East	SN03EBV	South Coast	SN11BUE	London
S815FVK	North East	SN03EBX	South Coast	SN11BUF	London
S816FVK	North East	SN03EBZ	South Coast	SN11BUH	London
S817FVK	North East	SN03ECA	South Coast	SN11BUJ	London
S818OFT	North East	SN03ECC	South Coast	SN11BUO	London
S819OFT	North East	SN03ECD	South Coast	SN11BUP	London
S820OFT	North East	SN03LDJ	South Coast	SN11BUU	London
S821OFT	North East	SN03LDK	South Coast	SN11BUV	London
S822OFT	North East	SN03LDL	South Coast	SN11BUW	London
S823OFT	North East	SN03LDU	South Coast	SN11FFZ	London
S824OFT	North East	SN03WKU	Metrobus	SN11FGA	London
S825OFT	North East	SN03WKY	Metrobus	SN11FGC	London
S826OFT	North East	SN03WLA	Metrobus	SN11FGD	London
S827OFT	North East	SN03WLE	Metrobus	SN12AAE	Metrobus
S828OFT	North East	SN03WLF	Metrobus	SN12AAF	Metrobus
S829OFT	North East	SN03WLH	Metrobus	SN12AAJ	Metrobus
S830OFT	North East	SN03WLL	Metrobus	SN12AAK	Metrobus
S831OFT	North East	SN03WLP	Metrobus	SN12AAO	Metrobus
S832OFT	North East	SN03WLU	Metrobus	SN12AAU	Metrobus
S833OFT	North East	SN03WLX	Metrobus	SN12AUM	London
S862ONL	North East	SN03WLZ	Metrobus	SN12AUO	London
S863ONL	North East	SN03WMC	Metrobus	SN12AUP	London
S864ONL	North East	SN03WMF	Metrobus	SN12AUR	London
S865ONL	North East	SN03WMG	Metrobus	SN12AUT	London
S866ONL	North East	SN03WMK	Metrobus	SN12AUU	London
S867ONL	North East	SN03WMP	Metrobus	SN12AUV	London
S894ONL	North East	SN03WMT	Metrobus	SN12AUW	London
S895ONL	North East	SN03WMV	Metrobus	SN12AUX	London
S977ABR	North East	SN03WMY	Metrobus	SN12AUY	London
S978ABR	North East	SN03YBA	Metrobus	SN12AVB	London
S979ABR	North East	SN03YBB	Metrobus	SN12AVC	London
SBL364	South Coast	SN03YBC	Metrobus	SN12AVD	London
SF10OXF	Oxford	SN03YBG	Metrobus	SN12AVE	London
SF56OXF	Oxford	SN03YBH	Metrobus	SN12AVF	London
SF61OXF	Oxford	SN03YBK	Metrobus	SN12AVG	London
SFO5KWM	South Coast	SN03YBR	Metrobus	SN12AVJ	London
SIB5373	South Coast	SN03YBS	Metrobus	SN12AVK	London
SIL7914	South Coast	SN03YBT	Metrobus	SN12AVL	London
SK07DWG	London	SN03YBX	Metrobus	SN51UAD	London

Reg	Operator	Reg	Operator	Reg	Operator
SN51UAE	London	SN60BZS	London	SN61DCV	London
SN51UAF	London	SN60BZT	London	SN61DCX	London
SN51UAG	London	SN60BZU	London	SN61DCY	London
SN51UAH	London	SN60BZV	London	SN61DCZ	London
SN51UAJ	London	SN60BZW	London	SN61DDA	London
SN51UAK	London	SN60BZX	London	SN61DDE	London
SN51UAL	London	SN60BZY	London	SN61DDF	London
SN51UAM	London	SN61BGE	London	SN61DDJ	London
SN51UAO	London	SN61BGF	London	SN61DDK	London
SN51UAP	London	SN61BGK	London	SN61DDL	London
SN51UAR	London	SN61BGO	London	SN61DDO	London
SN51UAS	London	SN61BGU	London	SN61DDU	London
SN51UAT	London	SN61BGV	London	SN61DDV	London
SN51UAU	London	SN61BGX	London	SN61DDX	London
SN51UAV	London	SN61BGY	London	SN61DDY	London
SN51UAW	London	SN61BGZ	London	SN61DDZ	London
SN51UAX	London	SN61BHA	London	SN61DEU	London
SN51UAY	London	SN61BHD	London	SN61DFA	London
SN51UAZ	London	SN61BHE	London	SN61DFC	London
SN53KKF	London	SN61BHF	London	SN61DFD	London
SN53KKG	London	SN61BHJ	London	SN61DFE	London
SN53KKH	London	SN61BHK	London	SN61DFF	London
SN53KKJ	London	SN61BHL	London	SN61DFG	London
SN53KKL	London	SN61BHO	London	SN61DFJ	London
SN53KKM	London	SN61BHP	London	SN62AVG	Konectbus
SN53KKO	London	SN61BHU	London	SN62AVO	Konectbus
SN53KKP	London	SN61BHV	London	SN62AVR	Konectbus
SN53KKR	London	SN61BHW	London	SN62AVY	Konectbus
SN53KKT	London	SN61BHX	London	T101DBW	Oxford
SN53KKU	London	SN61BHY	London	T102DBW	Oxford
SN53KKV	London	SN61BHZ	London	T103DBW	Oxford
SN53KKW	London	SN61BJE	London	T104DBW	Oxford
SN53KKX	London	SN61BJF	London	T105DBW	Oxford
SN54GPV	Metrobus	SN61BJJ	London	T106DBW	Oxford
SN54GPX	Metrobus	SN61BJK	London	T108DBW	Oxford
SN54GPY	Metrobus	SN61BJO	London	T109DBW	Oxford
SN54GPZ	Metrobus	SN61BJU	London	T110AUA	South Coast
SN54GRF	Metrobus	SN61BJV	London	T110DBW	Oxford
SN54GRK	Metrobus	SN61BJX	London	T111DBW	Oxford
SN56AWX	South Coast	SN61BJY	London	T113DBW	Oxford
SN56AYC	London	SN61BJZ	London	T114DBW	Oxford
SN56AYD	London	SN61BKA	London	T115DBW	Oxford
SN58CDY	London	SN61BKD	London	T116DBW	Oxford
SN58CDZ	London	SN61BKE	London	T117DBW	Oxford
SN58CEA	London	SN61BKF	London	T118DBW	Oxford
SN58CEF	London	SN61BKG	London	T119DBW	Oxford
SN58CEJ	London	SN61BKJ	London	T120DBW	Oxford
SN58CEK	London	SN61BKK	London	T128EFJ	Plymouth
SN58CEO	London	SN61BKL	London	T129EFJ	Plymouth
SN58CEU	London	SN61BKO	London	T130EFJ	Plymouth
SN58CEV	London	SN61BKU	London	T131EFJ	Plymouth
SN58CEX	London	SN61BKV	London	T132EFJ	Plymouth
SN58CEY	London	SN61BKX	London	T133EFJ	Plymouth
SN58CFA	London	SN61BKY	London	T134EFJ	Plymouth
SN58CFD	London	SN61BKZ	London	T135EFJ	Plymouth
SN58CFE	London	SN61BLJ	London	T136EFJ	Plymouth
SN58CFF	London	SN61BLK	London	T137EFJ	Plymouth
SN58CFG	London	SN61BLV	London	T138EFJ	Plymouth
SN58CFJ	London	SN61CZV	Konectbus	T139EFJ	Plymouth
SN60BXW	Oxford	SN61CZW	Konectbus	T140EFJ	Plymouth
SN60BZA	London	SN61CZX	Konectbus	T158ALJ	South Coast
SN60BZB	London	SN61CZY	Konectbus	T159ALJ	South Coast
SN60BZC	London	SN61CZZ	Konectbus	T160ALJ	South Coast
SN60BZD	London	SN61DAA	London	T165AUA	South Coast
SN60BZE	London	SN61DAO	London	T200CBC	Anglian
SN60BZF	London	SN61DAU	London	T216REL	South Coast
SN60BZG	London	SN61DBO	London	T217REL	South Coast
SN60BZH	London	SN61DBU	London	T218REL	South Coast
SN60BZJ	London	SN61DBV	London	T310SMV	Metrobus
SN60BZK	London	SN61DBX	London	T311SMV	Metrobus
SN60BZL	London	SN61DBY	London	T312SMV	Brighton & Hove
SN60BZM	London	SN61DBZ	London	T313SMV	Brighton & Hove
SN60BZO	London	SN61DCE	London	T400CBC	Anglian
SN60BZP	London	SN61DCO	London	T428LGP	North East
SN60BZR	London	SN61DCU	London	T438EBD	North East

Reg	Fleet	Reg	Fleet	Reg	Fleet
T518EUB	South Coast	TIL6718	South Coast	V327LGC	North East
T600BCL	South Coast	TIL6719	South Coast	V328KMY	Metrobus
T633AJT	South Coast	TIL6720	South Coast	V329KMY	Metrobus
T634AJT	South Coast	TIL6723	South Coast	V329LGC	North East
T635AJT	South Coast	TIL6724	South Coast	V330KMY	Metrobus
T636AJT	South Coast	TIL6725	South Coast	V330LGC	North East
T637AJT	South Coast	TIL6726	South Coast	V331KMY	Metrobus
T638AJT	South Coast	TIL6727	South Coast	V331LGC	North East
T639AJT	South Coast	TJI9462	South Coast	V332LGC	North East
T640AJT	South Coast	UEL489	South Coast	V334LGC	North East
T641AJT	South Coast	UF10OXF	Oxford	V335LGC	North East
T642AJT	South Coast	UF56OXF	Oxford	V336LGC	North East
T644AJT	South Coast	UF61OXF	Oxford	V337LGC	North East
T645AJT	South Coast	UFX852S	Konectbus	V338LGC	North East
T646AJT	South Coast	UJI2507	South Coast	V380HGG	Anglian
T647AJT	South Coast	UK59UCL	Brighton & Hove	V530GDS	North East
T648AJT	South Coast	USV115	South Coast	V531GDS	North East
T649AJT	South Coast	V161MEV	Anglian	V532GDS	North East
T669KPU	Brighton & Hove	V201ERG	North East	V533GDS	North East
T670KPU	Brighton & Hove	V202ERG	North East	V534GDS	North East
T671KPU	Brighton & Hove	V203ENU	Hedingham	V535GDS	North East
T672KPU	Brighton & Hove	V203ERG	North East	V536GDS	North East
T673KPU	Brighton & Hove	V204ERG	North East	V652DFX	South Coast
T675KPU	Brighton & Hove	V205ENU	Hedingham	V653DFX	South Coast
T677KPU	Brighton & Hove	V205ERG	North East	V654DFX	South Coast
T742JPO	South Coast	V206ERG	North East	V655DFX	South Coast
T743JPO	South Coast	V207ERG	North East	V656DFX	South Coast
T744JPO	South Coast	V208ERG	North East	V657DFX	South Coast
T745JPO	South Coast	V209ERG	North East	V658DFX	South Coast
T746JPO	South Coast	V209LGC	North East	V659DFX	South Coast
T747JPO	South Coast	V210ERG	North East	V660DFX	South Coast
T748JPO	South Coast	V210ERG	North East	V661DFX	South Coast
T749JPO	South Coast	V211ERG	North East	V662DFX	South Coast
T789XVO	Hedingham	V212ERG	North East	V663DFX	South Coast
T801CBW	North East	V213ERG	North East	V664DFX	South Coast
T801RFG	Hedingham	V214ERG	North East	V665DFX	South Coast
T802CBW	North East	V215ERG	North East	V667DFX	South Coast
T802RFG	Hedingham	V216ERG	North East	V669DFX	South Coast
T803CBW	North East	V217ERG	North East	V670DFX	South Coast
T804CBW	North East	V218ERG	North East	V671FEL	South Coast
T805CBW	North East	V218LGC	North East	V671RNP	South Coast
T806CBW	North East	V219ERG	North East	V672FEL	South Coast
T806RFG	Oxford	V220LGC	North East	V673FEL	South Coast
T807CBW	North East	V221ERG	North East	V674FEL	South Coast
T807RFG	Oxford	V226LGC	North East	V675FEL	South Coast
T808CBW	North East	V227KAH	Anglian	V676FEL	South Coast
T808RFG	Brighton & Hove	V228LGC	North East	V677FEL	South Coast
T809CBW	North East	V233LGC	North East	V679FEL	South Coast
T809RFG	Oxford	V250BNV	Hedingham	V680FEL	South Coast
T810CBW	North East	V284SBW	Oxford	V681FEL	South Coast
T811CBW	North East	V301LGC	Konectbus	V682FEL	South Coast
T812CBW	North East	V302LGC	North East	V683FEL	South Coast
T813CBW	North East	V303LGC	Konectbus	V684FEL	South Coast
T814CBW	North East	V304LGC	North East	V685FEL	South Coast
T814RFG	Hedingham	V305LGC	North East	V686FEL	South Coast
T815CBW	North East	V306LGC	North East	V710LWT	South Coast
T817RFG	Hedingham	V307LGC	Konectbus	V736OOF	South Coast
T819RFG	Brighton & Hove	V308LGC	North East	V801EBR	North East
T820RFG	Brighton & Hove	V310LGC	North East	V802EBR	North East
T866JBC	South Coast	V311LGC	North East	V803EBR	North East
T867JBC	South Coast	V312LGC	North East	V804EBR	North East
T868JBC	South Coast	V313LGC	North East	V816KGF	North East
T869JBC	South Coast	V314LGC	North East	V822ERG	North East
TDL856	South Coast	V315LGC	North East	V858EGR	North East
TF10OXF	Oxford	V317LGC	North East	V921KGF	North East
TF56OXF	Oxford	V319LGC	North East	V923KGF	North East
TF61OXF	Oxford	V322KMY	Metrobus	V966DFX	South Coast
TIL6710	South Coast	V322LGC	North East	V986ETN	North East
TIL6711	South Coast	V323KMY	Metrobus	V987ETN	North East
TIL6712	South Coast	V324KMY	Metrobus	V988ETN	North East
TIL6713	South Coast	V324LGC	North East	V989ETN	North East
TIL6714	South Coast	V325KMY	Metrobus	V990ETN	North East
TIL6715	South Coast	V325LGC	North East	VDL744	South Coast
TIL6716	South Coast	V326KMY	Metrobus	VF10OXF	Oxford
TIL6717	South Coast	V327KMY	Metrobus	VF56OXF	Oxford

Reg	Operator	Reg	Operator	Reg	Operator
VJI3968	South Coast	W488WGH	London	W829NNJ	Hedingham
VLT9	London	W489WGH	London	W830NNJ	Hedingham
VLT60	London	W491SCU	North East	W831NNJ	Brighton & Hove
VU02TTK	South Coast	W491WGH	London	W832NNJ	Brighton & Hove
VU03VVX	South Coast	W492WGH	London	W833NNJ	Brighton & Hove
VU03VVY	South Coast	W493WGH	London	W834NNJ	Brighton & Hove
VU52UEE	South Coast	W494WGH	London	W835NNJ	Brighton & Hove
VU52UEF	South Coast	W495WGH	London	W836NNJ	Brighton & Hove
VU52UES	South Coast	W496WGH	London	W837NNJ	Brighton & Hove
VUV246	South Coast	W497WGH	London	W838NNJ	Brighton & Hove
VX51RHZ	Konectbus	W498WGH	London	W839NNJ	Brighton & Hove
VX51RJZ	Konectbus	W501WGH	South Coast	W840NNJ	Brighton & Hove
W161RFX	South Coast	W502WGH	South Coast	W859PNL	North East
W162RFX	South Coast	W503WGH	South Coast	W861PNL	North East
W163RFX	South Coast	W504WGH	South Coast	W862PNL	North East
W164RFX	South Coast	W505WGH	London	W863PNL	North East
W165RFX	South Coast	W506WGH	South Coast	W864PNL	North East
W166RFX	South Coast	W507WGH	South Coast	W865PNL	North East
W174SCU	North East	W508WGH	South Coast	W866PNL	North East
W176SCU	North East	W509WGH	Plymouth	W901RBB	North East
W177SCU	North East	W511WGH	Plymouth	W902RBB	North East
W178SCU	North East	W512WGH	London	W903RBB	North East
W179SCU	North East	W513WGH	London	W904RBB	North East
W181SCU	North East	W514WGH	London	W905RBB	North East
W182CDN	South Coast	W516WGH	London	W906RBB	North East
W182SCU	North East	W516WGH	South Coast	W907RBB	North East
W183SCU	North East	W517WGH	London	W908RBB	North East
W184SCU	North East	W517WGH	South Coast	W908WGH	South Coast
W185SCU	North East	W518WGH	London	W909RBB	North East
W186SCU	North East	W518WGH	South Coast	W956WGH	London
W187SCU	North East	W519WGH	London	W996WGH	London
W188SCU	North East	W521WGH	London	W997WGH	South Coast
W189SCU	North East	W521WGH	South Coast	WA03BHW	Plymouth
W20FWL	North East	W522WGH	London	WA03BHX	Plymouth
W232CDN	South Coast	W522WGH	South Coast	WA03BHY	Plymouth
W254KDO	South Coast	W523WGH	London	WA03BHZ	Plymouth
W312CJN	Hedingham	W524WGH	London	WA03BJE	Plymouth
W334VGX	Metrobus	W526WGH	London	WA03BJF	Plymouth
W339VGX	Brighton & Hove	W527WGH	London	WA03CTK	South Coast
W399WGH	South Coast	W529WGH	London	WA03MGE	Plymouth
W401WGH	London	W531WGH	London	WA03MGJ	Plymouth
W402WGH	London	W532WGH	London	WA08LDF	Plymouth
W403WGH	London	W533WGH	London	WA08LDJ	Plymouth
W404WGH	London	W534WGH	London	WA08LDK	Plymouth
W408WGH	London	W536WGH	London	WA08LDL	Plymouth
W409WGH	London	W537WGH	London	WA08LDN	Plymouth
W411SCU	North East	W538WGH	London	WA08LDU	Plymouth
W415WGH	London	W539WGH	London	WA08LDV	Plymouth
W415WGH	South Coast	W541WGH	London	WA08LDX	Plymouth
W425WGH	London	W542WGH	London	WA08LDZ	Plymouth
W428WGH	London	W543WGH	London	WA08LEF	Plymouth
W435WGH	London	W578DGU	London	WA08LEJ	Plymouth
W457WGH	London	W601PLJ	South Coast	WA12ACJ	Plymouth
W458WGH	London	W602PLJ	South Coast	WA12ACO	Plymouth
W459WGH	London	W604PLJ	South Coast	WA12ACU	Plymouth
W461WGH	London	W649FUM	Hedingham	WA12ACV	Plymouth
W462WGH	London	W791VMV	Brighton & Hove	WA12ACX	Plymouth
W463WGH	London	W792VMV	Brighton & Hove	WA12ACY	Plymouth
W464WGH	London	W796VMV	Brighton & Hove	WA12ACZ	Plymouth
W466WGH	London	W798VMV	Brighton & Hove	WA12ADO	Plymouth
W467WGH	London	W799VMV	Brighton & Hove	WA12ADU	Plymouth
W468WGH	London	W806PNL	North East	WA12ADV	Plymouth
W469WGH	London	W816FBW	North East	WA51ACO	Plymouth
W471WGH	London	W817FBW	North East	WA51ACU	Plymouth
W472WGH	London	W818FBW	North East	WA51ACV	Plymouth
W473WGH	London	W819FBW	North East	WA51ACX	Plymouth
W475WGH	London	W821FBW	North East	WA51ACY	Plymouth
W476WGH	London	W821NNJ	Hedingham	WA54JVV	Plymouth
W479WGH	London	W822NNJ	Hedingham	WA54JVW	Plymouth
W482WGH	London	W823NNJ	Hedingham	WA54JVX	Plymouth
W483WGH	London	W824NNJ	Brighton & Hove	WA54JVY	Plymouth
W484WGH	London	W825NNJ	Konectbus	WA54JVZ	Plymouth
W485WGH	London	W826NNJ	Brighton & Hove	WA54JWC	Plymouth
W486WGH	London	W827NNJ	Brighton & Hove	WA54JWD	Plymouth
W487WGH	London	W828NNJ	Hedingham	WA54JWE	Plymouth

Registration	Location	Registration	Location	Registration	Location
WA56HHN	Plymouth	X204CDV	Plymouth	X687XJT	South Coast
WA56HHO	Plymouth	X223FBB	North East	X688XJT	South Coast
WA56HHP	Plymouth	X224FBB	North East	X702EGK	London
WA56OZM	Plymouth	X226FBB	North East	X705EGK	London
WA56OZO	Plymouth	X227FBB	North East	X707EGK	London
WA56OZP	Plymouth	X228FBB	North East	X745EGK	London
WA56OZR	Plymouth	X228WRA	Anglian	X822FBB	North East
WA56OZS	Plymouth	X229FBB	North East	X823FBB	North East
WA56OZT	Plymouth	X229WRA	Konectbus	X912WGR	North East
WA56OZU	Plymouth	X231FBB	North East	X913WGR	North East
WDL691	South Coast	X232FBB	North East	X914WGR	North East
WF10OXF	Oxford	X233FBB	North East	X915WGR	North East
WF56OXF	Oxford	X251NNO	Anglian	X916WGR	North East
WIL2574	South Coast	X309NNO	Anglian	X917WGR	North East
WJ52GNY	Plymouth	X319YEL	South Coast	X918WGR	North East
WJ52GNZ	Plymouth	X344YGU	Metrobus	X919WGR	North East
WJ52GOA	Plymouth	X384NNO	Anglian	X921WGR	North East
WJ52GOC	Plymouth	X386NNO	Anglian	X922WGR	North East
WJ52GOE	Plymouth	X492WGR	North East	X923WGR	North East
WJ52GOH	Plymouth	X501EGK	London	X924WGR	North East
WJ52GOK	Plymouth	X501WRG	North East	X925WGR	North East
WJ55HLG	Plymouth	X502WRG	North East	XAA299	South Coast
WJ55HLH	Plymouth	X503EGK	London	XAM152	South Coast
WJ55HLK	Plymouth	X503WRG	North East	XDL872	South Coast
WJ55HLM	Plymouth	X504EGK	London	XDL872	South Coast
WJ55HLN	Plymouth	X504WRG	North East	Y23OXF	South Coast
WJ55HLO	Plymouth	X506EGK	London	Y24OXF	South Coast
WJ55HLP	Plymouth	X506WRG	North East	Y167FEL	South Coast
WJ55HLR	Plymouth	X507EGK	London	Y169FEL	South Coast
WKZ8679	South Coast	X509EGK	London	Y171FEL	South Coast
WKZ8689	South Coast	X512WRG	North East	Y172FEL	South Coast
WKZ8689	South Coast	X513WRG	North East	Y173FEL	South Coast
WKZ8697	South Coast	X514WRG	North East	Y174FEL	South Coast
WLT516	London	X544EGK	London	Y199FEL	South Coast
WPH135Y	Hedingham	X546EGK	London	Y291HUA	South Coast
WV52AKY	South Coast	X547EGK	London	Y292HUA	South Coast
WV52FAO	South Coast	X548EGK	London	Y313NYD	Plymouth
WV52HTT	South Coast	X549EGK	London	Y314NYD	Plymouth
WX53WFP	South Coast	X551EGK	London	Y346YGU	Hedingham
X2OXF	Oxford	X551FBB	North East	Y346YGU	Hedingham
X3OXF	Oxford	X552EGK	London	Y347YGU	Hedingham
X4OXF	Oxford	X553EGK	London	Y359HMY	Metrobus
X5OXF	Oxford	X554EGK	London	Y361HMY	Metrobus
X6OXF	Oxford	X556EGK	Plymouth	Y362HMY	Metrobus
X7OXF	Oxford	X557EGK	Plymouth	Y363HMY	Metrobus
X8OXF	Oxford	X558EGK	Plymouth	Y364HMY	Metrobus
X13OXF	Oxford	X559EGK	London	Y365HMY	Metrobus
X28OXF	Oxford	X559EGK	South Coast	Y366HMY	Metrobus
X29OXF	Oxford	X561EGK	London	Y367HMY	Metrobus
X31OXF	Oxford	X562EGK	London	Y368HMY	Metrobus
X141CDV	Plymouth	X563EGK	London	Y369HMY	Metrobus
X142CDV	Plymouth	X564EGK	London	Y371HMY	Metrobus
X143CFJ	Plymouth	X566EGK	London	Y372HMY	Metrobus
X149FBB	London	X567EGK	London	Y373HMY	Metrobus
X151FBB	London	X568EGK	London	Y374HMY	Metrobus
X152FBB	London	X569EGK	London	Y376HMY	Metrobus
X153FBB	London	X571EGK	London	Y377HMY	Metrobus
X154FBB	London	X572EGK	South Coast	Y378HMY	Metrobus
X157FBB	London	X573EGK	South Coast	Y379HMY	Metrobus
X158FBB	London	X574EGK	South Coast	Y493ETN	North East
X159FBB	London	X575EGK	London	Y558KUX	North East
X161FBB	London	X576EGK	London	Y644NYD	Plymouth
X162FBB	London	X577EGK	South Coast	Y645NYD	Plymouth
X163FBB	London	X578EGK	London	Y646NYD	Plymouth
X164FBB	London	X589EGK	London	Y647NYD	Plymouth
X165FBB	London	X595FBB	North East	Y648NYD	Plymouth
X166FBB	London	X599EGK	London	Y703TGH	London
X167FBB	London	X605XFX	South Coast	Y704TGH	South Coast
X168FBB	London	X606XFX	South Coast	Y729TGH	London
X169FBB	London	X607XFX	South Coast	Y731TGH	London
X171FBB	London	X608XFX	South Coast	Y732TGH	London
X172FBB	London	X609WLJ	South Coast	Y733TGH	London
X201CDV	Plymouth	X615EGK	London	Y734TGH	London
X202CDV	Plymouth	X616EGK	London	Y735TGH	London
X203CDV	Plymouth	X656EGK	London	Y736TGH	London

Reg	Operator	Reg	Operator	Reg	Operator
Y737TGH	London	YG52CEF	South Coast	YM55SXF	Metrobus
Y738TGH	London	YG52CEJ	South Coast	YM55SXH	Metrobus
Y739TGH	South Coast	YG52CEN	South Coast	YM55SXO	Metrobus
Y741TGH	South Coast	YG52CLO	South Coast	YM55SXP	Metrobus
Y742TGH	South Coast	YG52CLV	South Coast	YM55SXR	Metrobus
Y743TGH	South Coast	YG52CLX	South Coast	YMW843	South Coast
Y744TGH	London	YG52CLY	South Coast	YN03DFA	Metrobus
Y745TGH	London	YG52CME	South Coast	YN03DFC	Metrobus
Y746TGH	South Coast	YG52CMF	South Coast	YN03DFD	Metrobus
Y747TGH	South Coast	YJ03PPF	South Coast	YN03DFE	Metrobus
Y748TGH	London	YJ03PPK	South Coast	YN03DFG	Metrobus
Y748TGH	South Coast	YJ03PPU	South Coast	YN03DFJ	Metrobus
Y782MFT	North East	YJ03PPV	South Coast	YN03DFK	Metrobus
Y801TGH	London	YJ03PPX	South Coast	YN03DFL	South Coast
Y802TGH	London	YJ05PXA	Konectbus	YN03DFP	South Coast
Y808MFT	North East	YJ05PXB	Konectbus	YN03DFU	Metrobus
Y808TGH	Plymouth	YJ05PXC	Konectbus	YN03DFV	Metrobus
Y809TGH	London	YJ05PXD	Konectbus	YN03DFX	Metrobus
Y811TGH	London	YJ05PXE	Konectbus	YN03DFY	Metrobus
Y812TGH	Plymouth	YJ05PXM	South Coast	YN03UPM	Metrobus
Y813TGH	Plymouth	YJ05PXN	South Coast	YN03UVM	Anglian
Y814TGH	London	YJ05XMR	South Coast	YN03UVP	Anglian
Y815TGH	London	YJ06FYB	South Coast	YN03UVR	Anglian
Y816TGH	London	YJ06FYC	South Coast	YN03UVT	Anglian
Y817TGH	London	YJ06FYD	South Coast	YN03UVU	Anglian
Y818TGH	London	YJ06FYE	South Coast	YN03UVV	Anglian
Y819TGH	London	YJ06FYU	South Coast	YN03UVY	Anglian
Y821TGH	London	YJ06FZP	South Coast	YN03UWJ	Anglian
Y822TGH	London	YJ07JTX	South Coast	YN03UWU	Metrobus
Y823TGH	London	YJ07JTY	South Coast	YN03UWY	Metrobus
Y824TGH	London	YJ09MHY	Konectbus	YN03WPP	Metrobus
Y825TGH	London	YJ09MHZ	Konectbus	YN03WPR	Metrobus
Y826TGH	London	YJ10MFA	Oxford	YN03WPX	Brighton & Hove
Y827TGH	Plymouth	YJ10MFE	Oxford	YN03WRF	Metrobus
Y828TGH	Plymouth	YJ10MFF	Oxford	YN03WRG	Metrobus
Y843GCD	Brighton & Hove	YJ10MFK	Oxford	YN03WRJ	Metrobus
Y844GCD	Brighton & Hove	YJ10MFN	Oxford	YN03WRL	Metrobus
Y845GCD	Brighton & Hove	YJ10MFO	Oxford	YN03WRP	Metrobus
Y846GCD	Brighton & Hove	YJ10MFP	Oxford	YN04ANU	Brighton & Hove
Y847GCD	Brighton & Hove	YJ10MFU	Oxford	YN04GHD	South Coast
Y848GCD	Brighton & Hove	YJ51XSK	Anglian	YN04GHG	South Coast
Y849GCD	Brighton & Hove	YJ51XSK	Anglian	YN04GHH	South Coast
Y851GCD	Brighton & Hove	YJ54UWN	South Coast	YN04GHJ	South Coast
Y852GCD	Brighton & Hove	YJ56FXW	Oxford	YN04GHK	South Coast
Y853GCD	Brighton & Hove	YJ56WUB	Oxford	YN04GJE	Brighton & Hove
Y854GCD	Brighton & Hove	YJ56WUC	Oxford	YN04GJF	Brighton & Hove
Y856GCD	Brighton & Hove	YJ56WUD	Oxford	YN04GJG	Brighton & Hove
Y857GCD	Brighton & Hove	YJ56WUE	Oxford	YN04GJJ	Brighton & Hove
Y858GCD	Brighton & Hove	YJ56WUL	South Coast	YN04GJK	Brighton & Hove
Y859GCD	Brighton & Hove	YJ56WUM	South Coast	YN04GJU	Brighton & Hove
Y861GCD	Brighton & Hove	YJ56WUO	South Coast	YN04GJV	Brighton & Hove
Y862GCD	Brighton & Hove	YJ56WVA	Konectbus	YN04GJX	Brighton & Hove
Y863GCD	Brighton & Hove	YJ56WVB	Konectbus	YN04GJY	Brighton & Hove
Y864GCD	Brighton & Hove	YJ56WVF	Metrobus	YN04GJZ	Brighton & Hove
Y865GCD	Brighton & Hove	YJ56WVG	Metrobus	YN04GKA	Brighton & Hove
Y866GCD	Brighton & Hove	YJ56WVS	Oxford	YN04GKC	Brighton & Hove
Y868GCD	Brighton & Hove	YJ56WVT	Oxford	YN04GKD	Brighton & Hove
Y869GCD	Brighton & Hove	YJ56WVU	Oxford	YN04GKE	Brighton & Hove
Y871GCD	Brighton & Hove	YJ56WVV	Oxford	YN04GKF	Brighton & Hove
Y926ERG	North East	YJ57EGX	Konectbus	YN04GKG	Brighton & Hove
Y927ERG	North East	YJ57EGY	Konectbus	YN04GKJ	Brighton & Hove
Y928ERG	North East	YJ58PGO	South Coast	YN04GKK	Brighton & Hove
Y929ERG	North East	YJ58PGV	South Coast	YN04LWP	Anglian
Y931ERG	North East	YJ58PGY	South Coast	YN04LWZ	South Coast
Y932ERG	North East	YJ60KGU	Anglian	YN05ATV	South Coast
Y933ERG	North East	YJ60KGV	Anglian	YN05ATY	South Coast
Y934ERG	North East	YM55SWU	Metrobus	YN05AUC	South Coast
Y935ERG	North East	YM55SWV	Metrobus	YN05AUK	South Coast
Y936ERG	North East	YM55SWX	Metrobus	YN05GZH	Brighton & Hove
Y975FEL	South Coast	YM55SWY	Metrobus	YN05GZJ	Brighton & Hove
Y983TGH	London	YM55SXA	Metrobus	YN05GZK	Brighton & Hove
Y986TGH	London	YM55SXB	Metrobus	YN05GZL	Brighton & Hove
Y987TGH	London	YM55SXC	Metrobus	YN05GZM	Brighton & Hove
YF56OXF	Oxford	YM55SXD	Metrobus	YN05GZO	Brighton & Hove
YG52CDZ	South Coast	YM55SXE	Metrobus	YN05GZP	Brighton & Hove

YN05GZR	Brighton & Hove	YN08DFX	Metrobus	YN55NFC	Brighton & Hove
YN05GZS	Brighton & Hove	YN08DFY	Metrobus	YN55NFD	Brighton & Hove
YN05HCA	Metrobus	YN08DFZ	Metrobus	YN55NFE	Brighton & Hove
YN05HCC	Metrobus	YN08DMY	London	YN55NFF	Brighton & Hove
YN05HCD	Metrobus	YN08JAU	Brighton & Hove	YN55NFG	Brighton & Hove
YN05HCE	Metrobus	YN08OAS	Metrobus	YN55NFH	Brighton & Hove
YN05HCF	Metrobus	YN08OAV	Metrobus	YN55NFJ	Brighton & Hove
YN05HCG	Metrobus	YN08OAW	Metrobus	YN55NFK	Brighton & Hove
YN05HFE	Anglian	YN08OAX	Metrobus	YN55NFL	Brighton & Hove
YN05HFF	Anglian	YN08OAY	Metrobus	YN55NFM	Brighton & Hove
YN05HFG	Anglian	YN08OAZ	Metrobus	YN55NFO	Brighton & Hove
YN05HFH	Anglian	YN08OBP	Metrobus	YN55NFP	South Coast
YN05HFJ	Anglian	YN08OBR	Metrobus	YN55PWJ	Metrobus
YN06CGO	South Coast	YN11LVE	Anglian	YN55PWK	Metrobus
YN06JWD	South Coast	YN11LVF	Anglian	YN55PWL	Metrobus
YN06JWE	South Coast	YN51MKV	North East	YN55PWO	Metrobus
YN06JWG	South Coast	YN51MKX	North East	YN55PWU	Metrobus
YN06JWJ	South Coast	YN53RXF	Metrobus	YN55PWV	Metrobus
YN06JWM	South Coast	YN53RXG	Metrobus	YN55PWX	Metrobus
YN06JWO	South Coast	YN53RXH	Metrobus	YN55PZC	Metrobus
YN06JWU	South Coast	YN53RXJ	Metrobus	YN55PZD	Metrobus
YN06JWV	South Coast	YN53RXK	Metrobus	YN55PZE	Metrobus
YN06JWW	South Coast	YN53RXL	Metrobus	YN55PZF	Metrobus
YN06JWX	South Coast	YN53RXM	Metrobus	YN55PZG	Metrobus
YN06JWY	South Coast	YN53RXO	Metrobus	YN55PZH	Metrobus
YN06JWZ	South Coast	YN53RXP	Metrobus	YN55PZJ	Metrobus
YN06JXR	Metrobus	YN53RXR	Metrobus	YN55PZL	Metrobus
YN06JXS	Metrobus	YN53RXT	Metrobus	YN55PZM	Metrobus
YN06JXT	Metrobus	YN53RXU	Metrobus	YN55PZO	Metrobus
YN06JXU	Metrobus	YN53RXV	Metrobus	YN55PZP	Metrobus
YN06JXV	Metrobus	YN53RXW	Metrobus	YN55PZR	Metrobus
YN06JXW	Metrobus	YN53RXX	Metrobus	YN55PZU	Metrobus
YN06JXX	Metrobus	YN53RXY	Metrobus	YN55PZV	Metrobus
YN06JXY	Metrobus	YN53RXZ	Metrobus	YN55PZW	Metrobus
YN06JXZ	Metrobus	YN53RYA	Metrobus	YN55PZX	Metrobus
YN06JYB	Metrobus	YN53RYB	Metrobus	YN56FDA	Metrobus
YN06JYC	Metrobus	YN53RYC	Metrobus	YN56FDC	Metrobus
YN06JYD	Metrobus	YN53RYD	Metrobus	YN56FDD	Metrobus
YN06JYE	Metrobus	YN53RYF	Metrobus	YN56FDE	Metrobus
YN06JYF	Metrobus	YN53RYH	Metrobus	YN56FDF	Metrobus
YN06JYG	Metrobus	YN53RYK	Metrobus	YN56FDG	Metrobus
YN06JYH	Metrobus	YN53RYM	Metrobus	YN56FDJ	Metrobus
YN06JYJ	Metrobus	YN53RYP	Metrobus	YN56FDK	Metrobus
YN06JYK	Metrobus	YN53RYR	Metrobus	YN56FDL	Metrobus
YN06JYL	Metrobus	YN53RYT	Metrobus	YN56FDM	Metrobus
YN06JYO	Metrobus	YN53RYV	Metrobus	YN56FDO	Metrobus
YN06NYK	Brighton & Hove	YN53RYW	Metrobus	YN56FDP	Metrobus
YN06NYL	Brighton & Hove	YN53RYX	Metrobus	YN56FDU	Metrobus
YN06SZW	Brighton & Hove	YN53RYY	Metrobus	YN56FDV	Metrobus
YN06SZX	Brighton & Hove	YN53RYZ	Metrobus	YN56FDX	Metrobus
YN06SZY	Brighton & Hove	YN53RZA	Metrobus	YN56FDY	Metrobus
YN06SZZ	Brighton & Hove	YN53RZB	Metrobus	YN56FDZ	Metrobus
YN07EWS	South Coast	YN53RZC	Metrobus	YN56FEF	Metrobus
YN07EWT	South Coast	YN53RZD	Metrobus	YN56FEG	Metrobus
YN07EXF	Metrobus	YN53RZE	Metrobus	YN56FFA	Brighton & Hove
YN07EXG	Metrobus	YN53RZF	Metrobus	YN56FFB	Brighton & Hove
YN07EXH	Metrobus	YN53USG	Metrobus	YN56FFC	Brighton & Hove
YN07EXK	Metrobus	YN53YGY	South Coast	YN56FFD	Brighton & Hove
YN07EXM	Metrobus	YN54AFK	South Coast	YN56FFE	Brighton & Hove
YN07EXO	Metrobus	YN54AFX	South Coast	YN56FFG	Brighton & Hove
YN07EZB	Anglian	YN54AJU	Metrobus	YN56FFH	Brighton & Hove
YN07LFU	Anglian	YN54AJV	Metrobus	YN56FFJ	Brighton & Hove
YN07LKF	Metrobus	YN54AJX	Metrobus	YN56FFK	Brighton & Hove
YN07LKG	Metrobus	YN54AJY	Metrobus	YN56FFL	Brighton & Hove
YN07UOF	Brighton & Hove	YN54AOM	Brighton & Hove	YN56FFM	Brighton & Hove
YN07UOG	Brighton & Hove	YN54AOO	Brighton & Hove	YN56FFO	Brighton & Hove
YN07UOT	Brighton & Hove	YN54AOP	Brighton & Hove	YN56FFP	Brighton & Hove
YN07UOU	Brighton & Hove	YN54AOR	Brighton & Hove	YN56FFR	Brighton & Hove
YN08DFJ	Metrobus	YN54AOT	Brighton & Hove	YN56FFS	Brighton & Hove
YN08DFK	Metrobus	YN54AOU	Brighton & Hove	YN56FFT	Brighton & Hove
YN08DFL	Metrobus	YN54AOV	Brighton & Hove	YN56FFU	Brighton & Hove
YN08DFO	Metrobus	YN54AOW	Brighton & Hove	YN56FFV	Brighton & Hove
YN08DFP	Metrobus	YN54AOX	Brighton & Hove	YN57FYA	Brighton & Hove
YN08DFU	Metrobus	YN54AOY	Brighton & Hove	YN57FYB	Brighton & Hove
YN08DFV	Metrobus	YN55NFA	Brighton & Hove	YN57FYC	Brighton & Hove

The 2012-13 Go-Ahead Bus Handbook

Reg	Operator	Reg	Operator	Reg	Operator
YN57FYD	Brighton & Hove	YR58RUU	Brighton & Hove	YX11CPN	London
YN57FYE	Brighton & Hove	YR58SNY	Metrobus	YX11CPO	London
YN57FYF	Brighton & Hove	YR58SNZ	Metrobus	YX11CPU	London
YN57FYG	Brighton & Hove	YSU875	South Coast	YX11CPV	London
YN57FYH	Brighton & Hove	YSU876	North East	YX11CPY	London
YN57FYJ	Brighton & Hove	YT09BKD	Metrobus	YX11CPZ	London
YN57FYK	Brighton & Hove	YT09BKE	Metrobus	YX11CTE	Metrobus
YN57FYL	Brighton & Hove	YT09BKF	Metrobus	YX11CTF	Metrobus
YN57FYM	Brighton & Hove	YT09BKG	Metrobus	YX11CTK	Metrobus
YN57FYO	Brighton & Hove	YT09BKJ	Metrobus	YX11FYS	London
YN57FYP	Brighton & Hove	YT09BKK	Metrobus	YX11FYT	London
YN57HPU	Anglian	YT09BKL	Metrobus	YX11FYU	London
YN57HPV	Anglian	YT09BKN	Metrobus	YX11FYV	London
YN57HPX	Anglian	YT09BKO	Metrobus	YX11FYW	London
YN57HPZ	Anglian	YT09BKU	Metrobus	YX11FYY	London
YN57HRA	Anglian	YT09BKV	Metrobus	YX11FYZ	London
YN58BCE	Brighton & Hove	YT09BKX	Metrobus	YX12FPA	London
YN58BCF	Brighton & Hove	YT09BKY	Metrobus	YX12FPC	London
YN58BCK	Brighton & Hove	YT09BKZ	Metrobus	YX12FPD	London
YN58BCO	Brighton & Hove	YT51EBF	Anglian	YX12FPE	London
YN58BCU	Brighton & Hove	YT59DYA	Metrobus	YX12FPF	London
YN58BCV	Brighton & Hove	YT59DYB	Metrobus	YX12FPG	London
YN58BCY	Brighton & Hove	YT59DYC	Metrobus	YX12FPJ	London
YN58BNA	Metrobus	YT59DYD	Metrobus	YX12FPK	London
YP09HWA	Brighton & Hove	YT59DYF	Metrobus	YX12FPL	London
YP09HWB	Brighton & Hove	YT59DYG	Metrobus	YX12FPN	London
YP09HWC	Brighton & Hove	YT59DYH	Metrobus	YX12FPO	London
YP09HWD	Brighton & Hove	YT59DYJ	Metrobus	YX12FPP	London
YP09HWE	Brighton & Hove	YT59DYM	Metrobus	YX12FPT	London
YP09HWF	Brighton & Hove	YT59DYN	Metrobus	YX58DXB	Metrobus
YP09HWG	Brighton & Hove	YT59DYO	Metrobus	YX58DXC	Metrobus
YP09HWH	Brighton & Hove	YT59DYP	Metrobus	YX58DXD	Metrobus
YP09HWJ	Brighton & Hove	YT59DYS	Metrobus	YX60DXT	London
YP09HWK	Brighton & Hove	YT59DYU	Metrobus	YX60DXU	London
YP09HWL	Brighton & Hove	YT59DYV	Metrobus	YX60DXW	London
YP09HWM	Brighton & Hove	YT59DYW	Metrobus	YX60EOE	London
YP09HWN	Brighton & Hove	YT59SFJ	South Coast	YX60EOF	London
YP09HWO	Brighton & Hove	YU02GHA	London	YX60EOG	London
YP09HWR	Brighton & Hove	YU02GHD	London	YX60EOH	London
YP09HWS	Brighton & Hove	YU02GHG	London	YX60EOJ	London
YP09HWT	Brighton & Hove	YU02GHH	London	YX60EOK	London
YP09HWU	Brighton & Hove	YU02GHJ	London	YX60EOO	London
YP52CTO	Metrobus	YU02GHK	London	YX60EOP	London
YP58UFV	Metrobus	YU02GHN	London	YX60EPO	London
YP58UGA	Brighton & Hove	YU02GHO	London	YX60EPP	London
YP58UGB	Brighton & Hove	YU52XVK	Metrobus	YX60EPU	London
YP58UGC	Brighton & Hove	YU52XVL	South Coast	YX60FBU	London
YP58UGD	Brighton & Hove	YU52XVM	South Coast	YX60FBY	London
YP58UGE	Brighton & Hove	YU52XVN	South Coast	YX60FBZ	London
YP58UGF	Brighton & Hove	YU52XVR	Metrobus	YX60FCA	London
YP58UGG	Brighton & Hove	YV03PZE	Metrobus	YX60FCC	London
YP58UGH	Brighton & Hove	YV03PZF	Metrobus	YX60FCD	London
YP58UGJ	Brighton & Hove	YV03PZG	Metrobus	YX60FCE	London
YP58UGK	Brighton & Hove	YV03PZH	Metrobus	YX60FCF	London
YP58UGL	Brighton & Hove	YV03PZJ	Metrobus	YX60FCG	London
YP58UGM	Brighton & Hove	YV03PZK	Metrobus	YX60FCL	London
YP58UGN	Brighton & Hove	YV03PZL	Metrobus	YX60FCM	London
YR02ZKV	South Coast	YV03PZM	Metrobus	YX60FCO	London
YR02ZKW	South Coast	YV03PZW	Metrobus	YX60FCP	London
YR02ZKX	South Coast	YV03PZX	Metrobus	YX60FCU	London
YR02ZKY	South Coast	YV03PZY	Metrobus	YX60FCV	London
YR02ZYK	North East	YV03PZZ	Metrobus	YX60FCY	London
YR02ZYM	North East	YV03RAU	Metrobus	YX60FCZ	London
YR10BCE	Metrobus	YV03RAX	Metrobus	YX60FDA	London
YR10BCF	Metrobus	YV03RBF	Metrobus	YX60FSN	London
YR10BCK	Metrobus	YV03RBU	Metrobus	YX60FSO	London
YR10BCO	Metrobus	YV03RBX	Metrobus	YX60FSP	London
YR10BCU	Metrobus	YV03RCY	Metrobus	YX60FSS	London
YR52VFH	London	YV03RCZ	Metrobus	YX60FSU	London
YR52VFJ	London	YX07HNO	Oxford	YX60FTO	Metrobus
YR52VFK	London	YX07HPJ	Oxford	YX60FTP	Metrobus
YR52VFL	London	YX11AGU	London	YX60FTT	Metrobus
YR52VFM	London	YX11CPE	London	YX60FTU	Metrobus
YR52VFN	London	YX11CPF	London	YX60FTV	Metrobus
YR58RUH	Brighton & Hove	YX11CPK	London		

Reg	Operator	Reg	Operator	Reg	Operator
YX60FTY	Metrobus	YX61BXB	London	YX61DVC	London
YX60FTZ	Metrobus	YX61BXC	London	YX61DVF	London
YX60FUA	London	YX61BXD	London	YX61DVG	London
YX60FUB	London	YX61BXE	London	YX61DVH	London
YX60FUD	London	YX61BXK	London	YX61DVJ	London
YX60FUE	London	YX61BXL	London	YX61DVK	London
YX60FUF	London	YX61BXM	London	YX61DVL	London
YX60FUG	London	YX61BXN	London	YX61DVM	London
YX60FUH	London	YX61BXO	London	YX61DVN	London
YX60FUJ	London	YX61BXP	London	YX61DVO	London
YX60FUM	London	YX61BXR	London	YX61DVP	London
YX60FUO	London	YX61BXS	London	YX61DVR	London
YX60FUP	London	YX61BXU	London	YX61EKF	London
YX60FUT	London	YX61BXV	London	YX61EKG	London
YX60FUV	Metrobus	YX61BXW	London	YX61EKH	London
YX60FUW	Metrobus	YX61BXY	London	YX61EKJ	London
YX60FUY	Metrobus	YX61BXZ	London	YX61EKK	London
YX60FVA	Metrobus	YX61BYA	London	YX61EKL	London
YX60FVB	Metrobus	YX61BYD	London	YX61EKM	London
YX60FVC	Metrobus	YX61BYF	London	YX61EKN	London
YX60FVD	Metrobus	YX61BYG	London	YX61ENC	Metrobus
YX60FVE	Metrobus	YX61DPF	London	YX61ENE	Metrobus
YX61BVY	London	YX61DPK	London	YX61ENF	Metrobus
YX61BVZ	London	YX61DPN	London	YX61ENH	Metrobus
YX61BWA	London	YX61DPO	London	YX61ENJ	Metrobus
YX61BWB	London	YX61DPU	London	YX61ENK	Metrobus
YX61BWC	London	YX61DPV	London	YX61ENL	Metrobus
YX61BWD	London	YX61DPY	London	YX61ENM	Metrobus
YX61BWE	London	YX61DPZ	London	YX61ENN	Metrobus
YX61BWF	London	YX61DSE	London	YX61ENO	Metrobus
YX61BWG	London	YX61DSO	London	YX61ENP	Metrobus
YX61BWH	London	YX61DSU	London	YX61ENR	Metrobus
YX61BWJ	London	YX61DSV	London	YX61ENT	Metrobus
YX61BWK	London	YX61DSY	London	YX61ENU	Metrobus
YX61BWL	London	YX61DSZ	London	YX61ENV	Metrobus
YX61BWM	London	YX61DTF	London	YX61ENW	Metrobus
YX61BWN	London	YX61DTK	London	YX61FYT	London
YX61BWO	London	YX61DTN	London	YX61FYU	London
YX61BWP	London	YX61DTO	London	YX61FYV	London
YX61BWU	London	YX61DTU	London	YX61FYW	London
YX61BWV	London	YX61DTV	London	YX61FYY	London
YX61BWW	London	YX61DTY	London	YX61FYZ	London
YX61BWY	London	YX61DTZ	London	YX61FZA	London
YX61BWZ	London	YX61DVA	London	YX61FZB	London
YX61BXA	London	YX61DVB	London	YX61FZZ	London

ISBN 9781904875 42 0   © Published by British Bus Publishing Ltd, September 2012

British Bus Publishing Ltd, 16 St Margaret's Drive, Telford, TF1 3PH

Telephone: 01952 255669

web; www.britishbuspublishing.co.uk
e-mail: sales@britishbuspublishing.co.uk